Social Development,
Social Inequalities,
and
Social Justice

THE JEAN PIAGET SYMPOSIUM SERIES

Series Editor:
Ellin Scholnick
University of Maryland

Available from LEA/Taylor & Francis

Overton, W.F. (Ed.): The Relationship Between Social and Cognitive Development.

Liben, L.S. (Ed.): Piaget and the Foundations of Knowledge.

Scholnick, E.K. (Ed.): New Trends in Conceptual Representations: Challenges to Piaget's Theory?

Niemark, E.D., DeLisi, R., & Newman, J.L. (Eds.): Moderators of Competence.

Bearison, D.J., & Zimiles, H. (Eds.): Thought and Emotion: Developmental Perspectives.

Liben, L.S. (Ed.): Development and Learning: Conflict or Congruence?

Forman, G., & Pufall, P.B. (Eds.): Constructivism in the Computer Age.

Overton, W.F. (Ed.): Reasoning, Necessity, and Logic: Developmental Perspectives.

Keating, D.P., & Rosen, H. (Eds.): Constructivist Perspectives on Developmental Psychopathology and Atypical Development.

Carey, S., & Gelman, R. (Eds.): The Epigenesis of Mind: Essays on Biology and Cognition.

Beilin, H., & Pufall, P. (Eds.): Piaget's Theory: Prospects and Possibilities.

Wozniak, R.H., & Fisher, K.W. (Eds.): Development in Context: Acting and Thinking in Specific Environments.

Overton, W.F., & Palermo, D.S. (Eds.): The Nature and Ontogenesis of Meaning.

Noam, G.G., & Fischer, K.W. (Eds.): Development and Vulnerability in Close Relationships.

Reed, E.S., Turiel, E., & Brown, T. (Eds.): Values and Knowledge.

Amsel, E., & Renninger, K.A. (Eds.): Change and Development: Issues of Theory, Method, and Application.

Langer, J., & Killen, M. (Eds.): Piaget, Evolution, and Development.

Scholnick, E., Nelson, K., Gelman, S.A., & Miller, P.H. (Eds.): Conceptual Development: Piaget's Legacy.

Nucci, L.P., Saxe, G.B., & Turiel, E. (Eds.): Culture, Thought, and Development.

Amsel, E., & Byren, J.P. (Eds.): Language, Literacy, and Cognitive Development: The Development and Consequences of Symbolic Communication.

Brown, T. & Smith, L. (Eds.): Reductionism and the Development of Knowledge.

Lightfoot, C., LaLonde, C., & Chandler, M. (Eds.): Changing Conceptions of Psychological Life.

Parker, J., Langer, J., & Milbrath, C. (Eds.): Biology and Knowledge Revisited: From Neurogenesis to Psychogenesis.

Goncu, A., & Gaskins, S. (Eds.): Play and Development: Evolutionary, Sociocultural, and Functional Perspectives

Overton, W., Mueller, U., & Newman, J. (Eds.): Developmental Perspectives on Embodiment and Consciousness

Wainryb, C., Turiel, E., & Smetana, J. (Eds.): Social Development, Social Inequalities, and Social Justice

Muller, U., Carpendale, J., Budwig, N., & Sokol, B. (Eds.): Social Life and Social Knowledge: Toward a Process Account of Development.

Social Development, Social Inequalities, and Social Justice

Cecilia Wainryb
University of Utah

Judith G. Smetana
University of Rochester

Elliot Turiel
University of California, Berkeley

LEA Lawrence Erlbaum Associates
Taylor & Francis Group

New York   London

Lawrence Erlbaum Associates
Taylor & Francis Group
270 Madison Avenue
New York, NY 10016

Lawrence Erlbaum Associates
Taylor & Francis Group
2 Park Square
Milton Park, Abingdon
Oxon OX14 4RN

© 2008 by Taylor & Francis Group, LLC
Lawrence Erlbaum Associates is an imprint of Taylor & Francis Group, an Informa business

Printed in the United States of America on acid-free paper
10 9 8 7 6 5 4 3 2 1

International Standard Book Number-13: 978-0-8058-5868-6 (Hardcover)

Library of Congress Cataloging-in-Publication Data

Social development, social inequalities, and social justice / [edited by] Cecilia
    Wainryb, Judith G. Smetana.
      p. cm. -- (The Jean Piaget symposium series)
    ISBN 978-0-8058-5868-6 (alk. paper)
    1. Social justice. 2. Equality. 3. Moral development. 4. Social ethics. I. Wainryb,
Cecilia. II. Smetana, Judith G., 1951-

HM671.S59 2008
305.23101--dc22   2007017118

Visit the Taylor & Francis Web site at
http://www.taylorandfrancis.com

To the memory of Terry Brown (1939–2005),
a remarkable Piagetian scholar, past president of
the Jean Piaget Society, and good friend.

CONTENTS

PREFACE

Economic, educational, and cultural resources affect children's and adults' lives and development. Most would agree with this statement; all contributors to this volume certainly do. Does that mean that children and adults are the product of social forces? For the most part, scholars who document the ways and extent to which social forces shape lives tend, implicitly, to answer this question in the affirmative. Therefore, and somewhat paradoxically, the rich literature bearing on the effects of social disparities and inequalities on human development has stood alienated from the constructivist literature on social development, a literature that has put forth a view of children and adults as actively engaged with and judging their social world. The resulting gap between the two bodies of research—the gap between the view of human development as constrained by social forces and the view of people as acting on and judging those same social forces—is not unbridgeable. In this volume we thus bring together the two bodies of scholarship and research bearing on social justice that have hitherto remained separate. In so doing we hope to broaden the understanding of the relations between social inequalities and social development.

In a provocative introductory chapter, Turiel sets the stage for thinking about the process of social development as entailing more than internalization of the external world. This idea—that even young children actively construct their understandings of the world—is not new and stems from a long tradition of constructivist scholarship originating in early work on moral judgment by Piaget (1932). More boldly, Turiel argues that in the process of making social and moral judgments, people, children included, scrutinize the social relationships, practices, and institutions that make up their social world, and often reject some as oppressive and unfair. In the second chapter, Helwig examines Piaget's early ideas about morality and relates them to the theme of this volume: social justice. He also brings Piaget's ideas into the present, describing current research on children's thinking about social rights.

The seven chapters that follow consider evidence obtained from research in developmental and social psychology, social policy, health research, and anthropological and philosophical inquiry to illustrate the many social inequalities characterizing the social relationships, practices, and institutions that frame children's and adults' development in the United States and across the globe. Each of the chapters offers unique observations on the nature of the relation between privilege and justice.

The chapters by Zigler and Styfco (chapter 3) and Gills, Schmukler, Azmitia, and Crosby (chapter 4) concern themselves with inequalities in educational opportunities in the United States and describe some of the ways in which political and legislative systems have and can be used to level the playing field and ameliorate social inequalities. The chapter by Goodman and Adler (chapter 5) tackles disparities in health and points to the interaction of social and biological factors in the development of disease. Two more chapters, by Horn (chapter 6) and Good and Aronson (chapter 7), discuss issues related to unequal rights, prejudice, and harassment, and their effects on sexual and racial minorities. The last two chapters, by Wikan (chapter 8) and Nussbaum (chapter 9), address problems of rights and gender as related to social hierarchy and describe, from international and cultural perspectives, the hardships and inequalities encountered by women.

What is unique about this set of essays is that in documenting the powerful ways in which social inequalities frame development, they also render visible the conflicts, discontents, and controversies that arise in the context of inequalities and that plague our own and other societies. They also illustrate the many ways in which children, adolescents, and adults across the world make judgments about such conditions and work to resist or change the practices and institutions they deem unjust.

Dissent is articulated and battles are fought by individuals and groups, some with and some without political clout. As the chapters in this volume illustrate, in some cases it is a teenage boy harassed at an American public school because of his sexuality or a destitute woman in India beaten by her husband, each giving voice to his or her own plight. In other cases it is a powerful president who harnesses riches and influence to wage a war against social injustice. Confrontations take place within the private confines of the family and in the public domain of schools, universities, and courts. At stake are educational and occupational opportunities, social and economic status and mobility, a sense of identity and integrity, a right to privacy and choice, and even physical health and life itself. In each case, the social inequalities that frame development are also the object of scrutiny and judgment.

Consistent with the developmental analysis provided by Turiel, these essays tell us that, in addition to being shaped by social forces, including unjust social forces, social development carries within it the possibility of change and social justice. We hope this convergence of scholarship on the topics of social justice, social equality, and social development will help define an agenda for further research and theorizing on these issues.

EDITORS

Cecilia Wainryb is a professor in the Department of Psychology at the University of Utah. She obtained her Ph.D. at the University of California, Berkeley, and held a post-doctoral fellowship in the Department of Psychology at Haifa University, Israel, where she conducted cross-cultural research on children's moral development. Her research has focused on children's understandings of moral conflicts in interpersonal contexts and, more recently, in the context of political violence, war, and displacement. Wainryb is also an affiliate professor at the Institute of Public and International Affairs and serves on the board of the Tanner Center for Nonviolent Human Rights Advocacy, both at the University of Utah.

Judith Smetana is professor of psychology and director of the developmental psychology Ph.D. program in the Department of Clinical and Social Sciences in Psychology at the University of Rochester. She obtained her B.A. at the University of California, Berkeley, her Ph.D. at the University of California, Santa Cruz, and held a post-doctoral fellowship in the Department of Psychology at the University of Michigan. While a professor at the Warner Graduate School of Education and Human Development at the University of Rochester, she held the Frederika Warner Chair in Human Development. Her research focuses on several topics, including adolescent–parent relationships in different ethnic and cultural contexts, the development of children's moral and social rule understanding, and parenting beliefs and practices. She has written numerous articles and chapters. She is the editor (with Melanie Killen) of the recent *Handbook of Moral Development* (Erlbaum, 2006);

she also the editor of *Changing Boundaries of Parental Authority During Adolescence* and *Parental Beliefs: Causes and Consequences,* both published by Jossey-Bass.

Elliot Turiel is professor in the Graduate School of Education at the University of California, Berkeley. He is also an affiliate in the Department of Psychology and a member of the Institute of Human Development. He obtained his Ph.D at Yale University. His research on social cognitive development includes analyses of the domains of morality and social convention. He has also researched relations of social development and culture. That research has examined conflicts stemming from social hierarchies framing relationships of dominance and subordination, as well as how people attempt to subvert and transform cultural norms and practices. He is the author of *The Development of Social Knowledge: Morality and Convention* and *The Culture of Morality: Social Development, Context, and Conflict* (both by Cambridge University Press). He is also the editor of *Development and Cultural Change: Reciprocal Processes* (Jossey-Bass), and co-editor of *Values and Knowledge and Culture, Thought and Development* (both by Erlbaum).

LIST OF CONTRIBUTORS

Nancy E. Adler, Ph.D
Health Psychology Program
University of California
San Francisco, California

Joshua Aronson, Ph.D.
Department of Applied
  Psychology
New York University
New York, New York

Margarita Azmitia, Ph.D.
Psychology Department
University of California
Santa Cruz, California

Faye Crosby, Ph.D.
Psychology Department
University of California
Santa Cruz, California

Joel Gills
Psychology Department
University of California
Santa Cruz, California

Catherine Good, Ph.D.
Psychology Department
Columbia University
New York, New York

Elizabeth Goodman, M.D.
The Floating Hospital for
  Children
Tufts-New England Medical
  Center
Boston, Massachusetts 02111

Charles Helwig, Ph.D.
Department of Psychology
University of Toronto
Toronto, Ontario
Canada

Stacey S. Horn, Ph.D.
College of Education
University of Illinois at Chicago
Chicago, Illinois

Martha Nussbaum, Ph.D.
University of Chicago Law School
Chicago, Illinois

Kristina Schmukler
Psychology Department
University of California
Santa Cruz, California

Judith G. Smetana, Ph.D.
Department of Clinical & Social
  Sciences
University of Rochester
Rochester, New York

Sally J. Styfco, Ph.D.
Zigler Center in Child
  Development and Social Policy
Yale University
New Haven, Connecticut

Elliot Turiel, Ph.D.
School of Education
University of California
Berkeley, California

Cecilia Wainryb, Ph.D.
Department of Psychology
University of Utah
Salt Lake City, Utah

Unni Wikan, Ph.D.
Department of Social
  Anthropology
University of Oslo
Oslo, Norway

Edward Zigler, Ph.D.
Department of Psychology
Yale University
New Haven, Connecticut

1

THE TROUBLE WITH THE WAYS MORALITY IS USED AND HOW THEY IMPEDE SOCIAL EQUALITY AND SOCIAL JUSTICE

Elliot Turiel

In *The Adventures of Tom Sawyer*, Mark Twain introduced readers to Huckleberry Finn, who was to become a main character, along with the runaway slave, Jim, in *The Adventures of Huckleberry Finn*. The escapades of Tom, with Huck and other boys about their age (13- or 14-year-olds), permeate the first *Adventures*. Tom, who lives with Aunt Polly, half-brother Sid, and cousin Mary, continually slips off at night seeking new adventures, plays hooky from school, gets into mischief at home and school, engages in hi-jinks at Sunday school, and occasionally gets lost for days on end. Usually, he runs away not out of anger with Aunt Polly, but to undertake another irresistible adventure. Mark Twain's portrayal of the boys' conflicts with adults and their rejection of society's mores is about their desires for fun and to pursue the personal pleasures of life. The boys rarely hurt people (their fights are benign), act unfairly, or deprive others of their just due. In Mark Twain's characterizations, the two boys who get into so much trouble with the parents, teachers, and ministers are portrayed as having a keen sense of sympathy for people and a strong desire to correct injustices. It is adults who are more often portrayed as engaging in moral affronts, including serious physical violence and in their treatment of slaves.

Huck Finn, who was the vagabond son of the town drunkard, "was cordially hated and dreaded by all the mothers of the town, because he was idle and lawless, and vulgar and bad—and because all their children admired him so, and delighted in his forbidden society" (*The Adventures of Tom Sawyer*, 1876, p. 61). Tom was under strict orders not to play with Huck, "so he played with him every time he got a chance." To use one of Mark Twain's favorite phrases, by and by (in one of the last adventures in *Tom Sawyer*), Huck acted the hero, with risk to his life and limb, to save the Widow Douglas from a murderous avenger. As it happened, Tom and Huck had also found a fortune during that adventure, which resulted in a new existence for Huck:

> Huck Finn's wealth and the fact that he was now under the Widow Douglas's protection introduced him into society—no, dragged him into it, hurled him into it—and his sufferings were almost more than he could bear. The widow's servants kept him clean and neat, combed and brushed, and they bedded him nightly in unsympathetic sheets that had not one little spot or stain which he could press to his heart or know for a friend. He had to eat with knife and fork; he had to use napkin, cup, and plate; he had to learn his book, he had to go to church; he had to talk so properly that speech was become insipid in his mouth; whithersoever he turned, the bars and shackles of civilization shut him in and bound him hand and foot.
>
> He bravely bore his miseries three weeks, and then one day turned up missing. (*Tom Sawyer*, pp. 278–279)

The worried adults looked everywhere for him, fearing the worst. But Tom knew where to find Huck: "Tom Sawyer wisely went poking among some old hogsheads down behind the abandoned slaughter-house, and in one of them he found the refugee." Huck protested Tom's efforts to bring him home:

> Don't talk about it, Tom. I've tried it, and it don't work; it don't work, Tom. It ain't for me; I ain't used to it. The widder's good to me, and friendly; but I can't stand them ways. She makes me git up just at the same time every morning; she makes me wash, they comb me all to thunder; she won't let me sleep in the woodshed; I got to wear them blamed clothes that just smothers me, Tom; they don't seem to let any air git through 'em, somehow; and they are so rotten nice that I can't set down, nor lay down, nor roll around anywher's; I hain't slid on a cellar-door for—well, it 'pears to be years; I got to go to church and sweat and sweat—I hate them ornery sermons! I can't ketch a fly in there, I can't chaw. I got to wear shoes all Sunday. The wider eats by a bell; she goes to bed by

a bell; she gits up by a bell—everything's so awful reg'lar a body can't stand it. (*Tom Sawyer,* pp. 279–280)

Tom's first ploy was to invoke convention: "everybody does that way." Huck retorted that he was not everybody, and blamed his entire predicament on the found fortune. He offered it all to Tom. But Tom would have none of that because "Tain't fair." Finally, Huck consented to try again with the Widow Douglas mainly because it was the only way he could join Tom and their friends in the "gang of robbers" and participate that night in the initiation rites.

Tom Sawyer and *Huckleberry Finn* are fiction, but they provide great insights into moral resistance, and the inner mental workings and social lives of children: one reason this is such good literature. (Perhaps a sign of Twain's insight is that *Huckleberry Finn* was banned in public libraries in Concord, Massachusetts, Denver, Colorado, and other towns.) Henry Nash Smith has written that *Huckleberry Finn* is "A great book, not only because it worked a revolution in American literary prose, but because of what it says—against stupid conformity and for the autonomy of the individual" (Introduction to *Huckleberry Finn*, p. xxix).

Moreover, Mark Twain has relayed in several places (Preface to *Tom Sawyer*; *Mark Twain's Autobiography*) that most of his characters were drawn from people he knew, as well as himself (his autobiography contains several examples of his relations with his mother and brother that parallel Tom's with Aunt Polly and Sid), and that most incidents had actually occurred. Some comments from *Mark Twain's Autobiography* (Volume 1, p. 100) are, "All the negroes were friends of ours, and with those of our own age we were in effect comrades. I say in effect, using the phrase as a modification. We were comrades, and yet not comrades; color and condition interposed a subtle line which both parties were conscious of and which rendered complete fusion impossible."

In that context, Mark Twain talks about a faithful and affectionate good friend, ally, and adviser in the warm, honest "Uncle Dan'l," who was represented as the runaway slave, Jim, in *Huckleberry Finn*. Huck Finn, Twain tells us, was based on Tom Blankenship, the son of the town drunkard where he lived as a child ("an exceedingly well defined and official office at the time"). Like Huck Finn, Tom Blankenship was constantly happy and sought out more than anyone else even though the adults forbade his company. As an adult Blankenship became a justice of the peace in a remote village in Montana, and was "a good citizen and greatly respected" (*Mark Twain's Autobiography*, p. 174).

Especially in *Huckleberry Finn*, Mark Twain concerned himself with issues of social inequality and social justice in the context of race and slavery. He drew a divide between society's ways and the desires and inclinations of individuals, I believe, for two purposes. One was to portray injustices at the societal level, and thereby critique society. The second purpose was to illustrate that children are often at odds with the expectations of adults and do not simply accommodate to societal ways. As an example, Twain's descriptions of Huck's predicament had to do with the myriad conventions and arbitrary restrictions imposed on children by adults who thought such restrictions necessary for civilization. Twain conveyed children's desires for enjoyment, fulfillment, adventures, play, and pleasures in areas that were part of their personal lives. And Twain made it abundantly clear that the children's distaste for the conventions and their pursuit of the pleasures of life did not interfere with their moral sense, feelings for the welfare of others, or a sense of fairness. Children's moral sense includes a rejection of societal practices they see as wrong.

In my view, Mark Twain's depiction of childhood is more discerning than depictions of childhood represented in characterizations of moral development as a process of socialization into society's values and norms. It is more discerning in that it portrays children as able to discriminate between the demands of convention and the requirements of justice. It also more accurately depicts individuals with abilities to scrutinize, critique, and attempt to transform societal arrangements embedding inequalities and injustices.

Socialization perspectives also draw a divide between children and society, but in a very different way. In most socialization perspectives, the divide is of the sort that Mark Twain put into the minds of parents, teachers, and ministers in his *Adventures*. That is, children must be reared to abandon their self-interests, needs, and desires, and learn to accommodate to society's ways. Therefore, socialization perspectives of various types fail to account for children's and others' opposition to society's injustices. Furthermore, psychological (and sociological) constructs regarding individuals' accommodation to society are used in ways that serve to reinforce inequalities and injustices. The concept of character is a case in point of how psychological constructs can be used to reinforce injustices.

CHARACTER AND MORAL DEGENERATION

I have used *Tom Sawyer* and *Huckleberry Finn* for illustrative purposes and to help frame a particular perspective on children. These sources do not provide us with research evidence. And I certainly believe that we must rely on research to formulate explanations of the inner mental worlds, and of the social and moral lives of children. However, there are many characterizations of children that go under the guise of social science that are almost equally devoid of research evidence (and devoid of Mark Twain's insights). Which gets me to the title of this piece, a title that might appear rather strange. How can morality impede social equality and social justice? Isn't social justice a moral matter? It certainly is! However, the idea of morality has been used for a variety of purposes, including as a means of controlling and suppressing people and thereby subjugating them to positions of inequality and subordination. Several terms have been used to these effects, including character, conscience, virtues, vice, sin, and moral degeneracy.

The term *character* is, of course, closely aligned with moral discourse. One view of children's acquisition of morality is that it entails the formation of an internal set of traits (Bennett, 1993, 1995; Bennett & Delattre, 1978; Ryan, 1989; Sommers, 1984; Wynne, 1986). In brief, the general proposition is that children must be taught in ways that lead them to acquire behaviors that are consistently applied and which reflect a set of internal dispositions of personality. Frequently, internal dispositions are labeled character traits, not only by social scientists, but also by educators, religious leaders, and politicians. Politicians often like to invoke the idea of character as a means of cajoling youth and others to shape up. As an example, George W. Bush made it a centerpiece of his inaugural presidential address in January of 2001. He proclaimed that the nation needed a "New commitment to live out our nation's promise through civility, courage, compassion, and character," and asked (presidents like to "ask" in inaugural addresses) the American people to be "Responsible citizens building communities of service and a nation of character."

President Bush touched upon some of the commonly listed traits and, as social scientists do, linked character to good citizenship and the need to instill a sense of community in children. As has been pointed out before (Kohlberg, 1968; Nucci, 2006), the particular set of traits deemed important varies somewhat in different presentations. The following set is likely to be represented: honesty, obedience, loyalty, friendship, responsibility, persistence, courage, and faith. Presumably, those with traits of character act by them consistently across situations and possess the self-control to withstand temptations to act in their own self-interest. Character traits are defined as nonrational dispositions that involve habits of behavior. These habits must be instilled in children through indoctrination (Bennett & Delattre, 1978; Wynne, 1986), direct instruction, and the transmission of society's traditions through stories and lived examples of good works. Anathema to people who hold this position are the ideas of relating to children by discussing moral issues and conflicts, using reasoning, or attempting to stimulate their thinking.

In subsequent sections I touch upon three aspects of morality and its development that point to shortcomings in the idea of character traits. One is that it is not always morally positive to act in accord with the traits. As examples, it is not always the morally preferable course of action to be obedient or loyal or truthful. In addition, it is not always the morally positive course to adhere to society's traditions or community standards. People recognize that acting in that way is not necessarily morally adequate because—and this is another aspect I discuss—they reason about moral and social issues and form judgments about social situations that involve drawing priorities about moral and other social goals. People make moral judgments that involve concerns with welfare, justice, and rights. Armed with such ideas, people scrutinize social relationships, societal arrangements, and practices. Often, people oppose existing practices because of perceived injustices. The idea of character traits does not account for the types of moral opposition, resistance, and efforts at change that stem from people's abilities to think about social relationships and social norms (Turiel & Perkins, 2004).

The flexibility of mind points to a third aspect I discuss: that children's development involves a process of construction of different domains of reasoning, including the moral, through their interactions with a multitude of social experiences. The character trait portrayal of children's moral development and moral education is inadequate because its proponents presume that development involves accommodation to, and inculcation of, the traditions of society.

Notions about character traits are often used to impede social justice by denying the validity of people's moral thought that can lead to opposition to injustices. Perhaps the most insidious and common means of control is through assertions that, in contrast with previous eras, society is in moral crisis and in danger of totally deteriorating morally. President Bush implied as much when he said that a new commitment was needed to live out the nation's promise. Other politicians have explicitly proclaimed the moral demise of American society and urgently called for changes toward less selfishness to correct the ship of state.

Most famously, in 1992 then vice-president Dan Quayle proclaimed that American society is in moral crisis as a consequence of a sharp increase in single-mother families, a breakdown in family structure, a paucity of family values, and an increase in permissiveness along with defiance of law and authority. Quayle's comments came in response to large-scale demonstrations, with rioting and looting, in the inner city of Los Angeles, which were in reaction to the outcome of a trial of four white Los Angeles policemen. The policemen had been tried on charges of severely beating a black man upon arresting him after a car chase. Although the beating had been captured on videotape and repeatedly shown on television, the policemen were acquitted of the charges. Politicians like Quayle failed to comment on the actions of the policemen, but were quick to accuse black and poor people of lacking moral values and precipitating a national moral crisis.

In recent times, claims of moral crisis in the land have been made by those who frame character in terms of individuals' traits (Bennett, 1992, 1998; Ryan, 1989; Wynne, 1986) and group dispositions such as national character (Bellah, Madsen, Sullivan, Swidler, & Tipton, 1985; Etzioni, 1993, 1996; Putnam, 2000). The common and recurring theme is that American society is in crisis because people are selfish and narcissistic. As a consequence, they pursue their own self-centered interests, overly stress rights of individuals, and lack commitment to community. This dire state of affairs is seen as a shift from previous times (e.g., 1920s, 1950s) in which people possessed the necessary moral commitments. The nation's youth are often blamed for this, as are minorities, women, and persons of lower socioeconomic classes. Implicit in many of these formulations is that minorities, the poor, and pockets of women (such as those taking part in feminist movements) have brought society to moral crisis through their self-interested behaviors and lack of respect for law and authority.

Those espousing the importance of character traits claim that people no longer value honesty and are willing to lie and cheat for selfish purposes (there is even talk about the "cheating culture"). Youth are blamed for both their dishonesty and for rebelliousness and defiance of authority. Others, who couch the issue in terms of national character, proclaim that because of the advent of radical individualism we must "reverse the slide toward the abyss" (Bellah et al., 1985, p. 284) by restoring traditions, and a sense of family, church, and community (see also Etzioni, 1993, 1996). For some, the moral crisis due to self-absorption and individualism is manifested in a sharp decline in group memberships (e.g., in civic, religious, and fraternal organizations) that presumably began to occur in the 1960s (Putnam, 2000); part of the solution lies in a renewed civic participation.

There are several inadequacies in the dual claims that contemporary society is undergoing moral crisis and that the current moral state represents a deterioration of a societal past that was morally superior. One problem is simply that every generation seems to make the same assessments of the present and past. As one example, during the 1920s similar complaints, with some of the same language, were voiced (see Fass, 1977, and Turiel, 2002, for more extensive discussions). It was said that the moral fabric of American society had deteriorated especially because the young became narcissistic, self-absorbed, and defiant of authority. At the time, permissive attitudes and child-rearing practices, along with the influences of jazz and life in New York City, were seen as some of the most prominent causes of the decline (Fass, 1977). The parallels to contemporary moral laments are striking. Now people blame permissiveness, as well as the influences of television, rap, and Hollywood.

The recurring theme, it seems, of every generation that one's own time is experiencing moral deterioration suggests that serious misattributions are being made. Apparently, people stereotype the past in ways discrepant with how people viewed society at the time. In addition, the view of the good old days ignores serious moral problems that may have existed in past times. For example, in the early part of the 20th century women were treated less equally to men than was the case in the latter part of the century. Women were not even able to vote, with many joining organizations to protest for women's suffrage. Another serious moral failing during the earlier period is evident in the treatment of minorities, especially black people. Until the enactment of civil rights laws in the 1960s there existed even greater racial discrimination than exists presently. In southern states racial segregation was widespread and black voters were disenfranchised. At the time, many beatings and lynching of black people occurred. Although serious inequalities and injustices with regard to women and blacks still exist, these are matters (as well as others, Turiel, 2002) that must be seen as entailing improvements in the moral state of American society.

Then and now, a focus of those who claim society is in moral crisis is on the perceived excesses of the young, along with their supposed rebelliousness and lack of respect for tradition and authority. Their focus on women is through the contention that women's demands for rights and work opportunities bring society down by undermining the traditional structure of the family (Bloom, 1987; Himmelfarb, 1994). Insofar as there is a concern with blacks, it is not on poverty or discrimination, but on the perceived inadequacies of the family structure and reactions to events such as the acquittal of those policemen from Los Angeles. Why is it that those lamenting the moral condition of present society and waxing nostalgic about the past ignore the obvious injustices inflicted on women and minorities? And why is it that those who lamented the moral condition of society in, say, the 1920s, did not do so because of the plight of women or blacks during those historical periods?

The recurring phenomenon of moral lament rests on stereotyping of society and historical periods. In stereotyping societies, little account is taken of injustices perpetuated in societal arrangements and little concern is given to making the situation more just. Rather, groups of people are targeted who may pose a threat to the status quo. All too often, the young—who are seen as insufficiently socialized into society's ways—are targeted because some are at the forefront of challenging both customary practices of a conventional kind and injustices in social practices. (Need I remind the reader of Tom Sawyer and Huck Finn?) Some of those most affected by injustices—women, minorities, the poor—are also among those most often targeted as causing moral crisis and decline.

Whether by conscious design or unwittingly, the misconceived and inaccurate proclamations of moral decline serve as a club, a powerful means of control. They denigrate groups of people as engaging in immoral activities that are so serious that they endanger the very fabric of society. The brush of moral crisis tars the actions and reactions of those with little power. Rarely is the brush of moral crisis used to tar or attempt to control people of status and power who engage in moral wrongdoing.

This was most evident in the reactions of politicians and in the absence of any reaction by social scientists to the recent spate of corporate scandals (e.g., Enron, Arthur Andersen, Tyco, WorldCom). People did not point to those scandals as further instances of the moral decline of American society. Those, like President Bush, who were not silent, made the opposite claim: that the wrongdoing of corporate executives was only due to a few bad apples in a morally sound society. In a well-publicized speech, Bush emphasized that most corporations are scandal free and that "the vast majority of businessmen and women are honest." He also maintained that the corporate world is in the hands of "leaders (who) … give the free enterprise system an ethical compass." (Contrast these reactions to how blacks in the civil rights movement of the 1960s, including Martin Luther King, Jr., were targeted by politicians and the F.B.I.)

SOCIALIZATION AND SOCIAL COMPLIANCE

It is important to reiterate that those who see moral crisis in the land maintain the position that social development is a process of accommodating to the traditions and values of society. For some, individual morality is defined as adherence to a set of character traits consistent with the traditions and standards of society. For others, individual morality is also defined as a commitment to community and group participation that displaces self-interested behaviors and goals. In all these approaches, moral shortcomings exist because individuals have failed to acquire, and comply with, the values of society. Issues of social justice, in the sense of unfair institutionalized traditions and practices that might be carried out by authorities, are not addressed.

As examples, the types of discrimination and harassment of homosexual boys and lesbian girls condoned by school authorities and implicit in the school rules and practices discussed by Horn (this volume) are not going to be treated as matters of social justice if morality is thought to reside in the traditional practices of society. Similarly, the problems of sex discrimination discussed by Nussbaum (this volume; also see Okin, 1989) are embedded in the practices of many societies and, therefore, would not be in the purview of problems of justice in conceptions of morality as accommodation to societal norms.

Not all who theorize that moral development involves processes of socializing children into the values of society or culture make claims about societal deterioration (e.g., Hoffman, 1984; Kochanska, 1993). Indeed, most of them do not comment on the moral state of society. Nevertheless, such theorists at best marginalize issues of social justice because the main criterion for morality is adherence to the values, standards, and practices of one's society or culture. By definition, morality is adherence to those values and practices and by implication noncompliance is contrary to morality. Therefore, explanations of moral development as accommodation and compliance leave issues of social justice by the wayside and have no explanatory means to account for opposition and resistance to societal ways or cultural practices (except by default to relegate them to nonmoral or immoral actions).

The story is a little different in accounts of the participation of individuals in traditional, usually non-Western, cultures that are hierarchically organized with different duties and roles prescribed to those in dominant and subordinate positions. In such accounts, non-Western cultures are said to be collectivistic in that they are organized around interdependence and the absorption of the individual into the group. Most often, females and those from lower social castes or classes are in subordinate positions and treated unequally to males or people of higher castes or classes.

Cultural practices around the duties and role expectations of people in subordinate positions do serve to control their behaviors in ways that benefit those in dominant positions. Women, for instance, are prohibited from activities that are accessible to men (e.g., education, work, leisure activities). Women are expected to fulfill roles in the family that entail subservience and obedience to their husbands and fathers (Shweder, Much, Mahapatra, & Park, 1997) and to follow practices (e.g., genital mutilation, polygamy for husbands) that may be harmful or unfair. Violations of their duties result in culturally sanctioned punishments (Shweder, Mahaptra, & Miller, 1987; Shweder et al., 1997). In some cases, the ultimate punishment of death is threatened and administered (see Wikan, this volume).

Both Nussbaum (this volume, 1999, 2000) and Wikan (this volume, 1996, 2002) document the dire consequences for women of these types of cultural practices. They also persuasively show how cultural practices serve to control women in ways that benefit men. Women who violate such cultural practices in order to assert their rights or in attempts to correct injustices are branded immoral, and said to dishonor the family (Wikan, this volume). Social scientists feed into the acceptance of inequalities in at least two ways. One is that they have relied almost exclusively on people in positions of power and privilege as their sources of information about cultural practices and the attitudes of members of the community (so-called informants). As Wikan (1991, p. 290) has stressed, it is the culture's "spokesmen" who are the informants, to the exclusion of "the poor, the infirm, and youths."

The second failure to sufficiently or adequately include the voices of people in subordinate positions has produced the, in my view, erroneous ideas that cultures are characterized by social harmony and that regardless of one's position in the social hierarchy, people accept the prescribed duties and roles. A common reason given for the idea that people would accept inequalities, injustices, and a denial of rights is that those in dominant positions compensate them through the protection and security insured. Wives, for instance, willingly accept obedience because of the protection received from their husbands (Shweder et al., 1997). As discussed below, the study of the perspectives of those in subordinate positions reveals that they are not accepting of inequalities or injustices.

THOUGHT AND DEVELOPMENT

The boys who populate Mark Twain's worlds of adventures are certainly not compliant with the mores that require them to live by a bell, dress properly, maintain cleanliness, keep to table manners, and sit still much of the time. The boys would not be seen to meet up to the requirements of character beloved by proponents of the view that morality consists of habits of behavior. The boys, most dramatically, are not accommodating to practices they see as unjust.

Leaving room for the poetic license of the novelist, I believe there is more evidence in support of Mark Twain's general portrayal of children than there is for the character formation and socialization positions I have just considered. I would say that Mark Twain's general portrayal of children is that they have their own perspectives on life and are constantly attempting to figure things out and make decisions about how to live, how to make the most of life, and how to relate to others. This points to a major failing of the character trait and socialization approaches, which do not account for what is fundamental to human beings: that, as Nussbaum put it, "Human beings are above all reasoning beings," (1999, p. 71) and that "All, just by being human, are of equal dignity and worth, no matter where they are situated in society, and ... the primary source of this worth is a power of moral choice within them, a power that consists in the ability to plan a life in accordance with one's own evaluations of ends" (1999, p. 57).

The psychological counterpart to Nussbaum's philosophical perspective on reasoning and moral choice is the proposition that children are autonomous in that moral standards are not accepted ready-made. As stressed by Piaget (1951/1995), children participate in the elaboration of moral norms. This points to another major failing in the character trait and socialization approaches, which is that they do not account for either the many different types of social experiences influencing development or the ways children are active in interpreting experiences and, thereby, constructing ways of thinking about the social world. In character trait and socialization approaches the primary emphasis in explanations of development, consistent with the ideas of accommodation and compliance, is on how adults influence children.

The two main settings presumed to influence children's acquisition of societal standards are the family and the school. Although there has been some concern with bidirectional influences between parents and children (Grusec & Goodnow, 1994), not much research of that sort has been undertaken on morality because of the emphasis on how children acquire values consistent with societal expectations.

Clearly, in Mark Twain's fictional world children and adolescents do not sit around absorbing what they are told about being good boys and girls or doing what they are directed to do. Research supports this view of children in several respects. A large number of studies show that by a fairly young age children draw distinctions between morality and the social conventions of the family, school, or society (Turiel, 1983, 1998). They understand that the customs and regularities of conventional kinds are variable, particular to social systems, and rest on particular rules and dictates of authority. At the same time, they form judgments about moral obligations that are not contingent on rules or what authorities dictate, and are not necessarily consistent with societal expectations.

A good deal of research also shows that children and adolescents do not accept what they consider morally unjustified directives from authorities (Laupa, 1991; Laupa & Turiel, 1986; Tisak, 1986). Consequently, their moral judgments are brought to bear on conditions in the social system, the plight of different groups in society, injustices at interpersonal levels, and oppression insofar as it exists. Children also distinguish moral claims from claims to arenas of personal choice, claims they assert in the face of people who might try to restrict personal choices (Nucci, 2001).

When I say that children do not simply sit around absorbing what they are told about being good boys and girls I do not mean that morality is not about the "good." Morality is about the good in the sense of cooperating with others and caring about others. However, children's developing sense of the good is based on, as Nussbaum stated it, equal dignity and worth connected to the power of moral choice. As such, morality also involves conflicts and social struggle. The dynamics of social interactions in childhood and beyond include a large measure of scrutiny of what people are told and the ways the social order is arranged.

We need to recognize that morality is "in the trenches" in two respects: in the activities associated with its development and in the ways it is applied under social conditions that involve injustices and failures to accord dignity and worth equally. With regard to development, children's moral judgments are most often not a consequence of how adults attempt to shape them. Rather, the development of morality involves the construction of judgments about welfare, justice, and rights through multiple social relationships and experiences. Much of children's everyday social experiences involve participating in and observing events of many types. Children participate in events that involve, as examples, people harming or helping each other, sharing or failing to share, excluding or including others, treating people equally or unequally. Children's lives are full of these types of experiences, about which they are neither unaware nor passive. Their observations and reflections of events are major sources of formation and changes of moral and social judgments.

Two types of studies have demonstrated the relevance of children's direct experiences with social interactions for moral and social judgments. In one type of study observations were made of children's interactions with other children and adults in the context of moral and social conventional transgressions. These studies, conducted with preschoolers (Nucci & Turiel, 1978; Nucci, Turiel, & Encarcion-Gawrych, 1983) and older children (Nucci & Nucci, 1982a, 1982b; Turiel, in press), show that interactions around moral transgressions are different from interactions taking place when conventional transgressions occur. Interactions around moral transgressions typically do not involve commands or communications about rules and expectations of adults (which do occur for conventional events), but are about feelings and the perspectives of actors, as well as communications about welfare and fairness.

The second type of study examined children's discussions, in narrative form, about events involving harm they had experienced as either perpetrators or victims (Wainryb, Brehl, & Matwin, 2005). The many narratives provided by the children showed that they focus on interactions and exchanges between people, the feelings evoked, and the effects of acts on self and others. The narratives also illustrate that children reflect upon their experiences. First consider some comments from preschoolers, who not surprisingly are briefer than older children. In talking about their experiences as victims, two preschoolers (one a boy and the other a girl) recalled the physical and emotional hurt involved (from Wainryb et al., 2005, p. 54):

> I remember one thing about um someone, um a friend hurting me. I, it was just little bit. He was a friend, his name was William, he hit me with his hammer in the middle of the head and it really hurt. It was plastic.

> My friend Sydney, ... when I came inside her house, she said she really didn't want to play with me and she um she hit me and um and I felt bad and so I asked her mom ... if I could go home and she said yes.

Similarly, a preschool boy recollecting a time he was a perpetrator expressed awareness of the harm his actions caused (p. 55):

> I was playing with my friend Adam and I said something that really hurt him and he said, "I don't like that." And I stopped. I also pushed him. And I said, "I'm sorry." Because he told me he didn't like it.

Older children were cognizant of the feelings involved and thought about the nature of relationships and mutual expectations. As a first-grade girl said when discussing a time she felt slighted by her "best friend" who referred to another child as her best friend (p. 56):

> And I kind of thought to myself that was kind of making me feel bad. So I wonder if I can go over there and tell her that I that that kind of hurt my feelings.... She's a best friend of mine and I just can't get it out of my mind because she, because, because whenever I walked home from her house at night time she would always give

me a hug and I would always do that and we would and I would never want to leave her house. Then at the birthday. ... I'm wondering if he's really her um best friend.

These types of concerns and reflections on social relationships were expressed by many children of various ages. I provide just one more example from the research by Wainryb and her colleagues, this time from a 10th-grade girl who talked about the time she evaded a planned evening with one of her best friends in order to spend time with other friends (pp. 59–60):

And I remember uh I kind of lied to her but I mostly like avoided her one night ... and then she figured it out and found out and she felt really bad and was hurt and so it wasn't good. 'Cause I bet she felt betrayed; maybe even she thought I don't care about her but I do um I didn't want to hurt her feelings because she was one of my best friends and so I know sometimes being honest is hard but it would definitely be worth it, but it was hard just because I felt so pressured like it happens a lot. I know it happens to a lot to people my age especially that you feel so pressured that you want to do something with one person but then you promised to another person and uh I don't know you want to be everywhere and you want to be everyone's friend and you don't want to hurt anybody but you also really just want to do what feels good, and that definitely was part of the situation. I wanted her to feel like okay. But I mean she got over it; we're friends and everything.

The second sense in which it is appropriate to say that morality is "in the trenches" pertains to how people deal with existing societal arrangements and cultural practices. In keeping with the basic idea that individuals do not simply accept moral propositions as ready-made, people struggle with perceived inequalities and injustices that are part of the institutionalized social order. Cultural practices are not pristine ways of doing things generally accepted no matter how they affect individuals or groups.

Indeed, the essays in this volume provide many examples of moral conflicts, controversies, and disputed matters. These include the issues of affirmative action and racial discrimination (Gills, Schmukler, Azmitia, & Crosby), the effects of racial stereotyping (Good & Aronson), problems of health maintenance and care for the poor (Goodman & Adler), poverty and education (Zigler & Styfco), issues of fairness and rights (Helwig), the rights and suffering of women (Nussbaum; Wikan), as well as those with nontraditional sexual orientations (Horn).

These are problems and conflicts within societies. I have stressed that in the process of development children often view the world differently from the ways it may be presented by parents, teachers, or in messages about society. A source of the discrepancy is their powers of reasoning and choice, along with the many experiences they process that go beyond adult dictates. Consequently, children (and adults) are not locked into habitual ways of thinking and acting. They possess a flexibility of mind with regard to life's experiences that often makes for opposition to and resistance of societal arrangements and cultural practices. This too was recognized by Mark Twain, especially in his portrayal of Huck Finn's struggles with the enslavement of human beings.

Huck Finn's defiant actions to free Jim from slavery were not without ambivalence and intense conflict. In Mark Twain's portrayal, the conflict and struggles were generated by feelings and thoughts about what is right to do as given in society's expectations and about what is right and good for individuals whose dignity and freedom are taken away. Mark Twain also recognized that the term *conscience* could be used to impede social justice. In writing about *The Adventures of Huckleberry Finn*, he said, "A book of mine where a sound heart & deformed conscience come into collision & conscience suffers defeat" (*Huckleberry Finn*, Introduction by Henry Nash Smith, p. xvi).

The collision comes to a head when Huck Finn is torn as to what to do about Jim and as to whether it would be better for Jim to go home or be free. First thinking that he should reveal Jim's whereabouts, Huck then thinks better of it because Jim would be punished and because "It would get all around, ... and if I was to ever see anybody from that town again, I'd be ready to get down and lick his boots for shame" (*Huckleberry Finn*, p. 178). However, the mental struggle continued as he thought better of it again: "The more I studied about this, the more my conscience went to guiding me, and the more wicked and low down ornery I got to feeling" (p. 178). Huck ponders the "plain hand of Providence," thinking that his wickedness of stealing a slave was being watched from heaven. His attempts to pray to be better were of no avail because he knew it would be a lie, "Because I was playing double."

So he writes a letter, yet not mailed, telling Miss Watson where to find Jim and feels much better knowing how close he came "to being lost and going to hell. And went on thinking." Now he thinks about Jim, about all they went through, about their sad and happy times, about their close friendship, and about how Jim cared for him. And conscience suffered defeat: "I was trembling, because I'd got to decide, forever, betwixt two things, and I knowed it. I studied a minute, sort of holding my breath, and then says to myself: 'All right, then, I'll go to hell'—and I tore it up" (p. 180).

THE POWER OF MORAL CHOICE:
OPPOSITION AND RESISTANCE

Conflicts and opposition to unjust societal arrangements and cultural practices are not only the stuff of novels or the province of special people with unique personal qualities. It is the stuff of everyday life. Sometimes, it is thought that moral opposition occurs only rarely and when the occasional courageous person with exceptional moral acuity appears on the scene. It is also thought that large numbers of people sometimes engage in moral opposition and resistance when they are energized by an exceptional person who leads them into it, especially through organized political movements.

This line of thinking perpetuates the idea that people (excluding the rare ones) do not have the power of moral choice and that others shape them in their moral outlooks. However, with the power of moral choice and the flexibility of mind to enable scrutiny and critique of what exists, human beings are energized by social inequalities and social injustices in their everyday world to engage in opposition and resistance in their everyday lives.

Nussbaum and Wikan (this volume, and Nussbaum, 1999, 2000; Wikan, 1996, 2002) have written extensively about resistance among women in nations such as Bangladesh, India, Egypt, and among immigrants in European nations. Nussbaum's observations stem, in part, from her work in the United Nations Development Programme (Nussbaum & Glover, 1995). She has discussed acts of resistance on the part of individuals in the family and work situations, as well as organized forms of resistance (e.g., the Self-Employed Women's Association with its 50,000 or more members interested in the improvement of the conditions of female workers).

In this volume, Wikan discusses females' reactions to the severe restrictions and violations of basic rights imposed on girls and women by cultural practices that greatly favor males. She has also conducted ethnographic studies in poor areas of Cairo, examining the reactions of females to male dominance, and of females and males to a government that fails to address the social and economic plight of those living in conditions of great poverty. She succinctly summarized her observations as follows: "These lives I depict can be read as exercises in resistance against the state, against the family, against one's marriage, against the forces of tradition or change, against neighborhoods and society—even against oneself" (Wikan, 1996, pp. 6–7).

Also on the basis of ethnographic studies, Abu-Lughod (1993) has documented opposition and resistance on the part of girls and women to the control exerted by males in a Bedouin hamlet in rural Egypt. Bedouin females typically use a variety of strategies, including elaborate schemes of deception, to counter traditional practices that restrain their activities. There is open and covert opposition to fathers, brothers, and husbands. There is opposition to practices such as arranged marriages, polygamy, and many restrictions in daily life on educational, work, and leisure activities.

I have written about similar activities from several sources. One source is public reports, especially in the media, of acts of opposition in recent years in places such as Iran, Afghanistan, India, Pakistan, and Egypt (Turiel, 2002, 2003; Turiel & Perkins, 2004). As an example, many people in Afghanistan acted deceptively in order to defy the bans imposed by the Taliban on many, many activities. After the fall of the Taliban in 2001, it was readily apparent that large numbers of people had hidden banned televisions, videos, musical instruments, art works, and much more. Women ran, in secret, schools for girls and worked as beauticians (both banned). Women also took great risks in efforts to expose the atrocities of the Taliban through covert activities as members of the Revolutionary Association of the Women of Afghanistan (a group formed in the 1970s and banned by the Taliban). Another set of examples comes from reports of the ways Iranians defied similar bans on recreational activities (on movies, music, alcohol, playing cards), women's dress, and relations between the sexes.

A second source is research we have conducted on the judgments of adolescent girls and women in traditional patriarchal cultures. These studies, which were conducted in the Middle East (Wainryb & Turiel, 1994), India (Neff, 2001), Colombia (Mensing, 2002), and Benin (Conry-Murray, 2005), show that females do not accept inequalities and power differences based on gender. The studies found that adolescent girls and adult women are quite aware that cultural practices are to the advantage of males over females. This is much more than implicit unreflective knowledge. Females struggle with their roles in the social system, worry about what they are denied, often judge cultural practices as unfair, and believe they should be changed. Here are some examples of statements in these regards (from Turiel & Wainryb, 2000):

> He is free. Even when a baby is born, people are glad if it's a boy, and less glad if it's a girl. We live in a conservative culture. Maybe

in the future I might want to treat my daughter in the same way as I would treat my son, but the culture wouldn't let me do it.... A boy is better than a girl; not better, but his status is higher. That's understood and you can't argue with it.... I believe in equality, but the culture would grant more to a male. (18-year-old female)

A man's life is simple. He works, he comes back home; he has no other responsibilities. I work too and I have kids and a home. He knows that when he comes back, everything will be ready for him. That's such a pleasure. When I come back home I have more work to do at home. So, who do you think deserves to get out a little and enjoy life? (adult female)

Males, who are the beneficiaries of the practices referred to by the women, are likely to endorse the entitlements they enjoy (Wainryb & Turiel, 1994). Males, however, are not oblivious to the inequalities. As one example, a fourteen-year-old Druze boy considered the situation for males and females in a reflective way:

Look, it would be better for me if it stayed this way. I can see from the viewpoint of a girl; she would like change, like equality with boys. She would like to have the same rights. But of course everyone wants what is best for themselves. And this situation, the way things are now, this is better for me; this is better for men. I can see, though, that for girls it would be much better if they had more freedom and more rights.

The reflections of children and adolescents go beyond gender inequalities. Research conducted in the United States shows that children and adolescents experience conflicts with siblings, peers, parents, and other adults in conjunction with concerns with the welfare and rights of others. The research documents that children form positive moral orientations to others, act cooperatively, and display emotions such as sympathy and empathy. The research also documents that children act in oppositional ways, get into conflicts with others, and defy prohibitions established by adults (Dunn, 1987, 1988; Dunn, Brown, & Maguire, 1995; Dunn & Munn, 1986, 1987; Dunn & Slomkowski, 1992). These seemingly opposite orientations do not reflect individual differences or how children approach relationships with different people. The same children take these orientations in relationships with the same people in different contexts involving different social and moral considerations (Turiel, 2006a, 2006b).

It is generally recognized that adolescents get into conflicts with parents and other adults. The conflicts are too often seen either as manifestations of failures on their part to meet moral ideals (part of the view of moral crisis discussed above) or a passing phase in the solidification of their identities and shifts into becoming adults. On the basis of research on judgments about deception (Perkins & Turiel, 2007; Turiel & Perkins, 2004), I believe that the conflicts and acts of opposition on the part of adolescents have a deeper moral source that reflects concerns with inequalities and power relationships. The research I am referring to was not aimed at documenting what is well-known—that adolescents lie to their parents—nor based on the presumption that lying is always morally wrong.

The research was designed to examine the circumstances in which adolescents believe lying is justified and their goals for doing so. Judgments were elicited about deception of parents or friends regarding a set of directives (that is, hypothetical situations depicting directives from parent or friend) about different types of activities. In the first place, the research shows that adolescents do not simply accept any kind of deception of parents. They believe that it is wrong to lie to parents or friends in order to cover up a misdeed. They also judge it wrong to lie to parents in order to get around their directives about matters that have to do with safety or the attainment of future goals, that is, prudential matters such as being told not to ride a motorcycle. Such parental directives are considered legitimate and deception about them is judged unacceptable.

However, there are parental directives that are not considered legitimate. These include parental directives, such as to engage in racial discrimination, that are perceived as morally wrong, as well as directives considered to be part of personal jurisdiction (such as who to date, what club to join). In both types of cases it is judged legitimate, as a last resort, to deceive parents. And these judgments have to do with the power and control that parents are able to exert over their children. As reflected in their reasons for its acceptance, deception is seen as a necessary means to get around social conditions of power and inequality. Moreover, deception of friends in those realms is seen as less acceptable than deception of parents because relationships with friends involve equality and mutuality.

These results indicate that deception by adolescents is not simply due to self-interest or moral failings. Their judgments and perspectives are much more nuanced than that. In these results we see at once the difficulties in views that morality involves consistent adherence to traits such as obedience or honesty. Obedience pre-empts moral opposition and resistance. Consistently acting honestly would ignore conditions in which honesty can result in various types of harm. Philosophers (see Bok, 1999) have long pointed out that honesty and prevention of grave harm can be in conflict (an example provided is whether one is obligated to tell the truth if a murderer asks where his intended victim has gone). One real-life example well illustrates the matter. Deception was often used to save Jews from German concentration camps during World War II. In a different context, research shows that physicians judge deception of insurance companies legitimate if it is the only means of obtaining treatments for serious illnesses (Freeman, Rathore, Weinfurt, Schulman, & Sulmasy, 1999).

These difficult issues surrounding honesty and deception provide examples of how people scrutinize social relationships, social hierarchy, and how groups of people are treated. They also provide examples of some of the ways in which opposition for moral ends occurs. Deception appears to be a common strategy put to these purposes across ages and cultures. Deception is not restricted to adolescence, which some see as a unique phase of opposition and conflict. In addition to adult physicians who regard deception as legitimate for the welfare of patients, American adults judge deception legitimate in marital relationships of unequal power as a means for wives especially to maintain fairness and a semblance of personal choice (Turiel & Perkins, 2004). Deception has also been one of the common strategies in places such as Iran and Afghanistan to combat perceived unjust restrictions imposed by those in power. It is also a strategy used by Bedouin women for similar ends.

All these examples have commonalities with how Mark Twain depicted adolescent boys. The research on adolescents' judgments about deception shows the same concerns with moral ends, a rejection of perceived illegitimate efforts by adults to control personal activities, and struggles over moral ends and social expectations (as in the type of struggle Huck Finn experienced when conscience suffered defeat). It is not only children and adolescents who are told to behave and stay in their place in the name of, say, conscience, character, or preserving the integrity of the culture. Adults, too, find themselves restricted by those in positions of power from enjoying the pleasures of life, exploring the world, and pursuing personal goals available to others. Particularly when such restrictions serve to reinforce the suppression of one group by another, the pursuit of personal goals becomes a serious moral matter.

A story told by Fatima Mernissi (1994), a sociologist from Morocco, in her memoirs of her childhood in the patriarchal culture of Morocco in the 1940s, is reminiscent of Mark Twain's portrayal of Tom Sawyer and Huck Finn and well illustrates how adults can come to treat leisure activities such as listening to music as serious matters requiring moral opposition. In Morocco, extended families lived together and women were confined to the walls of the compound. In Mernissi's family, women were denied access to a radio that could reach as far as Cairo, which was kept under lock and key in the men's salon. Nevertheless, when the men were away at work the women listened to music on that radio, "dancing away to its tunes, singing along with the Lebanese princess ... with no men in sight" (Mernissi, 1994, p. 7).

One day, when Fatima was nine years old, her father happened to ask what she had done that day. Fatima answered that they had listened to the radio. Upon learning this, the men became angry and dismayed at the prospect that the women might even go further in their subversive activities: "'If they made a copy of the radio key, soon they will make one to open the gate,' growled father" (p. 8). Although the men conducted an inquiry for two days as to where the key to the cabinet had been obtained, the women refused to acknowledge they had a key. Furthermore, the women made efforts to ensure that the children would not again give away their hidden activities, threatening to exclude them from their activities: "We defended ourselves by explaining that all we had done was tell the truth. Mother retorted by saying that some things were true, indeed, but you still could not say them: you had to keep them secret. And then she added that what you say and what you keep secret has nothing to do with truth and lies" (p. 8).

In Mernissi's account, resistance on the part of the women went beyond recreational activities because they desired other freedoms and rights, including the freedom to venture beyond the walls of the compound. Apparently, people of various ages act to right perceived wrongs in ways that are not captured by traits of obedience and honesty and that entail confronting those in positions of power and attempting to alter cultural practices. The desires of the women of Morocco to enjoy the pleasures of life and their willingness to engage in disobedience and deception in the pursuit of greater social equality and social justice would have been appreciated by Tom Sawyer and Huck Finn, and by Samuel Clemens.

REFERENCES

Abu-Lughod, L. (1993). *Writing women's worlds: Bedouin stories.* Berkeley: University of California Press.

Bellah, R. N., Madsen, R., Sullivan, W. M., Swidler, A., & Tipton, S. M. (1985). *Habits of the heart: Individualism and commitment in American life.* New York: Harper & Row.

Bennett, W. J. (1992). *The de-valuing of America: The fight for our culture and our children.* New York: Simon & Schuster.

Bennett, W. J. (1993). *The book of virtues*. New York: Simon & Schuster.

Bennett, W. J. (1995). *The children's book of virtues*. New York: Simon & Schuster.

Bennett, W. J. (1998). *The death of outrage: Bill Clinton and the assault on American ideals*. New York: Free Press.

Bennett, W. J., & Delattre, E. J. (1978). Moral education in the schools. *The Public Interest, 50,* 81–99.

Bloom, A. (1987). *The closing of the American mind: How higher education has failed democracy and impoverished the soul of today's students*. New York: Simon & Schuster.

Bok, S. (1999). *Lying: Moral choice in public and private life*. New York: Vintage Books.

Conry-Murray, C. (2005). Reasoning about gender hierarchy in Benin, West Africa: The role of informational assumptions and pragmatic concerns. Unpublished doctoral dissertation, University of California, Berkeley.

Dunn, J. (1987). The beginnings of moral understanding: Development in the second year. In J. Kagan & S. Lamb (Eds.), *The emergence of morality in young children* (pp. 91–112). Chicago: University of Chicago Press.

Dunn, J. (1988). *The beginnings of social understanding*. Cambridge, MA: Harvard University Press.

Dunn, J., Brown, J. R., & Maguire, M. (1995). The development of children's moral sensibility: Individual differences and emotion understanding. *Developmental Psychology, 23,* 791–798.

Dunn, J., & Munn, P. (1986). Siblings and the development of prosocial behaviors. *International Journal of Behavioral Development, 9,* 265–284.

Dunn, J., & Munn, P. (1987). Development of justification in disputes with mother and sibling. *Developmental Psychology, 23,* 791–798.

Dunn, J., & Slomkowski, C. (1992). Conflict and the development of social understanding. In C. U. Shantz & W. W. Hartup (Eds.), *Conflict in child and adolescent development* (pp. 70–92). Cambridge, UK: Cambridge University Press.

Etzioni, A. (1993). *The spirit of community: The reinvention of American society*. New York: Touchstone.

Etzioni, A. (1996). *The new golden rule: Community and morality in a democratic society*. New York: Basic Books.

Fass, P. S. (1977). *The damned and the beautiful: American youth in the 1920s*. New York: Oxford University Press.

Freeman, V. G., Rathore, S. S., Weinfurt, K. P., Schulman, K. A., & Sulmasy, D. P. (1999). Lying for patients: Physician deception of third-party payers. *Archives of Internal Medicine, 159,* 2263–2270.

Grusec, J. E., & Goodnow, J. J. (1994). Impact of parental discipline methods on the child's internalization of values: A reconceptualization of current points of view. *Developmental Psychology, 30,* 4–19.

Himmelfarb, G. (1994). *The de-moralization of society: From Victorian virtues to modern values.* New York: Vintage.

Hoffman, M. L. (1984). Empathy, its limitations, and its role in a comprehensive moral theory. In J. L. Gewirtz & W. M. Kurtines (Eds.), *Morality, moral development, and moral behavior* (pp. 283–302). New York: Wiley.

Kochanska, G. (1993). Toward a synthesis of parental socialization and child temperament in early development of conscience. *Child Development, 64,* 325–347.

Kohlberg, L. (1968). The child as a moral philosopher. *Psychology Today, 2,* 25–30.

Laupa, M. (1991). Children's reasoning about three authority attributes: Adult status, knowledge, and social position. *Developmental Psychology, 27,* 321–329.

Laupa, M., & Turiel, E. (1986). Children's conceptions of adult and peer authority. *Child Development, 57,* 405–412.

Mensing, J. F. (2002). Collectivism, individualism, and interpersonal responsibilities in families: Differences and similarities in social reasoning between individuals in poor, urban families in Colombia and the United States. Unpublished doctoral dissertation, University of California, Berkeley.

Mernissi, F. (1994). *Dreams of trespass: Tales of a harem girlhood.* Reading, MA: Addison-Wesley.

Neff, K. D. (2001). Judgments of personal autonomy and interpersonal responsibility in the context of Indian spousal relationships: An examination of young people's reasoning in Mysore, India. *British Journal of Developmental Psychology, 19,* 233–257.

Nucci, L. (2006). Education for moral development. In M. Killen & J. G. Smetana (Eds.), *Handbook of moral development* (pp. 657–682). Mahwah, NJ: Erlbaum.

Nucci, L. P. (2001). *Education in the moral domain.* Cambridge, UK: Cambridge University Press.

Nucci, L. P., & Nucci, M. S. (1982a). Children's reponses to moral and social conventional transgressions in free-play settings. *Child Development, 53,* 1337–1342.

Nucci, L. P., & Nucci, M. S. (1982b). Children's social interactions in the context of moral and conventional transgressions. *Child Development, 53,* 403–412.

Nucci, L. P., & Turiel, E. (1978). Social interactions and the development of social concepts in preschool children. *Child Development, 49,* 400–407.

Nucci, L. P., Turiel, E., & Encarcion-Gawrych, G. (1983). Children's social interactions and social concepts: Analyses of morality and convention in the Virgin Islands. *Journal of Cross-Cultural Psychology, 14,* 469–487.

Nussbaum, M. C. (1999). *Sex and social justice.* New York: Oxford University Press.

Nussbaum, M. C. (2000). *Women and human development: The capabilities approach.* Cambridge, UK: Cambridge University Press.

Nussbaum, M. C., & Glover, J. (Eds.). (1995). *Women, culture, and development: A study of human capabilities.* New York: Oxford University Press.

Okin, S. M. (1989). *Justice, gender, and the family.* New York: Basic Books.

Perkins, S. A., & Turiel, E. (2007). To lie or not to lie: To whom and under what circumstances. 78 *Child Development* 609–621.

Piaget, J. (1951/1995). Egocentric thought and sociocentric thought. In J. Piaget, *Sociological studies.* London: Routledge.

Putnam, R. D. (2000). *Bowling alone: The collapse and revival of American community.* New York: Simon & Schuster.

Ryan, K. (1989). In defense of character education. In L. P. Nucci (Ed.), *Moral development and character education: A dialogue* (pp. 3–18). Berkeley, CA: McCutchan.

Shweder, R. A., Mahapatra, M., & Miller, J. G. (1987). Culture and moral development. In J. Kagan & S. Lamb (Eds.), *The emergence of morality in young children* (pp. 1–83). Chicago: University of Chicago Press.

Shweder, R. A., Much, N. C., Mahaptra, M., & Park, L. (1997). The "big three" of morality (autonomy, community, and divinity) and the "big three" explanations of suffering. In A. Brandt & P. Rozin (Eds.), *Morality and health* (pp. 119–169). New York: Routledge.

Sommers, C. H. (1984). Ethics without virtue: Moral education in America. *American Scholar, 53,* 381–389.

Tisak, M. S. (1986). Children's conceptions of parental authority. *Child Development, 57,* 166–176.

Turiel, E. (1983). *The development of social knowledge: Morality and convention.* Cambridge, UK: Cambridge University Press.

Turiel, E. (1998). The development of morality. In W. Damon (Ed.), *Handbook of child psychology, 5th Edition, Volume 3:* N. Eisenberg (Ed.), *Social, emotional, and personality development* (pp. 863–932). New York: Wiley.

Turiel, E. (2002). *The culture of morality: Social development, context, and conflict.* Cambridge, UK: Cambridge University Press.

Turiel, E. (2003). Resistance and subversion in everyday life. *Journal of Moral Education, 32,* 115–130.

Turiel, E. (2006a). Thought, emotions, and social interactional processes in moral development. In M. Killen & J. G. Smetana (Eds.), *Handbook of moral development* (pp. 7–35). Mahwah, NJ: Erlbaum.

Turiel, E. (2006b). The multiplicity of social norms: The case for psychological constructivism and social epistemologies. In L. Smith & J. Voneche (Eds.), *Norms in human development* (pp. 189–207). Cambridge, UK: Cambridge University Press.

Turiel, E. (in press). Thought about actions in social domains: Morality, social conventions, and social interactions. *Cognitive Development.*

Turiel, E., & Perkins, S. A. (2004). Flexibilities of mind: Conflict and culture. *Human Development, 47*, 158–178.

Turiel, E., & Wainryb, C. (2000). Social life in cultures: Judgments, conflicts, and subversion. *Child Development, 71*, 250–256.

Twain, M. (1876/1936). *The adventures of Tom Sawyer.* New York: Heritage Press.

Twain, M. (1885/1958). *The adventures of Huckleberry Finn.* Cambridge, MA: Harvard University Press.

Twain, M. (1924). *Mark Twain's autobiography, volumes I & II.* (1924). New York: Harper & Brothers.

Wainryb, C., Brehl, B. A., & Matwin, S. (2005). Being hurt and hurting others: Children's narrative accounts and moral judgments of their own interpersonal conflicts. *Monographs of the Society for Research in Child Development, 70*, 3, Serial No. 281.

Wainryb, C., & Turiel, E. (1994). Dominance, subordination, and concepts of personal entitlements in cultural contexts. *Child Development, 65*, 1701–1722.

Wikan, U. (1991). Toward an experience-near anthropology. *Cultural Anthropology, 6*, 285–305.

Wikan, U. (1996). *Tomorrow, God willing: Self-made destinies in Cairo.* Chicago: University of Chicago Press.

Wikan, U. (2002). *Generous betrayal: Politics of culture in the new Europe.* Chicago: University of Chicago Press.

Wynne, E. A. (1986). The great tradition in education: Transmitting moral values. *Educational Leadership, 43*, 4–9.

2

THE MORAL JUDGMENT OF THE
CHILD REEVALUATED

Heteronomy, Early Morality, and Reasoning
About Social Justice and Inequalities

Charles C. Helwig

Piaget's *Moral Judgment of the Child,* published in 1932, is one of those foundational works that has achieved iconic status in its field. The influence of Piaget's book is apparent in virtually every subarea of the field of moral judgment that has emerged since Piaget published his monograph (for reviews of research inspired by Piaget's original studies, see Lapsley, 1996; Lickona, 1976; Turiel, 1983). Breathtaking in both scope and depth, Piaget's book has served as a touchstone for several generations of moral development researchers and will no doubt continue to do so. It is no exaggeration to say that, whatever one's interests in moral development, Piaget was in some important sense there already, and much is to be gained from an engagement with his thinking, no matter whether one ultimately agrees or disagrees with him. All the more impressive is that Piaget published his foray into moral development at a relatively early stage in his career, and apart from a few scattered papers brought together in the volume *Sociological Studies* (Piaget, 1995), did not revisit the topic in any systematic way, despite significant revisions to his general cognitive-developmental theory throughout his lifetime.

In this chapter, I offer a reappraisal of Piaget's theory of moral judgment, considered in light of some of the current perspectives and findings in moral development research. Piaget's work is used as a springboard for consideration of some of the broader issues that continue to have currency in the moral development literature, including definitions of morality, characterizations of moral development and its relation to other forms of social knowledge, and questions regarding the origins or precursors of morality in infancy and early childhood. This discussion is, of necessity, both selective and framed in part as a critique, to tease out some problematic aspects of Piaget's position, especially regarding his propositions about moral heteronomy, and to draw some lessons from contemporary research. The strengths and limitations of Piaget's theory in providing an account of the development of judgments and reasoning about social inequalities and social justice are considered.

PIAGET'S LEGACY: MORALITY AS JUSTICE AND ITS ROOTS IN SOCIAL INTERACTIONS

Piaget's (1932) exegesis builds upon two fertile insights that were largely novel to psychological theorizing of the time. The first is that morality, in its most advanced or equilibrated form, is a system of understanding that is based on ideal reciprocity and therefore distinct from received customs, social norms, and the injunctions of authorities or other respected persons. The second insight, deriving from his overall constructivist approach, is that moral understandings are constructed out of the particular and varying properties of social interactions that individuals experience in their daily lives.

Piaget's definition of more adequate or equilibrated morality stood in contrast to those of virtually every extant psychological theory at the time, although the roots of his thinking may be found in Aristotle's (1947) distinction between justice and convention and in Kant's notion of the autonomous moral will (Kant, 1964). The prevailing perspectives on moral development in Piaget's day (and still, to some extent, our own) defined morality in terms of a collection of societal standards that individuals come to internalize in the process of development (Durkheim, 1961; Freud, 1961; Watson, 1925). As a result of the external sources of morality proposed by these other perspectives, the content of morality is thus variable, both in fact and in principle. Accordingly, in these views there can be no inherent direction to moral development in ontogeny, beyond that of a straightforward accommodation to existing cultural norms as these norms are transmitted to individuals by the environment and subsequently internalized.

Piaget held that morality does, at times, take the form of an external orientation, but he saw this as descriptive of more primitive forms of morality (both ontogenetically and sociogenetically) that are grounded on respect for authority or tradition. Unlike these other approaches, however, Piaget (1932) distinguishes between a morality of constraint and a morality of cooperation:

> In all spheres, two types of social relations must be distinguished: constraint and cooperation. The first implies an element of unilateral respect, of authority and prestige; the second is simply the intercourse between two individuals on an equal footing. (p. 53)

Piaget identifies the morality of constraint with the more or less blind acceptance of tradition, custom, hierarchy, and authority, and thus he saw it as essentially nonrational in nature. In contrast, the morality of cooperation (or autonomy) is founded upon reciprocal interactions between individuals who are equal partners in the relationship. In the morality of cooperation, the individual freely participates in the elaboration of moral norms and thus consents to be bound by them. Relations of cooperation produce a morality of justice or reciprocity, in which there is mutual respect between individuals and a corresponding obligation to take the perspective of the other in social exchanges. Reciprocal perspective-taking, through which the interests and perspectives of individuals become coordinated and brought into equilibrium, is fundamental to sustaining systems of cooperation. Its analogue within more advanced forms of moral understanding is the notion of ideal reciprocity or justice, as reflected in the morality of the Golden Rule, or to "Do by others as you would be done by."

Piaget proposes that these two moralities, those of heteronomy and autonomy, are developmentally ordered. After an initial, premoral period in which there may be self-imposed habits or rituals in the child's behavior without any sense of obligation, the child enters into the period of heteronomous morality. The dual emotions of affection and fear that the child feels toward his or her parents tend to produce in the child an intense feeling of respect for these more powerful and loved adults. Rules emanating from adult authorities become imbued with the same feelings of reverence and respect, generating for the first time a moral obligation in the form of duty. This sense of obligation exists within an early level of thought that is permeated by egocentrism, or a failure to distinguish objective reality from the child's own subjective states.

As a result of the inability to understand how rules and obligations are generated and function within systems of reciprocity or perspective-taking, the heteronomous child will tend to reify any rules received from adults, treating them as indistinguishable from physical regularities. According to Piaget (1932), the young child's view of rules is global, undifferentiated, and characterized by the necessity of obedience:

> Any act that shows obedience to a rule or even to an adult, regardless of what he may command, is good; any act that does not conform to rules is bad. A rule is therefore not in any way something elaborated, or even judged and interpreted, by the mind; it is given as such, ready made and external to the mind. It is also conceived of as revealed by the adult and imposed by him. The good, therefore, is rigidly defined by obedience. (p. 106)

The sources of heteronomy, according to Piaget, lie in two interrelated processes. The first, noted above, is the young child's egocentrism. The second is the nature of the young child's social interactions with adults, which Piaget believed primarily to take the form of constraint. Adults are the source of a plethora of injunctions, commands, rules, and imperatives that are imposed upon children and which the young child, because of his or her egocentrism and cognitive immaturity, is incapable of understanding and therefore reifies (moral realism). Adults assert their power and demand compliance, not just to exercise control for its own sake, but also in part because of the limitations in the child's understanding resulting from egocentrism.

Piaget believed that a movement away from heteronomy toward a morality of autonomy and reciprocity was only possible with two mutually reinforcing developments. In later childhood and early adolescence, the child's social relations move from a preponderance of adult–child interactions toward increasing relations with peers. The more equal status among peers leads to a shift in which cooperation becomes the dominant form of social interaction during this time. In the cognitive realm, the child's growing ability to engage in perspective-taking enables the child increasingly to take advantage of these cooperative social interactions by engaging in truly reciprocal interchanges.

Through these experiences, the child comes to construct a rational morality of reciprocity based on mutual respect that supplants the earlier heteronomous morality of duty. Accordingly, the child's stance on tradition or custom is re-evaluated along with this development. The child at the autonomous phase can "dissociate custom from the rational ideal" (Piaget, 1932, p. 64) such that "the rational notions of the just and the unjust become regulative of custom" (Piaget, 1932, p. 66). Rules, authority, and duties, then, are seen as justified only to the extent that they are subjected to the norms of reciprocity and accepted by autonomous moral agents, who play equal roles in the construction or maintenance of the rules.

The interrelated claims that true morality is defined in terms of reciprocity and that it is rooted in cooperative social interactions enabled Piaget to resolve a central problem of moral development: How can a morality that is, in some important sense, socially constructed be compatible with individuals' capacity to take a critical orientation toward existing social norms or practices? Accounting for the ability of individuals to draw on conceptions of justice in order to evaluate social reality continues to be a problem faced by many contemporary models of moral development, especially those that rely primarily on social or cultural transmission as explanatory mechanisms (e.g., Shweder, 1999; Shweder, Mahapatra, & Miller, 1987).

The answer, for Piaget, was that the forms of reciprocity that individuals construct at the highest levels represent an abstraction (i.e., ideal reciprocity) from the social interactions that they experience, rather than a strict internalization of these norms from the environment. Reciprocity for Piaget is at once a moral norm and a psychological form of equilibrium that act in concert to transform psychological functioning in ontogenesis (Chapman, 1988). As Piaget (1932) states:

> … reciprocity has two aspects: Reciprocity as a fact, and reciprocity as an ideal, as something which ought to be. The child begins by simply practicing reciprocity, in itself not so easy a thing as one might think. Then, once he has grown accustomed to this form of equilibrium in his actions, his behavior is altered from within, its form reacting, as it were, upon its content. What is regarded as just is no longer merely reciprocal action, but primarily behaviour that admits of indefinitely sustained reciprocity. (p. 323)

Piaget employed this notion of equilibrium in order to explain how the child's thinking moves from more concrete versions of reciprocity (e.g., revenge) toward more sophisticated and abstract ideals, based on norms such as the Golden Rule or on a conception of justice as equity. Abstract conceptions of justice such as these are formal in nature and thus not attached to any particular form of social organization (although they may or may not be instantiated in particular social practices). Reciprocity, for Piaget, thus begins in concrete social interactions and exchanges, but is transformed on the plane of thought to become, ultimately, the standard by which individuals evaluate social interaction itself.

HETERONOMY: A PROBLEMATIC CONSTRUCT FOR PIAGET'S CONSTRUCTIVISM

Piaget's emphasis on morality as justice, along with his constructivist theory of how morality is acquired, had a transformative effect on the field of moral development whose influence endures to this day. Piaget's proposition of a morality of autonomy that is distinct from received social customs and conventions is an insight that continues to motivate a variety of different versions of contemporary constructivist theories of moral development (e.g., Kohlberg, 1981; Turiel, 2006).

Piaget's legacy of respect for the child's rational autonomy is so legendary, however, that it is easy to overlook what he said about the heteronomy of the young child. It is revealing to unpack some of Piaget's claims about early moral development—especially heteronomy—as a way of illustrating some important divergences that have emerged between Piaget's views and those of some contemporary moral development perspectives that have descended from his constructivist paradigm. In several respects, Piaget's account of early moral development appears to depart from some of the tenets of constructivism as we have come to know it today, in large measure through Piaget's own work in other areas. This discussion sets the stage for an evaluation of some of Piaget's key propositions about early moral judgment, in light of contemporary research findings and theorizing.

As mentioned, Piaget's book on moral development is an early work, and thus heavily influenced by his ideas about egocentrism and childhood realism. Not surprisingly, his views on moral judgments sometimes diverge from his later account of cognitive development in ways that reflect the subsequent evolution of his thinking. (Some of these divergences, as well, may be due to unique aspects of his moral theory.) These points may be illustrated by way of a brief contrast with Piaget's more mature account of logical development, as represented in a series of works (e.g., Piaget, 1963, 1971, 1962) published just a few years after the moral judgment book.

Shortly after publishing *The Moral Judgment of the Child*, Piaget became dissatisfied with his earlier body of work, in part because of its focus on verbal explanations at the expense of efforts to uncover the origins of concepts in the child's direct actions on objects (Chapman, 1988). Piaget was subsequently led to examine the origins of logic and other concepts in concrete actions, including manipulations of objects in infancy. This strategy enabled him to discover parallels between forms of logical relations implicit in action and found early in development, and later developing, more explicit, or reflective understandings. For example, in his mature theory of logical development, Piaget drew connections between a sensorimotor, action-based logic of classes and relations (proto-operations) found in infancy, and a later, representational logic of classes and relations (operations) emerging in childhood.

These parallels between early and later forms of logic, one sensorimotor, one representational, allowed Piaget to chart out the continuities in the development of logic as well as the transformations (discontinuities) between different developmental periods. By identifying structural parallels between different levels, Piaget thus was able to account for developmental transformations in structural terms, in contrast to his earlier functional explanation of intellectual development in terms of social aspects of the child's thought (Chapman, 1988). Subsequent work, building on that of Piaget (Langer, 1980, 1986), has traced the development of logical and physical cognition, respectively, to early forms of part–whole and means–ends relations exhibited in manipulations of objects in infancy.

Piaget's account of moral development, by contrast, is notable for its emphasis on the discontinuities in moral development and for its reliance on functional psychological explanations, such as the role of affect in early morality. As one example of discontinuity, at the earliest levels (in infancy) morality is not even present at all (there is only a consciousness of self-imposed regularities or habits). More significantly, discontinuities are stressed in the contrast between the heteronomous and autonomous moral levels. For example, although heteronomy and autonomy, as moral systems, both share a concept of obligation, the sources and nature of obligation at each level are distinct.

At the heteronomous level, the source of obligation is affect, in the feelings of respect that attach to adults arising out of a confluence of the child's feelings of fear and love for them. These emotional processes account for the child's acceptance of the norms and rules imposed upon the child by adults (Piaget, 1932, p. 383). In contrast, at the autonomous level, obligation is cognitive in nature and derived from the reciprocity inherent in thought (and constructed out of new forms of social relations of cooperation). Piaget here draws a stark contrast between these developmental periods: Autonomous morality is operational (grounded in perspectivism) and rational, whereas heteronomous morality occupies the opposite, nonrational extreme in that the content of morality is purely externally derived, transmitted by adults, and grounded, at least in part, in affective processes (albeit working in conjunction with egocentrism).

This set of propositions ultimately poses problems for a truly constructivist account of moral development. Piaget's moral theory contains unresolved tensions because it combines constructs from incompatible theoretical perspectives (e.g., social transmission as an explanation of some aspects of early morality, such as its content, versus cognitive assimilation as an explanation of other aspects, such as moral realism or egocentrism). These tensions result in an account of early morality that is heavily functionalist in its contours, in contrast to his predominately structural account of later morality.

Indeed, Piaget's description of a young child who receives external moral norms from parents who are both feared and loved would not be one that we today would associate with constructivist accounts of moral development. These aspects of Piaget's position on heteronomy are striking as they are shared with other, rival theoretical accounts, such as Freudian theory and behaviorism. In part, these problematic features of Piaget's account of moral development may be a result of engagement with some of the prevailing perspectives on morality of his time, especially that of Durkheim (1961). By acknowledging Durkheim's societal explanation of a morality of duty, but in viewing it as developmentally prior to moral autonomy, Piaget may have unwittingly incorporated aspects of Durkheim's approach (i.e., a socially transmitted morality and an affectively determined account of moral obligation) in his efforts to characterize Durkheim's position as a real but "disequilibrated" level of morality. As a consequence, Piaget ended up with positions that are in many respects antithetical to his own mature structuralism.

A second problem pertains to inconsistencies in how Piaget accounted for apparent instances of early forms of moral emotion and reciprocity, such as empathy and sharing, observed in young children's natural behavior. Consistent with his general approach, Piaget suggests that these forms of putative moral behaviors and sensibilities are to be explained by subsuming them within egocentrism or heteronomy. For example, Piaget (1932; see pp. 283–284, and p. 317) characterized these behaviors as capricious and motivated either by adherence to the wishes of adults, or by an egocentric personal desire that resides only in the moment (with no attendant sense of obligation).

On the other hand, Piaget sometimes speaks of a morality of autonomy developing in parallel with the morality of heteronomy and even appearing from the beginning in development. On these occasions, early forms of sympathy and mutuality, found in young children's social relations, are described as precursors to the more advanced forms of reciprocity that characterize moral autonomy. As Piaget (1932) states:

> The relations between parents and children are certainly not only those of constraint. There is a spontaneous mutual affection, which from the first prompts the child to acts of generosity, and

even of self-sacrifice, to very touching demonstrations which are in no way prescribed. And here no doubt is the starting point for that morality of good which we shall see developing alongside of the morality of right or duty, and which in some persons completely replaces it. (pp. 193–194)

However, these remain only suggestive asides in Piaget's overall account of moral development, and the relation between these earlier forms of morality and later reciprocity or mutual respect is never fleshed out, even briefly. Furthermore, although Piaget acknowledges that both autonomy and heteronomy can be found in the thought and behavior of the child throughout development, including at the earliest periods, his overriding focus is on showing how autonomy supplants heteronomy in development. He does not consider in any depth the complex and multifaceted continuities and discontinuities in development that a full appreciation of this heterogeneity in moral thinking and experience might be expected to generate. In sum, to the extent that important precursors to later forms of morality are identified, but their role in development unaccounted for, the explanation of morality is incomplete. Even more important, these moral "precursors" do not sit well within Piaget's general description of the heteronomous level (except, of course, by subsumption).

The next section examines some of Piaget's general claims about heteronomy in light of some contemporary research and theorizing on moral development. These recent approaches may be seen as occupied with taking up the other neglected strand in Piaget's own thinking, in which the possibility of important continuities between earlier and later moral understandings is postulated. These contemporary perspectives also raise questions about whether it is legitimate to account for issues such as authority, custom, and social convention in people's moral thinking through a broad and all-encompassing construct such as heteronomy. The implications of this recent theorizing and research for several of Piaget's key propositions about moral judgment and behavior are drawn out, beginning with Piaget's views on the distinction between justice and authority.

HETERONOMY, EARLY MORALITY, AND THE DISTINCTION BETWEEN JUSTICE AND AUTHORITY

As noted earlier, one of the most important distinctions that Piaget makes in his moral judgment book is between a morality of justice and a heteronomous morality of authority or duty. Piaget claims that this distinction is made only in late childhood and is tied to social interactions among peers whereby, through the dynamic exchange of viewpoints in cooperative social interactions, children come to construct a morality of reciprocity. Piaget's contention that justice and authority are undifferentiated in the mind of the child is most directly represented in two lines of inquiry described in *The Moral Judgment of the Child*. One is an examination of children's understanding of rules in the children's game of marbles, and the other is an investigation of children's judgments about hypothetical situations in which justice conflicts with the demands of authority.

Investigating morality in the context of children's games may seem a rather odd choice, but it follows from Piaget's definition of morality and, more directly, from his assumption of an impressionable heteronomous child who is under the influence of adult authority and traditions. Piaget (1932, p. 1) defined the essence of morality as "respect for a system of rules," with the primary developmental issue being to account for the how rules come to be respected. His focus, then, was on whether rules are upheld through unilateral respect or through a rational process of agreement and consensus (the particular content of rules is thus irrelevant).

In line with his assumptions about the young child's heteronomy, one of Piaget's major concerns, evident throughout *The Moral Judgment of the Child*, is with separating the influences of received moral knowledge from children's own self-constructive processes. Correspondingly, Piaget's inquiry into the understanding of rules was framed by an interrogatory into beliefs about the origins of rules in the game of marbles to determine whether rules are maintained by mutual respect or by blind obedience to tradition. Consistent with the overall characterization of heteronomy and autonomy, younger children believed the rules of marbles to originate in adults or to have existed throughout all time, whereas older children explicitly identified the rules as having their source in mutual consent and agreement among the participants.

In the other relevant line of investigation, children were asked about situations involving conflicts between justice and authority, as when one child in a family is asked by a parent to assume the other child's chores when the other child has gone out to play. Piaget found that younger children were more likely to say that the child should obey the authority, and many of them even regarded the adult's command as just, whereas older children focused on the inequity and viewed such commands as unfair (and even worthy of disobedience).

Piaget's conclusions, however, are in contradiction to those of a large body of research, conducted over the last 25 years, exploring children's ability to distinguish morality and social convention (Turiel, 1983, 2006). Research examining children's conceptions of different types of social rules has shown that even very young children (beginning around three years of age) distinguish moral rules, based on justice and concern for others' welfare, from social-conventional rules and customs (Turiel, 1983).

In this research, children were probed directly about the underlying basis of social rules (i.e., whether the rightness or wrongness of social rules and the acts they prescribe are viewed as contingent on punishment, authority, or the existence of explicit social sanctions). Moral rules involving harmful consequences or injustice toward others are viewed as necessary and generalized across social contexts (e.g., other countries), and the acts they regulate are viewed as wrong even in the absence of punishment, authority commands, or explicit social rules. In contrast, social-conventional rules (e.g., conventions and customs regulating behavior in social systems such as social-organizational rules, etiquette, forms of address, etc.) are viewed as variable across different social systems, and the wrongness of the acts they regulate are judged to be contingent on punishment, authority, and the existence of explicit social sanctions.

In addition to making these kinds of discriminations, children appeal to different types of issues when reasoning about these different kinds of rules. Moral rules are associated with justifications pertaining to the harmful consequences of actions for others or to explicit norms of fairness, whereas social-conventional rules are justified with reference to features of social organization, such as authority, punishment, and maintenance of social order.

It has been proposed that these different conceptions of rules are related to different domains of social understanding that children construct out of social interactions (Smetana, 2006; Turiel, 1983). The moral domain is comprised of concepts of harm, rights, and justice, and reflects children's reasoning about events entailing these kinds of consequences that they experience in their daily lives. In contrast, children develop concepts of social conventions as behavioral uniformities that coordinate human interactions in social organizations and ensure the smooth functioning of social systems. As part of the social-conventional domain, children construct understandings of a variety of issues pertinent to human interaction in social systems, such as authority, social-organizational rules and regulations, social roles, and status (Turiel, 1983). These social-conventional understandings are seen as separate from moral concerns with justice and human welfare, although they may be in tension with moral understandings in certain instances.

The research findings from social domain theory necessitate a rethinking of the origins of early moral and social-conventional understandings, as given in Piaget's account. For one, the origin of the distinction between justice and authority (or morality and social convention) does not appear to reside in late childhood or early adolescence, as Piaget thought. Furthermore, this distinction does not appear to rest solely on the establishment of complex cooperative systems of peer interaction, as described by Piaget, but happens during the time in which children's social life is heavily dominated by interactions with adults (along with the beginnings of significant interactions with peers).

Instead of portraying moral development in terms of the succession of two distinct, qualitatively different systems of understanding (heteronomy and autonomy), the contemporary research reveals important continuities between morality in early childhood and later on, calling for further consideration of the roots of morality in early social interactions. Research from a variety of other theoretical perspectives, discussed subsequently, has called into question other aspects of Piaget's characterization of heteronomy, including childhood egocentrism, the interpretation of early empathic reactions, and the role of adults in moral development.

Piaget's insight that moral development hinges upon the ability to distinguish self from other and to take the perspective of the other in social exchanges is shared by many contemporary accounts of early moral development (e.g., Hoffman, 2000). Because of the effects of egocentrism and heteronomy, however, Piaget did not describe these processes as relevant to the moral life of very young children. Several avenues of contemporary research, however, have challenged these conclusions.

Recent research has found that certain types of psychological perspective-taking develop much earlier than is suggested by Piaget's account of the egocentric young child. For example, research on children's developing theories of mind has shown that, beginning around two years of age, children distinguish between their own desires and those of others, and they are capable of reasoning about some of the implications that follow from this distinction when predicting others' behavior (Wellman & Bartsch, 1994). By three to four years of age, they begin to understand similar sorts of distinctions with respect to beliefs, including the role of false beliefs in predicting individuals' behavior.

These early perspective-taking abilities may facilitate the development of social understandings by giving young children access to the products of discursive interchanges with others, as pertaining to matters such as straightforward issues of truth or fact, psychological knowledge, and even early normative understandings (Tomasello &

Rakoczy, 2003). Piaget's proposition that dialogical exchanges of this sort are instrumental in enabling the child to decenter from his or her own viewpoint is supported by research examining the role of language in children's attainment of theory of mind. For example, Lohmann and Tomasello (2003) found that certain kinds of linguistic interactions, such as "perspective shifting discourse," in which adults point out contrasting perspectives on events, is associated with advances in the development of theory of mind.

Other research (Jenkins & Astington, 1996) has found that children with siblings attain a theory of mind at a faster rate than those without, presumably a result of the sustained psychological interactions more likely to occur between children in such families. These findings lend support to Piaget's general claims about the role of social interactions in overcoming childhood egocentrism, especially regarding discourse centering around the exchange of perspectives, although both peers and adults may contribute importantly to this process.

As noted, Piaget was skeptical about the part played by empathic reactions and early altruistic behaviors in the young child's moral life, because he did not see these reactions as genuinely motivated by a sense of obligation. However, the finding of true (i.e., obligatory) moral concepts in young children, based on concern for others' welfare, may have removed the major objection. Indeed, a recent comprehensive review (e.g., Eisenberg, 2000) of both experimental and naturalistic studies has concluded that children as young as two years of age experience genuine moral feelings of empathy, as evidenced by guilt reactions and unsolicited reparative behavior after transgressions. In other words, young children do not appear to be expressing empathy or altruism solely for egoistic ends or in order to please adults. These empathic reactions, along with the moral emotion of guilt, appear to be developing at around the same time that children are constructing understandings of psychological states of other people, as suggested by the theory of mind research.

It seems plausible, then, that children may be drawing on their perspective-taking and empathic capacities, in conjunction with their developing knowledge about psychological and physical harm, in constructing early moral understandings. Turiel (1983), for example, has suggested that young children may use their perspective-taking and counterfactual reasoning abilities to construct different inferences about moral and social-conventional events. From direct experience with consequences associated with moral events such as harm, a child may "Connect his or her own experience of pain (an undesirable consequence) to the observed experience of the victim" (Turiel, 1983, p. 43), leading to inferences about the undesirability of these acts. For moral events, the presence of an institutional system (rules, authority, etc.) is not necessary for the child to begin to make a moral judgment, although reflective processes such as perspective-taking and moral emotions such as empathy are likely components of this process.

The process of constructing social-conventional understandings may be somewhat different. Unlike moral acts, there is no intrinsic pre-scriptive basis for violations of social conventions (such as a child call-ing her teacher by her first name when there is a school rule requiring that children address their teachers by titles). Instead, the rightness or wrongness of these acts depends on the presence of a social-organiza-tional system with explicit rules, authoritative commands, and general expectations. Children's ability to connect the consequences of rule violations to these features of social systems (and thereby to recognize their contingent nature) underlies the capacity to construct social-con-ventional understandings (Turiel, 1983). Propositions such as these emphasizing children's active, rational processes in the formation of early social and moral concepts help to restore the focus on construc-tivism relegated to the background in Piaget's depiction of the heter-onomous young child.

In addition to these sources in inferences drawn from directly expe-rienced social events, contemporary research also has shown that the adult–child relationship may enhance or contribute to early moral development in ways not anticipated (or even precluded) within Piag-et's account. For example, in the context of moral interactions, children experience communications from both children (e.g., victims) and adults (parents, authorities) about these events. If young children are responsive to the features of moral events, it follows that adults also may play a genuine role in the development of moral judgments, for example, by providing information about the consequences of events, including pointing out unobservable psychological reactions, directing the child's attention to moral matters, and insisting that the child take these aspects of situations into consideration (Hoffman, 2000; Smetana, 2006).

Piaget was reluctant to give adult teachings a significant part in early moral development, because he believed that such communica-tions would be perceived by children as "lecturing" and constraint, and thus would only serve to reinforce heteronomy (Piaget, 1932, p. 133). Instead, Piaget believed that adults should interact with children as equals and instruct by example (Piaget, 1932, p. 194). However, results from numerous studies (reviewed in Eisenberg, 2000) examining the relation between parental socialization strategies and the development of moral internalization have shown that use of reasoning (termed "induction") is the most effective method in producing an internalized moral orientation, or conscience, in the child. (Other methods, such as simple power assertion, are associated with an externalized morality leading to obedience only in the face of threat of punishment). These findings are consistent with Piaget's propositions regarding the importance of reasoning and justification for morality, but they are inconsistent with the specific role that he gave to adults deriving from the assumption of childhood heteronomy.

As mentioned earlier, Piaget himself said that adult–child relations were not only characterized by constraint, but included mutuality, and yet he focused mainly on adult constraint in his account of moral development. However, other aspects of the adult–child relationship need to be examined and their role in the formation of early moral understandings accounted for. Recently, socialization researchers have begun to distinguish between types of adult–child interactions in ways that parallel some of Piaget's distinctions (and adding other types of relations that Piaget did not describe). For example, in a recent review, distinctions have been drawn between adult–child relations entailing hierarchy and power, mutuality and reciprocity, and relations of protection and care (Bugenthal & Grusec, 2006).

Some researchers have begun to explore the early forms of mutuality and reciprocity in adult–child interactions (even extending back to infancy), demonstrating, for example, positive linkages between adult–child mutuality and reciprocity in the toddler years, and later outcomes on various measures of morality (e.g., Kochanska & Murray, 2000). The reciprocity characterizing the early parent–child relationship may provide a context in which infants and very young children experience the earliest forms of mutual trust that serve as a foundation for the later construction of reflective conceptions of interpersonal trust and fairness (Watson, 2004).

Much of the relevant theorizing and research in these areas is motivated by other theoretical perspectives, such as attachment theory, evolutionary psychology, and socialization theory, but a constructivist reinterpretation of these findings is warranted. In general, these studies lend support to Piaget's propositions about the central role of social relations characterized by reciprocity in moral functioning and development, but not, however, to his claim that reciprocal relations in the peer context are the only or most significant ones for moral development.

CHILDREN'S SOCIAL AND MORAL JUDGMENTS: IMPLICATIONS FOR SOCIAL INEQUALITIES AND SOCIAL JUSTICE

Piaget's ideas about moral autonomy are highly relevant to judgments and reasoning about social inequality and social injustice. A strength of Piaget's distinction between the two moralities of autonomy and constraint is that it enabled Piaget to identify the negative effects of constraint on children's moral development, leading him to champion democratic forms of child rearing and education that emphasized the cultivation of children's rational autonomy and active participation. For example, Piaget was an early critic of authoritarian parenting, and in the more casual observations found in his moral judgment book he identified some of the negative effects of the use of power assertion in child discipline (see Piaget, 1932, pp. 190–191).

In the realm of education, Piaget's thinking has led to whole schools of constructivist pedagogy based on cooperative learning that have attempted to put his recommendations for a more democratic style of education into effect in the classroom, often with promising results (DeVries & Zan, 1994). Regarding moral education, Piaget was a major inspiration for Kohlberg's innovation of the "just schools," in which students are given a say, through a democratic social structure, in formulating and implementing school rules and policy (Power, Higgens, & Kohlberg, 1989). For Piaget, however, moral autonomy is something that is achieved and understood rather late in development. In contrast, the contemporary findings on early moral concepts reviewed earlier indicate that young children construct moral understandings in their daily experience that are genuine and not based on authority, punishment, or social convention (custom). In a sense, their moral world is more rational than Piaget anticipated, to the extent that young children's moral understandings are not determined by blind adherence to authority or tradition.

This conclusion has implications for children's capacity to take a critical perspective on social institutions and social organization, discussed in turn. However, it also may be said that children's social-conventional understandings are more sophisticated than Piaget has described. The contrast Piaget draws between a morality of justice and one of authority leads him to define social rationality exclusively in terms of morality (reciprocity), and thus to characterize hierarchical social formations based on authority, custom, and tradition as devoid of any rational basis. As others have suggested (Crittenden, 1990), Piaget's account seems to neglect a consideration of rational authority.

Piaget's underestimation of the rationality of hierarchical social organization may be seen through considering more recent research findings on children's developing understandings of social convention, social-organizational rules, and authority (Dodsworth-Rugani, 1982; Laupa & Turiel, 1986; Turiel, 1983). Children's conceptions of social conventions undergo a structural developmental progression in which understandings of the elements of social systems become increasingly abstract and sophisticated (Turiel, 1983). For example, at earlier levels, social-conventional rules are seen as maintaining social structure by controlling the behavior of individuals and defining their role obligations. At more advanced levels, social-conventional rules are seen as coordinating the interactions of individuals through shared understandings that allow members of the system to achieve their goals.

In a series of studies on children's conceptions of authority (summarized in Laupa, Turiel, & Cowan, 1995), young children were found to conceptualize and reason about adult authority with respect to the roles and functions of social systems. For example, young children believed that obedience to adults was contingent on the adult occupying a position within a social system (e.g., a teacher in a school, a parent in a family); adults who did not hold these positions did not have to be obeyed. In this research, children did not exhibit an undifferentiated view of adult authority, as implied by heteronomy, but saw authority as an embedded function existing within a defined social system with particular goals (e.g., education).

These findings have implications for the contrast Piaget draws between systems of social organization based on authority and those based on reciprocity or cooperation. As part of the dichotomy between reciprocity (cooperation) and constraint, Piaget defined moral rationality at the autonomous level as entailing democratic forms of cooperation (i.e., as in a society of equals based on mutual consent). The democratic model that Piaget used to illustrate his moral ideal, however, is probably both an idealized vision of the realities of peer interaction in adolescence, and a restricted model of legitimate social organization in general. Piaget's two poles—constraint-based hierarchy versus egalitarian democracy—do not fully take into account the multifaceted nature of social life, including that experienced by adults.

Individuals participate in a variety of social institutions having both hierarchical and democratic (egalitarian) structures, sometimes even within the same institution. To the extent that hierarchical social structures are seen as efficient means for meeting certain social-organizational goals, they may be upheld and accepted by individuals (provided that the implications of such hierarchy are not judged seriously to infringe upon individual autonomy or otherwise implicate injustices). Research on adults' conceptions of the legitimacy of social institutions has found that hierarchical institutions can be, and often are, viewed by adults as legitimate, as long as authorities within these institutions follow appropriate procedural justice mechanisms in dealing with subordinates and in handling conflicts (Tyler, 2001). Thus, justice may be compatible with (and not necessarily opposed to) hierarchy and authority in many circumstances.

In other instances, however, authority may conflict with the requirements of justice. Piaget investigated the relation between justice and authority in the context of conflicts in which an authority issues commands that have implications for justice (e.g., a parent commands that a child in a family assume the chores of another child). This methodology stems from Piaget's contention that authority is essentially nonrational, and hence the conflict is framed as one between heteronomy and justice. However, the findings of the research on social domains suggest that children develop notions of authority that are related to their conceptions of social systems, such as the division of roles and responsibilities within different social institutions, including the unequal role obligations that may hold within social hierarchies such as the family.

Thus, the types of situations used in Piaget's research may be seen from this perspective as implicating both social-organizational issues, such as the division of labor and role obligations within the family in the service of accomplishing goals as defined by authorities, as well as moral notions of fairness (e.g., equality in the distribution of role-related duties or obligations). In Piaget's research, young children were found to be more likely to judge that the commands of authorities in such situations should be followed, but it is unclear whether in these instances young children are merely prioritizing social-organizational goals over justice, or defining fairness in terms of obedience to authority, as Piaget suggests.

However, other research directly investigating young children's judgments about hypothetical instances in which authorities issue immoral commands indicates that even young children do not hold a view of the good as "rigidly defined by obedience." For example, research by Damon (1977) and Laupa and Turiel (1986) found that young children do not accept as legitimate adult commands to engage in acts that have moral consequences for others' welfare, such as theft or causing harm. Similarly, Helwig and Jasiobedzka (2001) found that six-year-old children take a critical perspective on societal laws that conflict with moral demands of fairness, such as hypothetical laws that discriminate against others on the basis of physical characteristics or income. Discriminatory laws such as these were viewed not only as unfair, but even as worthy of violation.

Interestingly, Piaget (1932, pp. 284–285) reports similar findings for one of his own studies examining judgments about the fairness of a common practice in children's experience of his day, that of shopkeepers making children wait while all the adults in the store were served first. The majority of six-year-olds, "with astonishing precocity," according to Piaget, judged this practice to be unfair, and maintained that children should be treated equally as adults. Piaget leaves these results largely uncommented on, and does not attempt to explain the discrepancy between this finding and those of his other studies of justice and authority. But one possibility, suggested by the social domain research, is that children are capable of distinguishing justice and authority—and even prioritizing justice—in situations in which there are no competing and rationally compelling social-organizational concerns. When salient moral and social-organizational goals are in conflict, however, the picture becomes more complex and the developmental patterns harder to predict.

How individuals construe and evaluate complex social reality in situations that entail potential conflicts between moral and social-conventional considerations is not a simple straightforward process. For example, individuals may either construe such situations exclusively in terms of one or the other social domains or attend to both aspects of complex situations but prioritize moral or social-conventional concerns in different ways in different situations.

All of this is potentially influenced by developmental factors (Turiel, 1983, 2006). Developmentally, then, there is no expectation that children's social reasoning necessarily would move from an emphasis on social-conventional aspects of social systems (authority, tradition, custom) at earlier ages toward a greater emphasis on moral concerns, including rights and justice later on. Instead, there may be complex patterns in which individuals at different ages alternately give priority to moral and social-conventional considerations, depending, in part, on conceptual development within each of these domains and on the development of abilities to successfully coordinate particular types of judgments and reasoning across these domains.

Recent research bearing on some of these issues has explored directly children's reasoning about their own autonomy in the context of judgments about different ways (democratic or authority-oriented) of making decisions in social groups (Helwig & Kim, 1999). In this research, conducted with Canadian elementary-school-aged children and adolescents, participants were asked to evaluate three different procedures for making group decisions involving children in a variety of social contexts: consensus (everyone agrees), majority rule (voting), and unilateral decision making by adult authorities (e.g., parents or teachers). The first two procedures (consensus and majority rule) may be seen as representing Piaget's model of autonomous, cooperative decision making, in which children are equal participants in the process.

The results of this research revealed that, across a wide age range, participants distinguished among social contexts and different decisions in deciding whether group decision making should take a democratic (egalitarian) or authority-oriented (hierarchical) form (Helwig & Kim, 1999). For example, decisions about school curriculum tended to be seen as best left up to teachers to decide, because of teachers' greater perceived competence and experience pertaining to goals in educational contexts (i.e., learning). In contrast, decisions about other matters, such as where a school class should go on a field trip, were seen as having a recreational component and best made democratically (e.g., by the vote of the class). These findings show that, even in hierarchical social contexts such as a school classroom, children sometimes endorse group decision making that emphasizes children's own autonomy.

Conversely, other findings from this research show that even in egalitarian peer contexts, children sometimes endorse hierarchical decision making favoring adult authority. For instance, when presented with an example of a group of children who were deciding on the choice of a movie to view together, many children and adolescents did not support children's autonomy to make these decisions by themselves. In these instances, concern over potentially harmful or age-inappropriate content in the media that children might be exposed to led individuals to prefer decision making by adults (e.g., parents). In general, the findings of this research reveal heterogeneity in reasoning, within and across social contexts, that cannot be interpreted in terms of a global orientation emphasizing either adult authority or child autonomy.

Moreover, the developmental patterns found in this research were not consistent with what might be expected from Piaget's account. There was no general progression, with age, toward greater endorsement of children's own autonomy in group decision making. In fact, the youngest children in this study (six-year-olds) were more likely than older children or adolescents to endorse democratic procedures, such as consensus, across the different types of social contexts and decisions. In other words, in judging diverse examples, younger children were more likely to consider exclusively children's need for input and autonomy, at the expense of other issues (e.g., goals of educational systems or the protection of children). Older participants, however, took into account not only children's need for autonomy and input but also their competence level and the goals of different situations in order to draw distinctions between occasions in which either democratic or authority-oriented decision making was believed to be appropriate.

Overall, these findings are consistent with a model of social reasoning that proposes the co-existence of diverse concerns of both a moral and social-conventional nature in individuals' thinking that become coordinated and applied to situations in increasingly sophisticated ways in development (Turiel, 2006). A similar pattern, in which children's autonomy is sometimes endorsed and sometimes subordinated to authority, has been found in research investigating the development of reasoning about children's rights to freedom of speech and religion (e.g., Helwig, 1997), and in reasoning about teacher-centered and child-centered educational practices in school classrooms (Helwig, Ryerson, & Prencipe, 2003).

The idea that even very young children possess moral understandings that may be in tension with social-conventional aspects of social systems has implications for another of Piaget's propositions: that of the effects of constraint. Piaget assumed that constraint was likely to reinforce heteronomy, especially in young children, who would reify adult commands and authority. (Piaget believed this would apply even to adults in very stratified, traditional cultures; see Piaget, 1932, pp. 334–341.) However, if children have genuine moral understandings that are separate from authority and customs, then the possibility arises that constraint may produce the opposite effect (i.e., an accentuation of feelings of unfairness). Note that it was the youngest children in Helwig and Kim (1999), presumably those who experience the highest amounts of adult constraint and have the least autonomy in school settings, who were most likely to endorse children's democratic participation regarding curriculum decisions in the classroom.

Interestingly, a similar result has been found in a cross-cultural replication of this study with adolescents from urban and rural regions of mainland China (Helwig, Arnold, Tan, & Boyd, 2003). In that study, Chinese adolescents, who experience a much more hierarchical educational system and have much less autonomy in academic decision making than adolescents in Western educational settings, were found to be more likely to prefer children's democratic input into curriculum decisions than were Canadian children and adolescents. Others have discussed at length the complexities pertaining to judgments of hierarchical practices that are perceived as unfair or overly restrictive, drawing on data from a variety of other cultural contexts (see Turiel, this volume; Wikan, this volume). The effects of constraint on moral judgments, either those of young children or those of adolescents and adults from traditional cultures, do not appear to be solely as Piaget suggested.

In sum, Piaget's postulate of two broad forms of morality that are systematically ordered in development, one nonrational in nature and based on hierarchy and acceptance of inequality and one rational in nature and based on democratic equality, fails to capture the heterogeneity of children's (and adults') social and moral understandings. The research from the social domain perspective has shown that children develop rational understandings of diverse aspects of social life, including concepts of hierarchical social organizations and systems as well as moral notions of justice, equality, and rights. Furthermore, by viewing the morality of authority (heteronomy) and the morality of justice (autonomy) as ordered phases in development, Piaget's model fails to account for younger children's ability to apply moral notions of justice to evaluate social organization.

CONCLUSIONS

Piaget's greatest and enduring contribution to the study of moral judgment is his insight that morality is more than merely the duties and requirements imposed by society, acquired through a copy model of development or internalized; morality is a system of justification of social actions that is defined by reciprocity and whose origin is in social relations of mutuality and cooperation. Nothing in this review of some of the research and theorizing that has transpired since Piaget's landmark study diminishes this fundamental insight, and much supports it.

In his fledgling book on moral judgment, however, Piaget simply did not carry this insight as far as he might have taken it, to explore the roots of morality in very early forms of social interactions having these properties, including those that young children experience with adults as partners. This would have led him to recognize the important ways in which even young children develop a moral perspective from which to critique authority and existing social organization.

On the other hand, in his effort to distinguish a rational morality of cooperation and reciprocity from a morality of duty based on authority, Piaget overdrew this distinction in a way that led him to subsume all of social rationality within moral rationality. He thereby failed to appreciate the other forms of social rationality found throughout development (such as those pertaining to reasoning about social-conventional systems). As argued here and illustrated in many findings from contemporary research, social rationality is of different types, of which moral rationality is but one, albeit highly important, form. Understanding the roots of early moral behavior and thinking is one unfinished strand of Piaget's work. Describing and explaining how moral understandings intersect throughout development in complex ways with other social concepts, such as authority and social convention, is yet another.

ACKNOWLEDGMENTS

Preparation of this chapter was supported by a grant from the Social Sciences and Humanities Research Council of Canada. I would like to thank John Gibbs and the editors for comments on an earlier version of the chapter.

REFERENCES

Aristotle. (1947). *Introduction to Aristotle*. New York: Random House.

Bugental, D. B., & Grusec, J. E. (2006). Socialization processes. In W. Damon and R. M. Lerner (Series Eds.) & N. Eisenberg (Vol. Ed.) *Handbook of Child Psychology*. Vol. 3: *Social, emotional, and personality development* (6th ed., pp. 366–428), New York: Wiley.

Chapman, M. (1988). *Constructive evolution*. Cambridge, UK: Cambridge University Press.

Crittendon, P. (1990). *Learning to be moral*. Atlantic Highlands, NJ: Humanities Press.

Damon, W. (1977). *The social world of the child*. San Francisco: Jossey-Bass.

DeVries, R., & Zan, B. (1994). *Moral classrooms, moral children: Creating a constructivist atmosphere in early education*. New York: Teachers College Press.

Dodsworth-Rugani, K. J. (1982). *The development of concepts of social structure and their relationship to school rules and authority*. Unpublished doctoral dissertation, University of California, Berkeley.

Durkheim, E. (1961). *Moral education*. Glencoe, IL: Free Press.

Eisenberg, N. (2000). Emotion, regulation, and moral development. *Annual Review of Psychology, 51*, 665–697.

Freud, S. (1961). *Civilization and its discontents*. New York: Norton.

Helwig, C. C. (1997). The role of agent and social context in judgments of freedom of speech and religion. *Child Development, 68*, 484–495.

Helwig, C. C., Arnold, M. L., Tan, D., & Boyd, D. (2003). Chinese adolescents' reasoning about democratic and authority-based decision making in peer, family, and school contexts. *Child Development, 74*, 783–800.

Helwig, C. C., & Jasiobedzka, U. (2001). The relation between law and morality: Children's reasoning about socially beneficial and unjust laws. *Child Development, 72*, pp. 1382–1393.

Helwig, C. C., & Kim, S. (1999). Children's evaluations of decision making procedures in peer, family, and school contexts. *Child Development, 70*, 502–512.

Helwig, C. C., Ryerson, R. H., & Prencipe, A. (2003, June). *Children's, adolescents', and adults' evaluations of different methods of teaching values.* Poster presented at the biennial meeting of the Society for Research in Child Development, Tampa, FL.

Hoffman, M. L. (2000). *Empathy and moral development: Implications for caring and justice.* Cambridge, UK: Cambridge University Press.

Jenkins, J. M., & Astington, J. W. (1996). Cognitive factors and family structure associated with theory of mind development in young children. *Developmental Psychology, 32*, 70–78.

Kant, I. (1964). *Groundwork of the metaphysic of morals.* New York: Harper & Row.

Kochanska, G., & Murray, K. T. (2000). Mother-child mutually responsive orientation and conscience development: From toddler to early school age. *Child Development, 71*, 417–431.

Kohlberg, L. (1981). *Essays on moral development. Vol. 1: The philosophy of moral development.* San Francisco: Harper & Row.

Langer, J. (1980). *The origins of logic: Six to twelve months.* New York: Academic Press.

Langer, J. (1986). *The origins of logic: One to two years.* New York: Academic Press.

Lapsley, D. (1996). *Moral psychology.* Boulder, CO: Westview.

Laupa, M., & Turiel, E. (1986). Children's conceptions of adult and peer authority. *Child Development, 57*, 405–412.

Laupa, M., Turiel, E., & Cowan, P. A. (1995). Obedience to authority in children and adults. In M. Killen & D. Hart (Eds.), *Morality in everyday life: Developmental perspectives* (pp. 131–165). Cambridge, UK: Cambridge University Press.

Lickona, T. (1976). Research on Piaget's theory of moral development. In T. Lickona (Ed.), *Moral development and behavior* (pp. 219–240). New York: Holt, Rinehart & Winston.

Lohmann, H., & Tomasello, M. (2003). The role of language in the development of false belief understanding: A training study. *Child Development, 74*, 1130–1144.

Piaget, J. (1932). *The moral judgment of the child.* London: Routledge & Kegan Paul.

Piaget, J. (1962). *Play, dreams, and imitation in childhood.* New York: Norton.

Piaget, J. (1963). *The origins of intelligence in children.* New York: Norton.

Piaget, J. (1966). *The child's conception of physical causality.* London: Routledge & Kegan Paul.

Piaget, J. (1971). *The construction of reality in the child.* New York: Ballantine.

Piaget, J. (1995). *Sociological studies.* London: Routledge.

Power, F. C., Higgins, A., & Kohlberg, L. (1989). *Kohlberg's approach to moral education.* New York: Columbia University Press.

Shweder, R. A. (1999). Why cultural psychology? *Ethos, 27,* 62–73.

Shweder, R. A., Mahapatra, M., & Miller, J. G. (1987). Culture and moral development. In J. Kagan & S. Lamb (Eds.), *The emergence of morality in young children* (pp. 1–83). Chicago: University of Chicago Press.

Smetana, J. G. (2006). Social-cognitive domain theory: Consistencies and variations in children's moral and social judgments. In M. Killen & J. G. Smetana (Eds.), *Handbook of moral development.* Mahwah, NJ: Lawrence Erlbaum.

Tomasello, M., & Rakoczy, H. (2003). What makes human cognition unique? From individual to shared collective intentionality. *Mind & Language, 18,* 121–147.

Turiel, E. (1983). *The development of social knowledge: Morality and convention.* Cambridge, UK: Cambridge University Press.

Turiel, E. (2006). Moral development. In W. Damon and R. M. Lerner (Series Eds.) & N. Eisenberg (Vol. Ed.), *Handbook of Child Psychology.* Vol. 3: *Social, emotional, and personality development* (6th ed., pp. 789–857). New York: Wiley.

Tyler, T. R. (2001). A psychological perspective on the legitimacy of institutions and authorities. In J. T. Jost & B. Major (Eds.), *The psychology of legitimacy* (pp. 416–436). Cambridge, UK: Cambridge University Press.

Watson, J. B. (1925). *Behaviorism.* Chicago: University of Chicago Press.

Watson, M. S. (2004). Trust, attachment theory, and moral education. *AME Newsletter, 20*(2), pp. 11–14.

Wellman, H. M., & Bartsch, K. (1994). Before belief: Children's early psychological understanding. In C. Lewis & P. Mitchell (Eds.), *Children's early understanding of mind: Origins and development* (pp. 331–354). Hillsdale, NJ: Lawrence Erlbaum.

3

AMERICA'S HEAD START PROGRAM
An Effort for Social Justice[*]

Edward Zigler and Sally J. Styfco

It is appropriate that the Head Start story be included in a volume centered on the theme of social justice. The birth of Head Start was part of a massive national effort to provide both social justice and parity to impoverished U.S. residents whose life circumstances had removed them from America's mainstream. These families lived in blighted urban centers as well as poor, rural areas where decent education and job opportunities were elusive. Their plight was made vividly clear in Michael Harrington's (1962) aptly named book, *The Other America*. The story of horrid poverty existing in one of the wealthiest nations on earth incited voters and their elected officials to do something about it.

The birth of Head Start also intersected with the civil rights movement of the 1960s, another visible effort in the pursuit of social justice. The demands for economic equity and for civil rights naturally intertwined, given the fact that a disproportionate percentage of families living in poverty were racial and ethnic minorities. Civil rights leaders including Martin Luther King, Jr. and Marian Wright Edelman were aware that achieving civil rights would be a meaningless victory if people remained trapped in poverty.

---

[*]This chapter is based on an address delivered at the Annual Meeting of the Jean Piaget Society in June 2004.

The battle for economic justice and social equality was led by a populist president, Lyndon Johnson, who hoped to complete the job begun by his role model, Franklin Roosevelt (Caro, 1982). Just as Roosevelt created his New Deal to address the Great Depression of the 1930s, Johnson envisioned his Great Society and announced a national War on Poverty to begin building it. To spearhead his effort, Johnson created the Office of Economic Opportunity (OEO), named in a manner consistent with Americans' value system. Middle-class or mainstream socioeconomic status could never be mandated or achieved through federal redistribution of wealth in this strongly democratic nation. In keeping with the values of independence and personal responsibility, individuals were to be given opportunities to help themselves get ahead, an approach that has resonated since America's founding days.

To lead his War on Poverty, Johnson selected a dynamic and visionary public servant, Sargent Shriver. Shriver had once served on the school board for the city of Chicago. Later, he led the very successful Peace Corps effort. He was married to Eunice Kennedy Shriver, the sister of the late President John Kennedy. The Kennedy family held a strong interest in the cause of children with mental retardation. President Johnson also had a background in education, which explains his receptivity to the Head Start program. Johnson came out of the hardscrabble hill country of Texas and planned to become a teacher, attending Southwestern Texas State Teacher's College (now Southwestern Texas State University). Like many Americans, Johnson saw education as the ladder enabling people to achieve higher social and economic well-being. He once told the first author, "If it weren't for education, today I'd be following the south end of a north-bound mule."

Thus, the Johnson administration was fully committed to reducing the social and economic inequalities apparent in the country, and education was treated as an important weapon in the War on Poverty arsenal. The battle cry of this period was, "No American child shall be condemned to failure by the accident of his birth" (Johnson, in Zigler & Valentine, 1997, p. 72). In addition to Head Start, Title I of the Elementary and Secondary Education Act was enacted to provide funds to the states to improve the education of poor children in schools throughout America (Arroyo & Zigler, 1993). Although most of the War on Poverty initiatives have long ago been dismantled, both Title I and Head Start continue to be major federal programs.

Another indication of President Johnson's personal commitment to the Head Start program was the decision to make his wife, Lady Byrd Johnson, the honorary chairperson. First Ladies are very selective in the projects they lend their names to and usually limit their involvement to one or two significant agendas. Not only did Mrs. Johnson work very hard at her Head Start task, but the two Johnson daughters also became active in the effort.

But what was Head Start to be? There was little said about Head Start in the bill that created OEO, and the program never had its own autonomous unit in that office. It was placed in the Community Action Program (CAP), which set up local community agencies to empower residents to improve their quality of life. These agencies became problematic in their efforts to mobilize the poor to gain political power and demand that local needs be addressed.

This social activism was met with considerable resistance, fueled by the fact that the federal funding stream bypassed state and local officials and went directly to community action agencies. What the social activists and community action leaders learned is that when you fight the system, the system quickly fights back. Furthermore, the CAP people had their own idea of what Head Start should be, even prior to any deliberation by the planning committee that was to design the new program. They saw the purpose of Head Start as changing the face of communities and as an instrument to empower the poor families living there (Greenberg, 2004; Schweinhart, 2003). Sargent Shriver had a different vision for Head Start, however, and the program was essentially his creation and that of the planning committee, not the Community Action agency under him.

The history of Head Start thus tells a story of efforts and obstacles in one of the major campaigns for economic justice and social equality undertaken during the last half of the 20th century. In telling the Head Start story, we include the personal perspective and first-hand experiences of the first author. (We use the convenience of referring to him by name in those accounts of his involvement.) Zigler was initially a member of the planning committee formed to design the program. Subsequently, he was appointed as the federal official responsible for the program when he served as the first director of the Office of Child Development within the Department of Health, Education and Welfare. A recounting of his experiences, we believe, adds to an understanding of decisions, events, and political struggles surrounding Head Start and its mission to address fundamental issues of social justice in a nation that has tried many ways to eradicate poverty.

A PROGRAM FOR POOR CHILDREN

Prior to Head Start there were a few experimental programs for preschoolers from poor families or children with mental retardation, who were overrepresented in the poor population. The goal of several of these programs was to improve the functioning and school readiness of participants. (The achievement gap between children in poverty and their more affluent counterparts was already well known in the 1960s.) One of the most famous and best researched of these efforts was directed by Susan Gray at Peabody College, a national center for the study of mental retardation and therefore a site of special interest for both Sargent and Eunice Shriver. Shriver was amazed by Gray's finding that children in her preschool program demonstrated greater improvements in IQ scores than children in a comparison group. These findings led him to surmise that if you could raise the IQ of a child with borderline mental retardation, you should be able to do the same for children without mental retardation who reside in poverty.

Another factor in the birth of Head Start came from a pie chart Shriver had constructed to illustrate the characteristics of the poor population. He discovered a fact that is true to this day, namely, that a large percentage of Americans residing in poverty are children. Being the astute politician that he was, Shriver was aware that his young agency was suffering a backlash as a result of the activism sponsored by the Community Action Programs. In fact, some places were refusing CAP funding, leaving him with the embarrassing possibility of having money left over in his budget. Shriver came to realize that many Americans have little sympathy for the poor, believing that people are poor because they are lazy, irresponsible, or unmotivated. (This viewpoint is sometimes referred to as blaming the victim, and it has considerable currency.) More generous thinkers make the distinction between the deserving poor, in poverty through no fault of their own, and the undeserving poor, whose circumstances are attributable to their own behavior.

Shriver's pie chart gave him an insight: The CAP should launch a program for children. Children who are born in poverty certainly cannot be blamed for their lack of money. Children are the innocent victims of poverty. Shriver thought that a program for poor children would be much more appealing to local leaders and citizens than the efforts targeting adults.

Of course, an insight is not a program, and a program must be conceptualized before any social action can take place. Shriver turned to a trusted family advisor and Johns Hopkins pediatrician, Dr. Robert Cooke, to chair a committee to design the new program. Cooke assembled a multidisciplinary team of experts that included pediatricians, developmental psychologists, a social worker, a nurse, and early childhood educators. This team had only three months to create the program eventually named Head Start.

The first author was the youngest member of the planning committee. He was invited to participate because his research had caught the attention of Dr. Cooke. Zigler's studies (reviewed by Zigler & Bennett-Gates, 1999) demonstrated that children with mental retardation often function below their intellectual capacity because of a variety of experiential factors, and that these same factors can attenuate the everyday performance of poor children who do not have mental retardation. One factor found to be particularly detrimental to children's performance was an inordinate number of failure experiences in the formative years. Cooke felt so strongly that frequent failure hinders poor children's school achievement that he suggested the new program be named "Project Success." He believed that success breeds success, so the program should provide poor children with multiple opportunities to achieve appropriate goals and develop a drive to succeed that would carry into elementary school.

The planning group quickly agreed on the two bedrock principles of Head Start that remain in place today: parent involvement and comprehensive services. The members, who hailed from various disciplines, listened to one another and discovered they all believed that children's lives and growth trajectories are determined in large part by their families. Because Head Start was to be a brief summer program, parents had to be enlisted as true partners with the Head Start staff so they could carry on the program goals throughout their children's school careers. Urie Bronfenbrenner was on the planning committee, and the inklings of what was to become his bioecological model were beginning to percolate. He believed that the community where the child and family lived also had a role in supporting child development. Thus Head Start should interface with other institutions and settings in the neighborhoods where the centers were located. This idea was also compatible with the community action emphasis found within OEO.

The multidisciplinary nature of the planning committee almost guaranteed the acceptance of the second bedrock principle. It was apparent then, and is apparent now (Rothstein, 2004), that the optimal development of preschool children requires more than preschool education. To succeed in school, children must be in good health, which includes adequate nutrition and sound mental health; have appropriate social-emotional skills; and live in families who have the knowledge and energies to devote to the important task of child rearing. Head Start therefore became the first program to provide comprehensive services, including support services for both children and their families. To this day, the field of early intervention is conflicted about whether efforts should be directed toward children or toward parents, with the goal of helping them to be better socializers of their children. Head Start's planners insisted both were necessary, and the two-generation approach to early childhood intervention was born.

The planning committee reached consensus on all of the major principles of Head Start early on except for two, one of which was more easily resolved than the other. The War on Poverty was obviously directed toward helping the poor, and Head Start was being designed as a special place reserved exclusively for poor children and their families. Modeling theory and all we knew at the time (e.g., the early writings of John Dewey [1916] on the purpose of education as a means of teaching students how to live in a democracy) led Zigler to argue that we should include more affluent children along with poor children in our Head Start centers. Other members of the planning committee felt that this would spend too much of Head Start's resources on children who were not poor and not in need of program services. A compromise was reached with the 90/10 rule that remains in place today. Grantees were permitted to have 10% of their enrollment be above the poverty line. (Because Head Start was never funded to serve all eligible children below poverty, the 10% figure has become more of a goal statement than a real operating principle.)

The second issue proved much more contentious. At the time, Zigler was a young and rigorous research scientist. He insisted that there had to be some type of evaluation of the new program to determine if it had benefits and indicate where changes were needed. The rest of the planning committee expressed their exasperation, pointing out that every feature of Head Start was positive in nature. There was no reason for an evaluation. Time was running out, as the program's inception was imminent. The debate continued until Julius Richmond (who was Head Start's first director) ended it. He called Zigler into the hall and said that although he agreed there should be an evaluation, there was simply no time to debate the issue. Furthermore, although making the decision to mount an evaluation, Richmond warned that time constraints were such that this could only happen if Zigler himself constructed the measures that would be needed.

Flushed with victory, and an excess of hubris, Zigler quickly returned to Yale and drafted a half dozen of his graduate students to assist in designing the research instruments. Although the final evaluation included a measure constructed by a long-time Richmond colleague, Bettye Caldwell, other measures had to be developed from scratch to assess myriad aspects of child development and family functioning, all in about two weeks time. Suffice it to say, this hurried effort was unquestionably the poorest evaluation in the history of behavioral research.

However, it did establish a principle that still exists today, namely, that Head Start would have a research and evaluation component. It should be remembered that this was a time before the concept of accountability became the mantra it is today.

The planning committee completed its assignment relatively free of political pressure. Shriver had convened a committee of experts because he wanted their expert opinion, so he stayed out of the deliberations. The members were occasionally harangued by the leaders of the Community Action Program and warned to be ever mindful that Head Start was part of their program. The experts on the planning committee, who were recognized leaders in their fields, generally paid little attention to CAP and pretty much went their own way. Thus, two very different views of the goals of Head Start were found within OEO. In the Community Action Program, the agenda was to change the face of American society by improving the conditions of the poor, and Head Start was one of many tools to accomplish this goal. The emphasis of the planning committee was on healthy child development and better school readiness.

A NAÏVE AND OPTIMISTIC ERA

Although today it is safe to say that the Head Start model of comprehensive, two-generation services has become accepted as the standard for effective intervention, the planners were not geniuses who knew exactly what to do. As noted above, there was little research or precedent to guide them. Secondly, the field of applied developmental science had not yet been invented. The committee consisted of applied workers and basic researchers, and neither group had ever paid much attention to the other. Nothing was more applied than Head Start, which was a real program that would serve over a half-million children and their families that coming summer. Each member of the committee brought to the effort the rich theoretical views of his or her respective discipline. However, looking back, our theories of human development were much more simplistic than they are today. In fact, they could be described as overly simplistic in light of the complex scientific thinking and research on early intervention available today, much of it inspired by the Head Start intervention.

To illustrate the growing sophistication of just one approach, when Zigler was a graduate student one-half century ago, explanations of human development focused almost exclusively on the mother/child dyad. The child was thought to be unidirectionally influenced by the actions of the mother, whereas the significance of fathers and other family members was minimally recognized. The bidirectional nature of mother/child interactions was not recognized until Richard Bell's (1968) seminal paper. The evolution of our thinking progressed to what has become developmental psychology's current leading paradigm, Bronfenbrenner's bioecological model. Yet the authors and others are now recognizing that this model, although a useful frame of reference, is much too complex and variegated to direct helpful childhood interventions (Zigler & Styfco, 2006). It is certainly true that families, schools, neighborhoods, employment opportunities, and local, state, and national policies have an impact on child development; however, no program could possibly target all of these systems. We have concluded that within the child's ecology, there are four major systems that should be the primary focus of our efforts to enhance child development. The first and by far the most important is the family, who not only socialize children but shape the environment they experience every day (Ayoub, 2006; Bradley, 2006). Next is the health care system, followed by the education system and the child care system, where so many American children spend the first five years of their lives before entering school.

Just as the field changed, so did Head Start. The optimism and rosy outlook at the program's birth lasted a relatively short period. Zigler remembers hearing Sargent Shriver on *Meet the Press* predict that poverty in America would end within 10 years. The future proved him wrong. The bulk of the poor remain mothers and their children. America today has the highest poverty rate of any of the world's industrialized nations. Yet the early 1960s was a foolishly optimistic era, a time when we actually believed poverty could be quickly eradicated and intelligence could be easily increased. Many social scientists had been seduced by the environmental mystique (Zigler, 1970). Joe Hunt's book, *Intelligence and Experience* (1961), emphasized the great malleability of the child and suggested that even small positive changes in the environment would result in enhanced cognitive development. At the same time, Benjamin Bloom (1964) was writing that the early years are a critical period when beneficial experiences can have particularly salutary consequences on development.

When Head Start opened in 1965, the program lasted six and in some places eight weeks during the summer before children entered elementary school. Forty years later, we have tome after tome demonstrating just how ravaging the experience of poverty can be to a child's development (Duncan & Brookes-Gunn, 1997; Huston, 2005). What possible magic did we think we possessed to mount a very short intervention and think it would offset the vast debilitating effects of living in poverty? A consensus now exists that there are two determinants of the effectiveness of any intervention. One is the quality of the services received, and the second is the intensity of the program (Zigler, Gilliam, & Jones, 2006). In the 1960s, many thought all we had to do was offer a program—any program—when children were young and this would do the trick.

Without question, at its inception Head Start was overhyped and oversold. It began at a meeting in the East Room of the White House chaired by Lady Byrd Johnson. Powerbrokers as well as caring citizens from all over the nation were invited to hear about this new Head Start program. Local communities were encouraged to apply for grants to put the program into place. Although we were still planning Head Start, the planning committee was there in force to act as informants for the audience.

Committee members did not give much thought to how many children should be served that first summer. Shriver dealt with this detail. He asked one of our nation's leading child psychologists, Jerome Bruner of Harvard, what he thought the initial enrollment should be. Bruner recommended 2,000, which sounded fine to the developmental scientists on the panel because at the time, most of our research studies were conducted with 30–60 children at most. However, President Johnson and Sargent Shriver were both larger-than-life individuals who thought big and acted big. The first number introduced by the political leaders was 25,000 children. That struck the planning committee as doable. However, following the White House meeting, Head Start took on a life of its own. Grant applications poured into Washington. These requests were processed by a hastily recruited group of substitute teachers. (See Zigler & Muenchow, 1992, for stories about this hectic process.) The 25,000 figure quickly became 100,000, then 200,000, and then 300,000.

The planning committee had qualms, but acquiesced. The members believed that nothing being proposed would endanger any child or have negative consequences. Head Start would offer nutritious meals and snacks, some educational services, some health care, and some parent education and involvement. Thus we could proceed with a clear conscience. The final number served that first summer was 561,000 children and their families. It must be remembered that this was shortly before the Vietnam War consumed our national spirit and wealth, and our nation was enjoying a fiscal surplus.

Later in the planning process, the first director of Head Start was named, a pre-eminent pediatrician, Julius Richmond, who was then the Dean of the School of Medicine at Syracuse University. (He would later become Surgeon General during the Carter administration.) Richmond's second in command was a bureaucratic wizard drafted from the Post Office Department, Jule Sugarman. After the planning committee had completed its recommendations, Shriver summoned Sugarman to his office and gave him exactly one day to lay out a roadmap for implementing the program (Moyers, 2004). This included the budget. Sugarman decided that federal funding of a few hundred dollars per child for a six- to eight-week intervention would be sufficient. (A leading developmentalist, Frances Horowitz, mounted a Head Start program in Lawrence, KS, where she was a faculty member at the University of Kansas. She told the first author that she wrote to the Head Start branch at OEO to complain that the money allotted could not possibly fund a good quality program. The reply she received essentially stated that the government was not interested in a quality program, but rather a Head Start program.)

The reviewers of the grant applications were of necessity both quick and lenient. Head Start was to have five components, and if these hastily hired substitute teachers saw any mention that each component was included, the program was funded. Zigler complained to Sugarman and his deputy, Dick Orton, that we were unquestionably funding some totally inadequate programs. They agreed but said they had a plan. Right now they just needed to get the programs opened; later they would visit them, and any sites found to be below an acceptable quality threshold would lose their funding. Although this made a certain amount of sense, at the time no one realized that quality problems were being built into the Head Start structure that would plague the program for decades.

The planning committee members personally visited Head Start sites that first summer to get some sense of how matters were proceeding. Overall, they found a great deal of commitment and enthusiasm for the program, but a mixed picture of what the children were actually experiencing. Two of those trips stand out in Zigler's memory. On a visit to Los Angeles, violence broke out in the city and police cars appeared everywhere. The next day we realized we had been in the middle of the Watts riots. Fortunately, the Head Start program in Watts experienced no problems, because the community felt that Head Start was inviolable. It is interesting to note that many years later, during the riots in mid-central Los Angeles, Head Start sites were attacked along with everything else in the neighborhood. In 1965, though, Head Start was brand new and definitely had a considerable patina. It was seen as an island of hope for the future.

The second memorable event from that summer took place during visits to New Orleans. Zigler chatted with the director of the Head Start program, a well-known early childhood educator and old friend.

She complained about the local Community Action Agency that was receiving the federal money for the program. This particular agency was forcing her to hire people to work in the center who, in her words, "should never be within 100 miles of a child." We see in this episode the difference between the planning committee and the CAP in their goals for Head Start. The Community Action workers saw Head Start as a weapon in the War on Poverty, to be used to provide people with paying jobs to empower them and improve their standard of living. Like all federal programs, jobs were used as part of a patronage system to reward individuals who supported the Community Action organization. The planning committee saw Head Start as a means of preparing children to escape the poverty that encumbered their parents.

Federal officials, witnessing the popularity of Head Start across the nation, simply declared victory on both fronts in this particular battle in the War on Poverty. This is obvious in a triumphant statement made by President Johnson: "This program this year means that 30 million man-years—the combined lifespan of these youngsters—will be spent productively and rewardingly, rather than wasted in tax-supported institutions or in welfare-supported lethargy" (in Zigler & Valentine, 1997, p. 68). That all of this could be attributed to a six-week intervention is preposterous on its face and simply reflects the unbridled enthusiasm and optimism of that time. Today, we are incredulous that Americans were so willing to believe that the fight for social justice and equality had already been won for the next generation.

ALIGNING HEAD START WITH REALITY

With the election of President Richard Nixon in 1968, the War on Poverty was essentially over. Donald Rumsfeld was dispatched to OEO with the task of eventually dismantling the agency. But what was to be done with Head Start? The program remained extremely popular among the citizenry and policymakers. The Nixon administration made the decision to move Head Start from the endangered OEO into the Department of Health, Education and Welfare (HEW). The Office of Child Development (OCD) was created within HEW with responsibility for Head Start, the Children's Bureau, and other children's programs. OCD later became the Administration on Children, Youth and Families in the U.S. Department of Health and Human Services, where the office of Head Start is located today.

In 1970, Edward Zigler became the first director of OCD, making him the federal official responsible for the Head Start program as well as the new chief of the venerable Children's Bureau. He inherited some of the old OEO Head Start staff, many of whom were still wedded to the empowerment goals of the Community Action Program. The social activism funded by CAPs across the nation was in opposition to the views of the Nixon administration. Head Start parents began writing their congressmen to complain that their Head Start centers (typically under a CAP grantee) were spending a lot of money to mobilize them for local activism rather than on the children. This created a backlash against social activism in Head Start on the part of Congress, which had never been enamored with that aspect of the CAP. Zigler ordered that no Head Start money would be spent on these mobilization practices. Head Start would be the program the planning committee envisioned, serving children and their families for the ultimate purpose of improving school readiness.

There was much foot–dragging in carrying out these orders, basically among OEO holdovers still loyal to the Community Action plan for Head Start. This was when Zigler became conversant with an issue that he had never encountered in the world of academia. He was constantly being asked whether this or that individual was "loyal" to him. To the college professor that he was, loyalty is an irrelevant attribute. Mentors do not want their students to be loyal; rather, we want them to take issue and argue with us. It is through such dialogue that learning and knowledge building take place. Washington and its bureaucracies are far different. Loyalty is considered the sine qua non of effective civil servants. In the real world, employees are expected to do what their boss tells them to do. In Washington, staff may or may not support their leader. If not, they may not try too hard to carry out requests or accomplish goals, and they might even sabotage these efforts. Learning how the system worked, Zigler soon brought his own people into OCD and weeded out the recalcitrant holdovers from OEO. Then he began the work of making Head Start an effective child development program.

Quality Issues

The heterogeneity in the quality of Head Start programs that the planning committee members observed when they visited centers the first summer continued unabated for the next five years. By the time Zigler assumed responsibility for the program, there were still too many classrooms where the "teachers" hadn't the slightest idea of what to do with the children. Students had breakfast, lunch, snacks, and a nap, but they wandered around in unstructured play for the remainder of the day. Quality improvement became Zigler's top goal and has remained the authors' top priority for the past 40 years. Although there was no research to prove it in 1970, by now there is ample evidence demonstrating that the outcomes of any program are highly dependent on the quality of the services provided.

Zigler recalled the earlier conversation with Sugarman and Orton when he questioned what would be done with the inadequate programs. Dick Orton was now reporting to Zigler, who invited Orton to his office for a discussion. Zigler reminded Orton of his promise to conduct an evaluation of the Head Start programs after funding them, and to do away with those found to be doing a poor job. Zigler pointed out that it was now five years later and questioned how many programs had been shut down and their funds redirected. Orton told Zigler there were none, but one center had almost been closed. Apparently Head Start officials had received complaints that the children at this center were being hit with sticks by the staff. A full investigation was made, but it was found that the parents wanted their children to be hit with sticks when they needed discipline. Orton explained that because parents have such a leading voice in Head Start, the feds had no choice but to comply. Zigler, an adamant foe of corporal punishment, disagreed, pointing out that the ultimate responsibility for Head Start practices lay with us. Instead of abdicating to parents' views on such critical issues, the staff's role was to teach them about less punitive forms of discipline. Zigler immediately issued a memorandum to all centers stating that no Head Start child will be subjected to corporal punishment.

At the heart of the Head Start quality issue was the weakness of the preschool education component, which seemed to have worsened over time. When Head Start was a summer program, many certified elementary school teachers used their time off to teach in Head Start. As more programs adopted an academic-year calendar, these trained teachers were not available. Furthermore, with its origins in the CAP, the precedent had been set that Head Start should serve as an employment and training ground for participating families. Thus parents were often hired as teachers, even those with minimal education and no experience in the classroom.

The poor quality of the early education component was underlined by an incident Zigler and Jeanette Valentine encountered when they were editors of the first book on the birth of Head Start (1979). They invited leading figures in the various fields represented in Head Start to write about each component of the program. They asked a well-known early childhood educator and past president of the National Association for the Education of Young Children (NAEYC), Eveline Omwake, to assess the education component. She initially declined the invitation, explaining that she would have little if anything positive to say. The editors insisted they needed that contribution, because the best hope for improving the quality of Head Start was to make clear its shortcomings. Omwake bluntly wrote, "For some children no Head Start would be better than what they are getting" (1979, p. 222). She blamed the quality of the preschool education component, which she found to be inconsistent, directed toward unrealistic or lax goals, and often inappropriate for the ages of the young students. Her recommendation was for Head Start directors to focus more on hiring professionally trained teachers and less on being an employment office for jobless neighborhood residents. Her chapter may be read today (Zigler & Valentine, 1997).

In regard to the preschool education component, one of Zigler's inventions proved to be counterproductive. Early in Head Start's history, the White House Conference on Children designated the need for good quality child care as the most pressing problem for children and families in America. The number of women in the out-of-home workforce had been steadily climbing over the years, as it continues to do today. Much of the child care available in the 1970s was provided by untrained individuals and was frequently nothing more than custodial care. As chief of the U.S. Children's Bureau, Zigler had a responsibility dictated by law to do something about it. He thought it was important to develop a large cadre of child care workers who met a minimal level of qualifications. With the help of the NAEYC, the Child Development Associate (CDA) credential was created. The basic concept of this training was that the child care worker would learn enough about child development and how to meet children's needs to demonstrate competence in a prescribed set of performance standards. There are now tens of thousands of CDAs, and the credential is recognized in every state in the nation.

The reason we say the idea was counterproductive in Head Start is that the CDA was meant to be a minimal indicator of proficiency in working with young children. It was not meant to be a substitute for higher levels of education such as an AA or BA degree in early childhood education. However, the Head Start budget did not have the funds to hire appropriately trained teachers, so many centers hired CDAs as lead teachers. Although CDA training can qualify someone to be a very good assistant teacher, it does not provide the level of knowledge required of a lead teacher in a preschool program.

Preschool education in Head Start has improved greatly since the early 1990s, when Congress set aside quality improvement funds, half of which were dedicated to staffing issues. In the 1998 reauthorization, Congress mandated that half of the lead teachers in Head Start must have at least an AA degree. Although this requirement has been met, it is widely recognized that the high-risk children who attend Head Start need highly qualified teachers to prepare them for school. Middle-class children are routinely taught by a BA-level teacher with certification in early childhood education, but many Head Start children still have teachers with CDAs, AAs, or none of the above. As this chapter is being written, Congress is considering mandating that at least half of the lead teachers in Head Start have BAs. These good intentions will have little impact unless funds for salaries are increased along with the required levels of training. Head Start teachers who earn degrees often move to jobs in the public school system, where pay and benefits are higher.

Although social justice might seem to dictate that Head Start accommodate the employment needs of the poor populations it serves, the children's needs for high-quality preschool education must take precedence. There is plenty of room in Head Start for parents to participate, and training should be available to help them meet the qualifications of many job titles. To be an effective teacher, however, requires a considerable amount of formal academic training.

The uneven quality rampant in Head Start led Zigler to initiate the development of a set of performance standards to dictate the minimum content of services all centers must provide. The Program Performance Standards were written by the Head Start Bureau and implemented in 1975. Every grantee was required to provide yearly reports to their regional office to show they were meeting the standards. Centers were also visited and assessed every three years by a team of reviewers. Those found to be out of compliance were given extra training and technical assistance (TTA) to correct their problems. Over time, lack of funding led to reductions in TTA and site visits. Quality slid (Chafel, 1992), until a major program expansion in the 1990s forced Congress to dedicate funds for improvements. Part of this effort was the revision of the original performance standards, which was ordered by the Clinton administration to reflect changes in best practices and the population served, particularly the inclusion of younger children. The revised standards became effective in 1998 and remain Head Start's primary quality control tool.

Integration

Zigler also attempted to correct social inequities in Head Start. Children with developmental disabilities were routinely excluded from Head Start classrooms, just as they were from public schools. (This was before the passage of what is now called the Individuals with Disabilities Education Act, or IDEA.) One reason is that most Head Start workers were not trained to meet the needs of children with handicapping conditions. Zigler set a goal that at least 10% of enrollment be reserved for children with disabilities, meaning that staff had to make a special effort to recruit families of children with special needs. A technical assistance effort was put into place to train staff to serve these children. It is unfortunate that this approach was not used when the forerunner of the current IDEA (Public Law 94-192) was passed in 1975, mandating that children with disabilities have access to public schooling. Teachers with little training in special education were overwhelmed at first and were as much in need of extra training as Head Start staff. In recent years, children with disabilities have comprised 12–13% of Head Start enrollment and in many places are the only children served who are above the poverty line.

This brings up another type of segregation that was built into Head Start. To be eligible for the program, children have to live in families with incomes below the federal poverty line. (There are a few exceptions, including disability.) This created a social environment where poor children go to one preschool setting and wealthier children to another, painting class lines at an early age. As the federal official responsible for Head Start, Zigler attempted to end this segregation. He developed a plan to open Head Start to all children, with parents above poverty paying a fee calibrated to their income. Families below the poverty line would continue to receive Head Start at no charge.

To Zigler's surprise, the biggest foes to this plan came from within the Head Start community. Opponents argued that wealthier parents would take over roles in the program and poor parents would lose their voice. Zigler found this argument to be weak, because he had been very impressed with the intelligence and dedication of the many parents residing in poverty he had met at Head Start centers across the country. The coup de grace to the plan was a forceful editorial in the *New York Times* that referred to Zigler as a "reverse Robin Hood," robbing from the poor to give to the rich.

Zigler wrote a letter in defense in which he pointed out how the idea was based on sound pedagogical and developmental knowledge. He cited evidence that poor children profit from being in learning centers with more affluent classmates, and that the progress of the wealthier children is not impeded. The motivation for the plan was not to give a hand-out to parents who could afford to pay for preschool but to enhance the development of the poor children who attend Head Start and possibly their middle-class peers as well.

With almost universal opposition to the idea, Head Start has remained a program where children are segregated on the basis of socioeconomic status. The authors believe this particularly troublesome issue will become moot in coming decades as the states continue progressing toward universal preschool education. Two states, Georgia and Oklahoma, already have this system in place, and several others are rapidly moving to offer prekindergarten to all children. A full discussion of this movement can be found in a recent book (Zigler et al., 2006).

Defining Parents' Roles

The next task undertaken was to clarify the role of parents in Head Start. The Economic Opportunity Act of 1964 that launched the War on Poverty contained the wording, "maximum feasible participation" of the poor in antipoverty programs. This battle cry was unevenly interpreted by various Head Start grantees, just as it was within the other War on Poverty programs. Zigler worked with a very effective staff member, Bessie Draper, to develop a clear and important role for Head Start parents. This led to the creation of the Head Start policy councils, half of whose members must be current and former parents of Head Start children. These policy councils became the top governing body of each Head Start center and remain in place to this day.

After the rules for the new policy councils were issued, Zigler learned once again that no good deed goes unpunished. At the time, about 20% of Head Start programs were housed in public schools. (The percentage is higher today.) Almost immediately after the mandate was published, school superintendents began to complain that no school administration could give parents the type of authority granted by the policy councils. Many threatened that if Zigler persisted in this order, they would be forced to close their Head Start programs. Again the first author stood firm, and the schools managed to live with the policy councils. This incident illustrates in one more way that Head Start was ahead of its time. Today we have evidence that parent involvement in their children's education has a positive impact on school performance. In fact, Congress has mandated parent involvement in several major education laws, including the IDEA, Title I of the Elementary and Secondary Education Act, and the Educate America Act. As this chapter is being written, Congress is taking a fresh look at the role of the policy councils as they form the Head Start reauthorization bill.

Clarifying Head Start's Goals

Prior to the founding of OCD, most evaluative studies of Head Start had assessed its merit in terms of IQ improvement, or lack thereof. Raising IQ scores was never mentioned in the planners' conception of Head Start. Yet the results of early studies and the enthusiasm of political leadership soon made IQ changes the desirable goal of the program.

For example, Leon Eisenberg reported a 12-point increase in IQ among Head Start participants, which he attributed to the then six-week Head Start session. Given Shriver's belief that IQ improvement was a legitimate expectation of Head Start attendance, federal officials inquired whether Zigler could calculate the total number of IQ points that had been gained by all children attending Head Start that first summer.

Zigler, who had been studying mental retardation and the difficulty of improving IQ all of his professional life, refused to assert that Head Start had actually raised any child's intelligence. With Herbert Birch, a senior and respected worker in the field of mental retardation, Zigler argued that it was an error to consider change in the most stable measure that behavioral science had ever invented as the ultimate goal of any program. To make this point, he and his colleagues conducted a series of studies (Zigler, Abelson, Trickett, & Seitz, 1982; Zigler & Butterfield, 1968) that demonstrated the IQ gains reported by Eisenberg and others were not due to a true improvement in cognitive functioning, but rather reflected a variety of motivational factors and improved test-taking abilities following the Head Start experience—for example, less wariness of the test situation, more confidence, better familiarity with items on the test, and so on. In other words, children's intelligence had not really changed, but they were able to use their innate abilities more fully. This achievement is not as exciting as big gains in IQ, but it can have a meaningful impact on learning and school performance.

Head Start was put into place to prepare children for school entry, not to boost their scores on intelligence tests. To refocus attention, Zigler decided that the program needed a clearer goal statement. He chose the term "everyday social competence" as the official goal of Head Start, but it turns out this was not clear enough. The federal government invested substantial time and money on conferences, work groups, and contractors to define social competence and to develop a set of measures through which the construct could be operationalized (Raver & Zigler, 1991). The effort was later abandoned during the Reagan administration. The components of social competence seemed rather straightforward: physical and mental health, social and emotional skills, and cognitive development (Zigler & Trickett, 1978). Measuring these domains is what proved tricky. The entire matter became moot with the 1998 reauthorization, where Congress specified school readiness as the stated goal of Head Start. At the age of school entry (five), social competence and school readiness are essentially the same thing. The term "school readiness," however, is more easily understood by laypersons and was a good choice of words.

A National Laboratory

To discover ways to improve Head Start services (and to deflect attention from unrealistic expectations of IQ gains), Zigler moved Head Start in the direction of becoming a national laboratory (Henrich, 2004). He envisioned the program as a place to mount and test new models of intervention, in the spirit of Campbell's (1969) experimenting society. The first intervention tried under the Head Start banner was Healthy Start. Admittedly, this project was not based on any scientific theory or evidence but was a solution to a conundrum presented to Zigler arising from his naiveté regarding the true ways of Washington.

One of the first congressional hearings that Zigler testified at was before a powerful House subcommittee, chaired by Carl Perkins of Kentucky. These hearings are generally conducted in two parts. First, the witness reads a formal statement that is actually prepared by the Office of Management and Budget. This guarantees that the witness will present the administration's position, and not "leave the reservation." During the second part of the hearing, committee members question the witness, so answers are spontaneous and may vary from the administration's stance. For this reason, unknown members of the administration are in the audience and report back to the witness's superior on his or her performance.

Perkins was a well-known and ardent supporter of Head Start, and his committee had oversight responsibilities for the program. Thus, the federal official responsible for Head Start had to answer to both his superiors in the administration and to the oversight committee during this hearing. During the question and answer period, Perkins nodded with pleasure and agreement with each of Zigler's replies. One of his questions was what Zigler thought of the recently released Westinghouse Report that was so critical of Head Start. Zigler quoted the many critics of the report, including the great Donald Campbell, and concluded that the report was a weak study, done in a hurried fashion, and should not be taken too seriously as an evaluation of the merits of Head Start. This also pleased Perkins, who informed Zigler that he could not agree more. Instead of leaving well enough alone, Zigler made the mistake of adding a caveat that there was one finding in the report with which he agreed. Graduates of the Head Start summer programs had shown no improvements, whereas those in the academic-year programs showed a few modest positive outcomes. Zigler added that it was extremely unlikely that a six-week program could have any effects and recommended that Congress convert to all full-year programs to serve children in poverty with more than a tokenistic effort.

Zigler was not at all prepared for the congressman's reaction. Perkins became livid and threatened Zigler with serious consequences if he closed so much as one summer program. This totally mystified Zigler, because he was being ordered to waste taxpayers' money on an inadequate program when a better model was available. He questioned many individuals before fully appreciating Chairman Perkins's motivations. Many employees in the summer program were school teachers. These same teachers worked the telephones in getting the vote out for Congressman Perkins. These summer jobs were patronage to the teachers for the work they did on his behalf. Such are the ways of Washington, making it necessary to learn how to navigate the community in order to do one's job.

Because the summer programs were untouchable, Zigler worked with his staff to ascertain how to modify them so they would have a real benefit to children and their families. The result is that some summer programs became Healthy Start, which focused on the physical and mental health care of Head Start–eligible children. The program involved health screenings and follow-up services, with the goal of placing each child into a permanent medical home. We tried this for a couple of summers, but the program proved to have no add-on benefit to what was delivered in the typical Head Start summer program. With this evaluation in hand, Healthy Start was terminated. After Zigler left Washington, the summer Head Start program continued for several more years until it was finally phased out.

Other efforts under the Head Start national lab banner were much more successful. The Home Start program was created to serve children who live in rural and other isolated areas. An evaluation of this model proved positive, and it continues today under the name Head Start Home-Based Services.

In those early days, few states had widespread kindergarten programs. Head Start served three-, four-, and five-year-old children and their families. It was soon recognized that many three-year-olds entered Head Start as troubled and difficult children, their development already compromised by the experience of poverty. It thus became clear that it was a mistake to ignore children before they reached preschool age. The Parent–Child Centers were launched to serve poor children from birth to the age of three. These centers were the forerunners of today's Early Head Start program, which has been in existence for 10 years. This program is the subject of an ongoing rigorous evaluation that thus far has demonstrated broad benefits to children and families (Love et al., 2002).

Zigler felt that even a one-year program was not sufficient to offset the negative effects of growing up in poverty. Furthermore, it was obvious there was great heterogeneity among individuals living below the poverty line in terms of their social resources and needs. Rather than requiring parents to force themselves into the Head Start model, a network of demonstration sites called the Child and Family Resource Program (CFRP) was put into place to offer more individualized services. The program was available to families with children from birth to age eight and incorporated a wide variety of services they could select from depending on their needs. This program was actually one of the earliest family support programs in existence. The program engendered considerable enthusiasm and praise. In fact, the U. S. Comptroller General (1979) conducted an objective evaluation and concluded that the CFRP represented the wave of the future. Unfortunately, the program was soon terminated, probably for no other reason than that it was a complicated and demanding effort that was difficult for bureaucrats to embrace. Yet it inspired the widespread family support movement that now numbers thousands of programs across America.

A final demonstration that we mention here is the Education for Parenthood program. Assuming the role of parenthood is a demanding process, and many people are unprepared for the experience. As the nation has become more mobile and adults are separated by great distances from their extended families, they have limited resources to help them with the travails of child rearing. Zigler thought a good preventive strategy would be to teach adolescents about the principles of child development and give them opportunities to interact with young children in Head Start and child care centers. The Education for Parenthood program was implemented by some 6,000 high schools across the nation. An evaluation showed considerable benefits to students, but this federal program was also dismantled. The concept survives in a number of similar programs offered in schools, as well as in the thousands of home visiting and parent education programs that operate across the country.

CHANGING NOTIONS OF SOCIAL JUSTICE

Prior to the George W. Bush administration, Head Start had rarely been subjected to intense partisan debate. Historically, both parties have contributed to the development and growth of Head Start, and both have taken pride in the program. This history took a sharp u-turn with the election of President George W. Bush. During his first presidential campaign, Bush made it clear that he thought Head Start did not sufficiently emphasize preschool education, particularly literacy. He vowed to move Head Start to the Department of Education to give it a more academic focus. What candidate Bush did not state, and what most people do not know, is that the Department of Education does not directly manage programs the size of Head Start. The department's modus operandi is to develop funding formulas and block grant (devolve) federal programs to the states. In the case of Head Start, instead of a homogeneous program with uniform performance standards, the result would be 50 different state programs that would vary in content, model, and quality. In other words, Head Start as we know it would cease to exist. It should be noted that governors are usually eager to gain federal money and control of federal programs, and that they have always been unhappy with Head Start's federal-to-local funding stream that bypasses state officials altogether.

After being elected, Bush found little enthusiasm among the power brokers in relocating Head Start to the Department of Education. During the recent Head Start reauthorization process, his administration developed a compromise plan that proposed an "experiment" of block granting Head Start to a maximum of eight states. The rationale was that this arrangement would better coordinate Head Start with the myriad early childhood programs at the state level. The administration's argument was summarized in a paper by Wade Horn (2004), the federal official currently responsible for Head Start.

Zigler and many others actively opposed the eight-state plan, arguing that coordination could be achieved through less risky and Draconian means. The primary issues against devolution were that there would be diminution in quality without national performance standards, parent participation would be weakened, and that the content would turn to academics rather than preparing the whole child for school. The authors laid out these issues in a paper (Zigler & Styfco, 2004b) that was widely read on Capitol Hill. Nevertheless, the eight-state plan was included in the House reauthorization bill, which was essentially written by Republican members only. For the first time, Head Start became a partisan issue.

In most prior reauthorizations, both parties have asked for Zigler's input on the legislative proposals. In fact, he has worked with every administration, Republican and Democrat, since that of Lyndon Johnson. And even though he has been at odds with the Bush administration on several Head Start issues, he nevertheless continues to work with the officials managing the program. He has never been viewed as a political ideologue, but rather as a knowledgeable scholar devoted to the goal of making Head Start as effective as possible. However, for the 2004 reauthorization Zigler presented his views before a large number of Democratic congressmen, but not a single Republican requested his input.

The Senate's effort to write the companion reauthorization piece in 2004 was quite different. There appeared to be a genuine bipartisan effort to write a bill directed solely toward improving Head Start. (This is the historical purpose of reauthorization: Changes are made to enhance a program, not to dismantle or rebuild it.) Both parties requested Zigler's advice in shaping the bill, which eventually was written without the eight-state provision. Progress on the reauthorization was delayed by the national elections and then dropped by the lame duck Congress. Both the House and the Senate had to begin at square one in writing a reauthorization bill in 2005–2006.

This effort was markedly less partisan, and both parties directed their efforts toward genuinely improving the quality and function of Head Start. Neither the House nor the Senate's bill proposed block granting Head Start to even one state. Both bills contained the good feature of increasing the number of BA-level teachers in Head Start. However, neither bill provided the funds necessary to permit Head Start to actually compete in the open market in hiring well-qualified preschool teachers by paying them what they are worth. This appears to be little more than an unfunded mandate.

There is no secret in how to improve the quality of Head Start and the outcomes of children experiencing the program: (1) Every lead teacher should have a BA and certification in early childhood education, and every assistant teacher should have an AA or CDA. (2) Children should attend Head Start for two years rather than for a single academic year. The evidence is clear that more intense services are needed by children who face the risks of Head Start enrollees (e.g., Reynolds, 2004). Alas, both suggestions for improvement simply cost too much money to be considered. Poor children and their families are a relatively powerless group and, unlike the period when Head Start was born, the plight of poor children is not of huge national concern.

Children who live in poverty experience myriad barriers to optimal development. Head Start has always taken a whole-child approach to prepare students for the social and academic expectations of school. The Bush administration has taken a contrary view, focusing primarily on literacy and math skills as the key to school readiness. This thrust became apparent early in his administration when Mrs. Bush chaired a White House conference on cognitive development. The conference did not even encompass all of cognitive development but rather concentrated on literacy. The conference was actually masterminded by a mid-level bureaucrat whose own scholarly contribution centered on the effectiveness of phonetic instruction in literacy development.

In testimony before a committee chaired by Senator Kennedy, Zigler argued that literacy was just one part of cognitive development, and that cognitive development was just one part of human development. Although endorsing the importance of literacy, Zigler argued that a much broader approach must be taken to enhance a child's reading readiness. Learning to read requires much more than knowing the ABCs. Children must have good health, emotional self-regulation, and the social skills necessary to adjust to the learning environment.

This advice fell on deaf ears. The Bush administration bypassed congressional approval by issuing mandates through the Head Start Bureau. For example, training and technical assistance were refocused to provide training in reading instruction. (Previously this unit offered centers help with meeting all of the performance standards.) Head Start staff were trained in the use of Landry's literacy enhancing circle curriculum, which is now required for all centers.

There is no question that the Head Start Bureau in any administration must determine policy and issue mandates necessary to fulfill its duties and obligations. However, in the past these mandates were generally issued in close communication with the Head Start community, and there was never an adversarial relationship between the programs and the bureau. There was a sense that all were working together toward the same goal, namely, to help every child in Head Start prepare for school. The Bush administration changed this cooperative style to a top-down management style in which Head Start programs follow federal instructions rather than each grantee adapting its own program, within the guidelines of the performance standards and with the help of what is now the office of Head Start and regional offices.

The marked divergence of the Bush administration from Head Start's past can be seen in the implementation of a hastily developed evaluation program called the National Reporting System (NRS). The NRS consists of four basically cognitive tests administered at the beginning and end of the Head Start year to all participants who will enter kindergarten the following fall. This system has created a huge controversy not to mention a lot of animosity. A letter to the Head Start Bureau criticizing the scientific basis and appropriateness of the measures was signed by 300 scholars.

The Head Start community was befuddled by the NRS, never having been told its purpose or how the results were supposed to be used. They were already using a number of assessment tools and did not see the value added by the NRS. Many had adopted an evaluation system developed during the Clinton administration, which had also been concerned about accountability and how to measure the program's success in preparing children for school entry. Helen Taylor, the Head Start Bureau chief at the time, worked with scholars, the Head Start community, and the schools to develop a performance-based outcome system. The framework focused on outcomes in eight developmental domains including, but not limited to, literacy and math skills. Not only did Head Start practitioners see the NRS as redundant to this broader system they already had in place, but they complained that the money provided to defray the cost of administering the tests was insufficient. Many grantees were forced to subsidize the testing costs with other program money, thus reducing the services their children received.

Scholarly criticisms of the NRS focused on critical issues such as poor psychometric properties and the appropriateness of using standardized tests with such young children. Professionals also criticized the narrow cognitive focus of the NRS, which ignored physical and mental health, social-emotional development, parent involvement, and many other features that have a profound impact on school readiness (e.g., Meisels & Atkins-Burnett, 2004; Zigler & Styfco, 2004a). A formal report has now been written by Capitol Hill's own Government Accountability Office (2005) that roundly criticizes the NRS. At this writing, plans are to add measures of social-emotional skills and to improve the system's scientific properties. Furthermore, one House reauthorization bill mandates that the NRS evaluation be critiqued by the National Academy of Sciences, and another bill simply ends it.

Head Start and the entire field of early intervention have long been plagued with the expectation of unrealistic goals. This is a recipe for failure, because if you set a goal you cannot reach, of course you will fail. The salience of this issue can be seen in a report issued by the Bush administration (U. S. Department of Health and Human Services, 2003) that suggests Head Start is a failure because children who graduate from the program are not as school ready as middle-class children. To believe that a nine-month, half-day program (which is what a large percentage of participants receive) can impart the same benefits of five optimal years of development that middle-class children have before they enter school is, as a leading author asserted, to believe in magic (Brooks-Gunn, 2003). Rothstein (2004) presented a very convincing argument that neither the Head Start program, nor the schooling that follows it, will ever be able to close completely the achievement gap between middle- and low-income children. The causes of poor school readiness, and subsequent poor academic achievement, are simply bigger than any early intervention or school system can tackle.

On the brighter side, it is true that Head Start and higher-quality schooling can decrease the achievement gap. In fact, solid evidence now exists that high-quality preschool programs are an excellent investment (Heckman, 2000; Zigler et al., 2006). Furthermore, the early results of the first rigorous national evaluation of Head Start have now been reported. They show positive effects that are modest but apparent across a broad array of outcome measures (Puma, Bell, Cook, Heid, & Lopez, 2005; Yoshikawa, 2005). As this longitudinal study progresses, we will learn if these small changes in a variety of domains grow over time.

The documented benefits of high-quality early intervention may not balance the scales of social justice or level the playing field for children of the poor. But they clearly indicate we are on the right track by providing young children who live with economic disadvantage the opportunities to prepare for the long years of schooling that lie ahead. It is certainly more just to have these opportunities than not.

REFERENCES

Arroyo, C. G., & Zigler, E. (1993). America's Title I/Chapter 1 programs: Why the promise has not been met. In E. Zigler & S. J. Styfco (Eds.), *Head Start and beyond: A national plan for extended childhood intervention* (pp. 73–95). New Haven, CT: Yale University Press.

Ayoub, C. (2006). Adaptive and maladaptive parenting: Influence on child development. In N. Watt, C. Ayoub, R. Bradley, J. Puma, & W. LeBoeuf (Eds.), *The crisis in youth mental health. Critical issues and effective programs. Volume 4. Early intervention programs and policies* (pp. 121–143). Greenwich, CT: Praeger.

Bell, R. Q. (1968). A reinterpretation of the direction of effects in studies of socialization. *Psychological Review, 75*, 81–95.

Bloom, B. S. (1964). *Stability and change in human characteristics.* New York: Wiley.

Bradley, R. H. (2006). The home environment. In N. Watt, C. Ayoub, R. Bradley, J. Puma, & W. LeBoeuf (Eds.), *The crisis in youth mental health. Critical issues and effective programs. Volume 4. Early intervention programs and policies* (pp. 89–120). Greenwich, CT: Praeger.

Brooks-Gunn, J. (2003). Do you believe in magic? SRCD *Social Policy Report, 17*(1).

Campbell, D. (1969). Reforms as experiments. *American Psychologist, 24*, 409–429.

Caro, R. (1982). *The years of Lyndon Johnson* (2 Vols.). New York: Knopf.

Chafel, J. A. (1992). Funding Head Start: What are the issues? *American Journal of Orthopsychiatry, 62*, 9–21.

Dewey, J. (1916). *Democracy and education.* New York: Free Press.

Duncan, G., & Brooks-Gunn, J. (Eds.) (1997). *The consequences of growing up poor.* New York: Russell Sage.

Government Accountability Office. (2005, May). *Head Start. Further development could allow results of new test to be used for decision making.* (GAO-05-343). Washington, DC: Author. http://www.gao.gov/new.items/d05343.pdf

Greenberg, P. (2004). Three core concepts of the war on poverty: Their origins and significance in Head Start. In E. Zigler & S. J. Styfco (Eds.), *The Head Start debates* (pp. 379–396). Baltimore, MD: Paul H. Brookes.

Harrington, M. (1962). *The other America: Poverty in the United States.* New York: Macmillan.

Heckman, J. (2000). Policies to foster human capital. *Research in Economics, 54,* 3–56.

Henrich, C. (2004). Head Start as a national laboratory. In E. Zigler & S. J. Styfco (Eds.), *The Head Start debates* (pp. 379–396). Baltimore, MD: Paul H. Brookes.

Horn, W. F. (2004, March 25). Statement before the Subcommittee on Labor, HHS, Education and related agencies, Committee on Appropriations, U. S. House of Representatives. Washington, DC.

Hunt, J. McV. (1961). *Intelligence and experience.* New York: Ronald Press.

Huston, A. (2005). Connecting the science of child development to public policy. SRCD *Social Policy Report, 19*(4).

Love, J. M., et al. (2002, June). *Making a difference in the lives of infants and toddlers and their families: The impacts of Early Head Start.* Washington, DC: U. S. Department of Health and Human Services. http://www.acf.hhs.gov/programs/opre/ehs/ehs_resrch/reports/impacts_exesum/impacts_execsum.pdf

Meisels, S. J., & Atkins-Burnett, S. (2004, January). The Head Start National Reporting System: A critique. *Beyond the Journal: Young Children on the Web,* 1–4.

Moyers, B. (2004). *Sarge: The life and times of Sargent Shriver.* Washington, DC: Smithsonian Books.

Omwake, E. B. (1979). Assessment of the Head Start preschool education effort. In E. Zigler & J. Valentine (Eds.), *Project Head Start: A legacy of the War on Poverty* (pp. 221–228). New York: Free Press.

Puma, M., Bell, S., Cook, R., Heid, C., & Lopez, M. (2005, June). *Head Start impact study first year findings.* Washington, DC: U. S. Department of Health and Human Services.

Raver, C. C., & Zigler, E. (1991). Three steps forward, two steps back: Head Start and the measurement of social competence. *Young Children, 46*(4), 3–8.

Reynolds, A. J. (2004). Dosage-response effects and mechanisms of change in public and model programs. In E. Zigler & S. J. Styfco (Eds.), *The Head Start debates* (pp. 379–396). Baltimore, MD: Paul H. Brookes.

Rothstein, R. (2004). *Class and schools.* New York: Teachers College Press.

Schweinhart, L. J. (2003). The three types of early childhood programs in the United States. In A. J. Reynolds, M. C. Wang, & H. J. Walberg (Eds.), *Early childhood programs for a new century* (pp. 241–254). Washington, DC: CWLA Press.

U. S. Comptroller General. (1979). *Early childhood and family development programs improve the quality of life for low-income families.* (HRD-79-40). Washington, DC: U. S. General Accounting Office.

U. S. Department of Health and Human Services. (2003, June). *Strengthening Head Start: What the evidence shows.* Washington, DC: Author.

Yoshikawa, H. (2005). *Placing the first year findings of the National Head Start Impact Study in context.* Washington, DC: Society for Research in Child Development.

Zigler, E. (1970). The environmental mystique: Training the intellect versus development of the child. *Childhood Education, 46,* 402–412.

Zigler, E., Abelson, W. D., Trickett, P. K., & Seitz, V. (1982). Is an intervention program really necessary to raise disadvantaged children's IQ scores? *Child Development, 53,* 340–348.

Zigler, E., & Bennett-Gates, D. (Eds.). (1999). *Personality development in individuals with mental retardation.* New York: Cambridge University Press.

Zigler, E., & Butterfield, E. C. (1968). Motivational aspects of changes in IQ test performance of culturally deprived nursery school children. *Child Development, 39,* 1–14.

Zigler, E., Gilliam, W. S., Jones, S. M., & colleagues. (2006). *A vision for universal preschool education.* New York: Cambridge University Press.

Zigler, E., & Muenchow, S. (1992). *Head Start: The inside story of America's most successful educational experiment.* New York: Basic Books.

Zigler, E., & Styfco, S. J. (2004a). Head Start's National Reporting System: A work in progress. *Pediatrics, 114,* 858–859.

Zigler, E., & Styfco, S. J. (2004b). Moving Head Start to the states: One experiment too many. *Applied Developmental Science, 8,* 51–55.

Zigler, E., & Styfco, S. J. (2005). Epilogue. In N. Watt, C. Ayoub, R. H. Bradley, J. E. Puma, & W. A. LeBoeuf. (Eds.), *The crisis in youth mental health. Critical issues and effective programs. Volume 4. Early intervention programs and policies* (pp. 347–371). Greenwich, CT: Praeger.

Zigler, E., & Trickett, P. (1978). IQ, social competence, and evaluation of early childhood intervention programs. *American Psychologist, 33,* 789–798.

Zigler, E., & Valentine, J. (Eds.). (1979). *Project Head Start: A legacy of the War on Poverty.* New York: Free Press.

Zigler, E., & Valentine, J. (Eds.). (1997). *Project Head Start: A legacy of the War on Poverty* (2nd ed.). Alexandria, VA: National Head Start Association.

4

AFFIRMATIVE ACTION AND ETHNIC MINORITY UNIVERSITY STUDENTS

Enlarging Pipelines to Support Success

Joel Gills, Kristina Schmukler, Margarita Azmitia, and Faye Crosby

In the United States today, as never before, education holds the key to prosperity. The bachelor's degree now strongly serves a gating function. In 2004, for example, those who had graduated from college earned on average twice as much as those whose education stopped at the end of high school (U.S. Department of Labor, 2004).

Many institutions of higher learning take very seriously their role in helping America fulfill its identity as the land of opportunity. One function of public universities is to promote social and economic mobility for talented young citizens. Public universities seek to serve all the state's citizens, not just those who have grown up in affluence. Given the American commitment to equality of opportunity, persistent demographic differences in educational attainments are deeply disappointing. In 2003, 34% of European-heritage high school graduates went on to graduate from a four-year college, whereas only 10% of Latinos and 18% of African Americans did (National Center for Education Statistics, 2003). How can the achievement gap be closed? Some believe that the gap may never close (Thernstrom & Thernstrom, 1997). Others look to minority communities to make changes in their own behavior (Johnson, 2004; Steele, 1990). Still others insist that schools themselves must take affirmative steps to make sure that a college education is open equally to those from privileged and underprivileged backgrounds (Tierney, Colyar, & Corwin, 2005).

Whenever a school takes positive steps to assure equality, it engages in one form or another of affirmative action. The American Psychological Association defines affirmative action as occurring when "an organization expends energy to make sure that there is no discrimination in employment or education and, instead equal opportunity exists" (1996, p. 5). The more energy expended, the more vigorous the affirmative action.

American colleges and universities have used three major forms of affirmative action. First, some schools have provided exclusive fellowships and special programs for students from underrepresented groups. Second, many schools have expended more resources on locating and attracting students of color than they spend on locating and attracting European-heritage students. Third, some colleges and universities have made adjustments to the admissions requirements, favoring some groups (e.g., African Americans) as an expedient way of compensating for the unfair disadvantages that have faced the group at earlier moments in their educational development.

It can be argued that many of our nation's social inequalities stem from the educational disadvantages that plague ethnic minority and low-income youth. Educational inequalities result in social inequalities. When those with the education and power to make important decisions do not reflect the populations for whom they are making decisions, social inequalities are bound to result. Affirmative action serves to foster the education of youth and adult citizens from all backgrounds who will have the knowledge and opportunity to hold positions of power and thereby to reflect the broader society that they serve. Thus, affirmative action in education attempts to ameliorate impending social inequalities by ensuring that children and adolescents from all backgrounds have the opportunity to succeed and contribute to the betterment of society.

In this chapter, we look at two forms of affirmative action in higher education. First, we describe outreach practices. Second, we turn to the issue of race-sensitive admissions policies, showing how they have evolved and articulate what we know from social scientific studies about the problems—real and imagined—of race-conscious admissions policies. Unlike critics of affirmative action, we argue that empirical data show that race-sensitive admissions policies do far more good than harm. Nonetheless, the published studies leave unanswered a related question. In the final section of our chapter, we pose the following question: How could race-sensitive admissions practices function even more effectively than they do at present?

Relying on qualitative data from ongoing research being conducted at UC Santa Cruz, we conclude that thoughtful interventions, especially during the first year of college, can be quite instrumental in enhancing the college experience of students from educationally disadvantaged backgrounds. Throughout the chapter, we integrate the perspectives of social psychology and developmental psychology. Social and developmental psychologists have long researched and theorized about the educational pathways of educationally disadvantaged students. Unfortunately, their research and theories have not often been integrated. By collaborating on this chapter, we hoped to not only contribute to our fields of social (Crosby and Schmukler) and developmental (Gills and Azmitia) psychology, but also to educational policies and programs that benefit minority children and adolescents.

OUTREACH

Among all forms of affirmative action in higher education, outreach programs typically provoke the least controversy (Crosby, 2004). In California and other states, academic outreach programs have been created to equip students and their families with the social capital that is associated with academic success. These programs vary in scope, size, and location, the targeted developmental period, whether they are selective, the level of expected familial involvement, and the strategies used to distribute social capital—knowledge, social networks, and resources for education—to their participants. However, for all programs the overarching goal is to increase college attendance and graduation among educationally disadvantaged students.

Many of the state and federal academic outreach programs were established in the 1960s and 1970s in response to the civil rights movement and local, state, and federal efforts to diversify universities. Most academic outreach programs initially targeted high school students because of developmental and educational research showing that this is a time when adolescents are actively constructing their educational and career identities in addition to the alarming statistics on the low high school graduation rates of African American and Latino students. In the early 1980s, however, developmental and educational psychologists in conjunction with K–12 teachers began to highlight middle school as a key turning point in disadvantaged students' educational pathways. This recognition led to the expansion of many extant academic outreach programs into the middle school years and to the creation of academic outreach programs that focus exclusively on this developmental period (Gándara & Bial, 2001).

As theoretical frameworks and empirical evidence about the academic pipeline accumulated, academic outreach programs were established at community colleges because many disadvantaged students were not eligible to attend a four-year university after graduating from high school. Thus, they were unable to pursue this route to higher education. In turn, these outreach programs focused on helping students become eligible to transfer to four-year universities. More recently, based on evidence that a significant widening of the achievement gap between disadvantaged students and their peers occurs between third and fourth grades, academic outreach efforts have extended to elementary schools. At the elementary school level, outreach focuses on familiarizing students and their families with the university, providing after-school help with academic skills, and providing professional development opportunities for teachers [Gándara & Bial, 2001; Policy Analysis for California Education (PACE), 1997].

Outreach programs are justified by two general observations. First, many institutions of higher learning are unfamiliar to youth from educationally disadvantaged backgrounds and in particular to ethnic minority youth from groups that have been historically underrepresented in higher education. Thus, these institutions are viewed with suspicion. A certain amount of effort is needed to make the school feel like a safe and welcoming environment. Second, disadvantaged families are often unable to provide their youth with the social capital of most college-bound youth (Coleman, 1988; Stanton-Salazar, 2004). Social agencies including schools should, therefore, hold out a helping hand to disadvantaged youth who have talent and high aspirations.

One outreach program that serves youth across the country is *I Have a Dream* (IHAD), which was established in New York City in 1981 by Eugene Lang, a businessman who adopted the sixth-grade class at his former elementary school and promised to pay the college tuition of all the students who graduated from high school. Today, participants attend workshops after school, on weekends, and over the summer. The program monitors participants through several school transitions and still provides college scholarships to those participants who graduate from high school. Currently there are IHAD programs in 27 states. The program has served 13,500 students and has been so successful that it served as the model for *Gear Up*, the nationwide program funded by the U.S. Department of Education to help disadvantaged students transition successfully into and beyond middle school.

IHAD's effectiveness derives primarily from the caring and trusting relationships that are developed among the program's coordinators, schools, and the students involved. Evaluators have commented on the apparent lack of family involvement in the IHAD agenda (Gándara & Bial, 2001). Following some social capital theorists (Coleman, 1988; Stanton-Salazar, 2004), IHAD believes that the transmission of educational resources is most effective when it moves directly from the institution to the student. IHAD and related programs emphasize friendships because the program recognizes that having friends in the program will not only keep adolescents involved but also create a community of peer scholars who value education and help each other succeed (see also Azmitia & Cooper, 2001).

The IHAD vision has spawned several local programs. The Cabrillo Advancement Program (CAP) is one such program in the county of Santa Cruz, California, our home community. Founded in 1995, CAP annually serves 500 students in nine schools. Selection into the program occurs on the basis of an essay about the future that is assigned by middle school teachers in the participating school districts.

CAP differs from IHAD in three important ways. First, CAP is small and operates with very limited resources, whereas IHAD is large and relatively well funded. From the first difference springs a second: CAP only provides a small scholarship ($1000) to its high school graduates to be redeemed only at a specific community college. Finally, unlike IHAD, CAP has a strong family component. The developers of CAP believe that both the transmission of social capital and the construction and maintenance of a college-going identity are strengthened by family involvement and support, especially as a safeguard against competing peer activities in middle school. Family involvement also increases the possibility that students will remain in the program during middle school and high school despite competing peer activities and employment (Azmitia & Cooper, 2001).

These two outreach programs focus on the transition to middle school because, as mentioned earlier, considerable research has shown that this is a key turning point in disadvantaged students' educational pathways (Azmitia & Cooper, 2001; Larson & Rumberger, 1995; Seidman, Aber, Allen, Mitchell, & Feinman, 1994). In their landmark study, Simmons and Blyth (1987) found that many adolescents' grades, academic motivation, school attendance, and self-esteem declined from elementary to middle school. Researchers have proposed that the decline occurred because this school transition coincides with many changes in young adolescents' lives. For many adolescents, the transition to middle school coincides with puberty, shifts in cognitive skills, and changes in their relationships with family and peers.

Middle schools are also very different from elementary schools: A larger student body and the variety of teachers with whom students interact daily increase students' feelings of isolation and alienation (Eccles et al., 1993). Academic tracking, which was less transparent in elementary school, also begins in earnest. Educationally disadvantaged students are more likely to be tracked into remedial classes and to perceive their teachers as unsupportive. This adds to the risk that they will disengage from school and "leak out" of the educational pipeline to high school graduation and college (Oakes, 1985).

Several school-based academic outreach programs focus on untracking educationally disadvantaged students from noncollege pathways. The Advancement Via Individual Determination (AVID) program, for example, focuses on the high school years, a critical time for solidifying college-going identities. Each year since AVID's founding in 1980 in San Diego, California, the California State Department of Education has provided grants to schools to develop academic enrichment programs for educationally disadvantaged incoming high school students who have high achievement test scores but low junior high school grades. The program takes students who were previously in vocational tracks and places them alongside educationally advantaged students in college track classes. This strategy is coupled with additional classes on writing, note taking, inquiry, and collaborative work strategies.

Although AVID seeks to create and sustain college-going identities among its participants, the program also attempts to highlight to its participants the importance of retaining their ethnic and cultural identities by going on field trips and bringing in motivational speakers from the community (Mehan, Hubbard, & Villanueva, 1994). At present, 30,000 students have completed the AVID program, with 93% of these students enrolling in college after high school graduation (California State Department of Education, 2005).

RACE-SENSITIVE ADMISSIONS POLICIES

Outreach programs appeal greatly to the sense of individualistic striving that is often seen as the hallmark of America, but outreach programs are expensive and serve relatively few students. Whereas the numbers of students affected each year by outreach are in the thousands, the numbers affected by race-sensitive admissions policies are in the millions.

Race-sensitive admissions policies evoke strong feelings, usually negative. To many people, they appear both unfair and ineffective. Although outreach programs are under constant threat of budget cuts from the state or federal government, no one has yet brought a lawsuit against an outreach program. In contrast, many people have used the courts to try to dismantle race-sensitive admissions policies.

Two rationales for race-sensitive admissions procedures have been identified (Tierney, 1997): diversity and fairness. In a nutshell, the diversity argument posits that higher public education exists to serve the purposes of the state. With education being a central feature of democracy, one goal of the state is to have an educated electorate. Limited public resources mean that the demand for places at public universities exceeds the supply of available spaces. How is the state to choose among the many applicants? First, it must devise ways to distinguish between those who are capable of doing university-level work and those who are not. Even restricting consideration to the first group, there are too many applicants for the available spaces. The state must then use criteria to make selections from among the qualified applicant pool.

One way to choose students is to make sure that university students reflect the demographic basis of the state in terms of sex, ethnicity, location (e.g., north or south), and type of community (e.g., urban, suburban, rural). Such diversity assures that people from all backgrounds have an opportunity for upward mobility. Diversity also benefits those students who are admitted to the university—majority as well as minority, men as well as women, suburban as well as rural or city-dwellers—because student engagement and learning is known to be enhanced by coming into close contact with dissimilar others (Gurin, 2004).

Somewhat different is the fairness argument used to justify race-sensitive admissions policies. According to the fairness argument, race-sensitive admissions policies function primarily as expedient adjustments to systems, which are themselves expediencies, and imperfect ones at that. Admission criteria that appear to be neutral and unbiased may, in unanticipated ways, put applicants from some backgrounds at a special disadvantage. What can appear on the surface to be preferential treatment is actually just extra effort needed to counterbalance the pervasive "baked in the skin" preference so customarily given to European-heritage people, to males, and to people from affluent backgrounds, that it remains largely outside of conscious awareness.

Legal Battles

Since being put into place in the 1960s, race-sensitive admissions policies have provoked resistance. Some European-heritage applicants have bristled at what they see as a policy of reverse discrimination. Preferential treatment, they say, is preferential treatment, whether it favors the hegemonic group or a disadvantaged group. Twice, legal battles over race-sensitive admissions policies have reached the Supreme Court.

In 1978 the Supreme Court decided the case of *The Regents of the University of California v. Bakke* (1978), which had originated in the rejection of a European-heritage student by the medical school at the University of California Davis (UCDMS). The admissions policy at UCDMS had set aside 16% of its places for applicants of color, who were evaluated relative to each other but not relative to the 84% majority. Such a policy, said the Court, was unconstitutional.

The Court in *Bakke* clearly articulated the principle of "strict scrutiny," by which the state or any of its agencies may make distinctions among people on the basis of race or ethnicity only if the procedure passes "strict scrutiny." To pass strict scrutiny, the state or its agents must demonstrate that (a) there is a compelling state interest involved in the actions and (b) its actions are "narrowly tailored" to the situation. A narrowly tailored solution might, for example, have a sunset clause in it.

Although clearly articulating the principle of strict scrutiny, the *Bakke* decision generated confusion in other ways. In subsequent years, appellate courts differed in their interpretations of *Bakke*. The Ninth Circuit decided that *Bakke* had established the principle that the state has a compelling interest in assuring diverse student bodies; however, the Fifth Circuit declared that it was only one individual, Justice Powell, who felt that student diversity constituted a compelling state interest (Smith & Crosby, in press).

It was, therefore, with trepidation that civil rights activists learned in 2002 that the Supreme Court had agreed to hear the famous Michigan cases: *Gratz v. Bollinger* and *Grutter v. Bollinger.* Jennifer Gratz had been rejected from the undergraduate college at the university, and Barbara Grutter had been rejected from the law school. Both rejected applicants were European-heritage, and both resented the fact that students of color who had lower scores than themselves had been accepted.

The rulings in the Michigan cases provided mixed news for the future of affirmative action in college admissions policy (Crosby, 2004; Stohr, 2004). In the case of the undergraduate College of Literature, Science and the Arts (*Gratz v. Bollinger*, 2003), the Court ruled that the point system used by the university was unconstitutional because it was not narrowly tailored. Yet in the case of *Grutter v. Bollinger* (2003), the Court supported the university (Crosby, 2004; Stohr, 2004), finding that the holistic approach of the graduate admission policy was narrowly tailored.

In both *Gratz* and *Grutter*, the Court affirmed that diversity was a compelling state interest. Writing the Grutter majority decision, Judge O'Connor claimed *Bakke* as a precedent. O'Connor referred to social science research that showed the importance of having a critical mass of minority students to make the university experience beneficial to both minority and majority students. In order for minority students to feel comfortable expressing their own views without being stereotyped, there needs to be a critical mass of minority students. Once critical mass is met, European-heritage students will be able to see diverse views among minority students, and will abandon essentialist beliefs that all ethnic minority students are fungible in their attitudes (*Grutter v. Bollinger*, 2003).

The majority opinion in *Grutter* also saw the state's interest in diversity as compelling because diversity seemed to be a way to keep the peace. The Supreme Court held that "In order to cultivate a set of leaders with legitimacy in the eyes of the citizenry, it is necessary that the path to leadership be visibly open to talented and qualified individuals of every race and ethnicity" (*Grutter v. Bollinger*, 2003). As Lehman (2004) has pointed out, by referencing the role of institutions of higher education in American society, the Court signaled that such institutions could be judged not only on the basis of what their students learned, but also on the basis of how they appeared to society at large. Public institutions exist not only for their own sake or for the pleasure of their professors and students, but also for the greater good of society. Recognition of the role of colleges and universities in maintaining a just society is an extraordinarily important legacy of the Michigan cases.

Effects of Race-Sensitive Admissions Policies: How Bad Are the Consequences?

What are the consequences of race-sensitive programs in education for the intended beneficiaries, for other students, and for society at large? Opponents warn against negative consequences. Proponents see the consequences as positive.

Is Attrition a Consequence?   An early outspoken critic of affirmative action was Shelby Steele (1990), twin brother of the famous social psychologist and advocate of affirmative action, Claude Steele. In a beautifully crafted and widely cited book, *The Content of Our Character*, Shelby Steele (1990) opined that race-sensitive admissions policies were harming those whom they pretended to help. By allowing underprepared minority students to enter the university, such policies, said Steele, set students up for failure and then further crippled them by implicitly inviting them to blame the system when they flunked out of school.

The evidence for Steele's dire conclusions came from what he had seen at San Jose State University, where he taught English. The evidence was, in short, unsystematic and anecdotal. But it struck a chord and thus instigated a set of studies that sought to test his assertions in systematic ways.

The first hard evidence about the consequences of race-sensitive admissions policies came roaring onto the scene in 1998 with the publication of the authoritative *Shape of the River* (Bowen & Bok, 1998). Bowen and Bok combed through the longitudinal records of over 80,000 students who had matriculated in 1951, 1976, and 1989 at 28 elite colleges and universities. The book's major conclusion was that when people of color are admitted to a college or university with lower scores on admission criteria than others, they nonetheless tend to perform as well as majority students in terms of graduation rates, matriculation in graduate or professional school, and professional life. The "special admits" do, however, earn lower grades than others in college and in professional or graduate school, and they also prove distinctive in terms of their civic engagement as adults, giving many more hours in volunteer commitments than do other graduates.

Lempert, Chambers, and Adams (2000a, 2000b) reached similar conclusions from a survey they conducted of the graduates from the classes of 1970 through 1996 of the University of Michigan Law School. Using stratified random sampling, the study included over 1,000 participants. Lempert et al. (2000a) found that LSAT scores and undergraduate grade point average (GPA) predicted grades in law school but not other measures of success. Minority graduates in the sample were not distinct from European-heritage graduates in terms of passing the bar, current income, or reported satisfaction with their education.

Additional studies (Brown, Charnsangavej, Keough, Newman, & Rentfrow, 2000; Van Laar & Levin, 2000) have supported the findings that ethnic minority students admitted under race-sensitive admissions policies do earn lower grades than majority students. Nonetheless, the between-group differences in college GPA are consistently smaller than the between-group differences in scores on the entrance examinations. The latter finding gives weight to Jencks's (1998) observation about selective system bias.

The preponderance of evidence refutes Shelby Steele's worry about the pernicious effects of affirmative action in education; however, a recent study by UCLA law professor Richard Sander (2004) reminds us not to become complacent. Closely analyzing data from 27,000 young men and women who had entered law school in 1991 and who were tracked until 1997, Sander shone a spotlight on some disturbing patterns. First, Sander found that ethnic minority students were accorded preferential admissions. He also noted that the ethnic minority students ended up being disproportionately represented among the lowest segments of their law school classes, among dropouts, among those who failed the bar exam on the first attempt, and among those who did not pass the bar by the end of the study. Although several experts (Ayres & Brooks, 2005; Chambers, Clydesdale, Kidder, & Lempert, 2005; Wilkins, 2005) have warned against inferring causal connections on the basis of co-variation, Sander's analysis provides a sobering reminder of ethnic differences in terms of graduation from law school and passing the bar exam.

Is Self-Esteem Adversely Influenced?   Even if there proves, in the end, to be no evidence for differential attrition rates, it may still be that race-sensitive admissions policies have the negative effect of undermining the self-confidence of those whom they seek to help. A number of prominent ethnic minority men have written and spoken about the threat that they personally felt to their self-esteem when they were tagged as members of a disadvantaged group (e.g., Carter, 1991; Rodriquez, 1982). A series of laboratory studies have shown that persons who think they have been selected for a position simply to fill a quota feel critical of themselves and of others like them (e.g., Heilman, Block, & Lucas, 1992; Heilman, Block, & Strathatos, 1997).

Although quite plausible, the notion of diminished self-esteem turns out to be incorrect. Several surveys (e.g., Elizondo & Crosby, 2004; Schmermund, Sellers, Mueller, & Crosby, 2001; Truax, Wood, Wright, Cordova, & Crosby, 1998) of ethnic minority college students show that they endorse affirmative action and retain a sense of pride in their abilities as students, thereby demonstrating no apparent negative impact on their self-esteem. They sometimes feel unwelcome in their college environment and sometimes express less self-confidence than European-heritage students, but they do not express this as being a result of affirmative action.

Why is self-esteem not harmed when ethnic minority students gain access to colleges and universities from which they were previously excluded? We can only speculate, but two factors seem important. First, there is strong evidence from the laboratory of Madeline Heilman (e.g., Heilman et al., 1992; Heilman et al., 1997) and others (summarized in Crosby, 2004, pp. 147–157) that the pernicious effects of preferential selection only occur when people are unsure of their capabilities. When people know that they are capable, they are unaffected by being told that they had gained a position partially or wholly due to some demographic characteristic. Consistent with the laboratory evidence are the results of several surveys that show that it is the ethnic minority students who are most insecure about their capabilities or most unsure of their ethnic identity who give affirmative action the least support (Elizondo & Crosby, 2004; Schmermund et al., 2001; Truax et al., 1998). Second, ethnic minority students may refuse to be stung by any disapproval from European-heritage peers and professors if they believe that the disapproval springs, at least in part, from pre-existing racial prejudices (Ayers, 1992).

Is Intergroup Hostility Augmented? It might seem logical to assert that race-sensitive policies will ignite racial divisions. Some judges have cited interethnic hostility as an almost inevitable outcome of race-sensitive admissions policies (Crosby, 2004). Surveys of the general population show that many people of European-heritage are unsympathetic to either affirmative action or to the ethnic minorities whom it seeks to serve (Crosby, 2004). Negative opinions about race-sensitive policies in education give rise to a suspicion of ethnic backlash.

Again, systematically collected data do not confirm what seems intuitively likely. Neither Bowen and Bok (1998) nor Lempert et al. (2000a, 2000b) found any evidence that White students disliked interacting with students of color or resented their presence on campus. Similarly, in a set of studies conducted under the direction of Patricia Gurin, researchers found that White students valued the contact with ethnically dissimilar others and concluded that they had benefited by being educated at schools that valued diversity (Gurin, 2004).

Is Learning Negatively Affected? Gurin's research, which was critical to the success of the University of Michigan case, helped psychologists better understand how students learn in multicultural and monocultural situations. Gurin and associates recognized that the University of Michigan would be a monocultural environment were it not for affirmative action, and they hypothesized that student learning would suffer. To test their theory-based prediction that encounters with diverse others benefit both European-heritage students and students of color, Gurin and associates conducted three interrelated studies (Gurin, 2004, Gurin, Dey, Hurtado, & Gurin, 2002).

One study analyzed a longitudinal dataset of nearly 12,000 students who matriculated in 184 colleges and universities in 1984 and who were surveyed again in 1989 and 1994. The second study involved detailed questionnaires given to all students of color and a representative sample of European-heritage students at the University of Michigan who were tracked throughout the four years of undergraduate study. Nearly 1,600 students participated in the second study. Embedded in the second study was a third that contained a subsample of 174 students.

Half of these students had participated in a semester-long Program on Intergroup Relations (IGR). The other half comprised the comparison group, matched to the IGR group in terms of gender, ethnicity, precollege residency, and on-campus residence hall.

Gurin and her associates found reliable and consistent relationships between diversity experiences, on the one hand, and various measures of educational engagement and learning. The connections existed across all ethnic and gender groupings and were equally visible nationally as in the University of Michigan studies. Diverse learning environments also enhanced students' readiness to participate in a pluralistic democracy. The more students interacted with other students from different groups, the more they felt comfortable tackling difficult issues about the democratic process and civil dissent. Students who had a lot of contact with individuals from other groups understood that divergence of viewpoints can strengthen, not threaten, group functioning and that polite dissent is at the core of a well-functioning democracy (Gurin, Nagda, & Lopez, 2004; Zuniga, Nagda, & Sevig, 2002).

Gurin's results were consistent with findings of other scholars in different educational settings using different measures (Antonio et al., 2004; Chang, Astin, & Kim, 2004; Orfield & Whitla, 2001). Conversely, a group of conservative scholars (Rothman, Lipset, & Nevitte, 2003) published what they conceived of as counterevidence and gained notoriety at the time of the Michigan court cases, but subsequent analyses proved their study to be deeply flawed (Gurin, 2004).

In Sum   Outspoken critics of race-sensitive admissions policies have foreseen dire results from the policies. Systematic studies have, by and large, not substantiated the negative view of "hard" affirmative action policies. On the contrary, studies conducted by numerous researchers have now shown that race-sensitive policies help America achieve its egalitarian ideals more than do so-called color-blind policies.

DO OUTREACH AND RACE-SENSITIVE ADMISSIONS SUFFICE?

To claim that various forms of affirmative action prove beneficial is not to claim that such policies are beyond improvement. Work at the University of California Santa Cruz on students' transition to college life has convinced us that it is not enough to bring educationally disadvantaged students to the university. Rather, institutions and students benefit when the institutions also exert energy trying to make the newcomers feel valued and at home. Although the need to devote efforts to retention and graduation of disadvantaged students has long been recognized and has led to the creation of a variety of support programs and services, many educationally disadvantaged students still leave the university, especially in their first year. Reductions in the state and federal monies for outreach have also led universities to attempt to determine what works to retain and graduate educationally disadvantaged students. The transition to college project emerged from these efforts. The project was a collaboration between a faculty-led (Azmitia) team of researchers and university staff (the Educational Opportunity Programs [EOP], the admissions office, and student services).

The Transition to College Project

The transition to college is often the first time adolescents move away from their families and home communities. This a fertile time for adolescents to explore their identities and start to figure out who they want to become as adults. Considerable attention has been paid to the transition to college as a marker of emerging adulthood and life-long educational, career, and by implication, social class trajectories (Cooper, Jackson, Azmitia & Lopez, 1998; Gándara, 1995; Tierney et al., 2005). Whereas the number of late adolescents attending college in the United States has increased steadily over the last decades, European- and Asian-heritage adolescents are significantly more likely to attend college and graduate than Latino-, African-, and Native American adolescents (Cabrera & La Nasa, 2000; O'Hare & Pollard, 1998; Tierney et al., 2005).

To understand divergent trends in college attendance and retention among students from diverse backgrounds, one of us (Azmitia) and her students (Gills, Radmacher, Syed, Reis, Tonyan, and McLean) began a two-year longitudinal study in 2002 of students enrolled at the University of California (UC) Santa Cruz. The goal of the study has been to examine what experiences are common for most adolescents in the adjustment to college and what experiences are unique to educationally disadvantaged adolescents. About half of the sample of 216 adolescents consisted of educationally disadvantaged students designated as underrepresented by UC: Chicano/Latino-, African-, Filipino-, and Native American-heritage students and low-income European-heritage students who were the first in their families to attend college. The remaining participants were from European and Asian (Chinese and Japanese) descent, two groups who have done well at UC. Sixty-five percent of the sample was female.

The educationally disadvantaged and Asian-heritage students were randomly selected from a list of all entering ethnic minority first-year students supplied by the university. One hundred students (50 males and 50 females) from each ethnic group were randomly selected and received letters inviting them to participate the summer prior to their enrollment in the university. Because there were less than 100 African- and Native American-heritage students on the list, all the members of these groups were sent the invitation letters. Students indicated their interest in participating by returning a postage-prepaid postcard; between 30 and 50% of the members of each ethnic group returned the postcards. Due to their large number, the university did not provide a list of entering European-heritage students; these participants and additional ethnic minority participants were recruited through flyers posted in dorms and bus stops, a recruitment table placed in the student commons, and by word of mouth.

Participants individually completed a survey and an interview during the first five weeks of the fall, winter, and spring quarters of their first year of college and during the spring quarter of their sophomore year. The survey included measures of social support, mental health (self-esteem and depression), self-efficacy, identity, and involvement in university activities. The interviews gathered information about the students' high school; home communities; families; friends; academic and nonacademic activities at the university; their perceptions of the university and their professors; their adjustment to college; their overall identity exploration; their ethnic, gender, and social class identities; their perceptions of the diversity of the campus; and their goals for the future.

Lessons From the Study

Reviewing interviews conducted with educationally disadvantaged students, we were struck by three observations that have implications for helping affirmative action to be more effective. The first has to do with students' feelings of discontinuity with their backgrounds and distancing from their home community. The second concerns the benefits of a summer immersion program, and the third relates to issues of ethnic visibility and invisibility.

Distancing From Home   When they go to college, adolescents usually leave their families, friends, and communities. For most adolescents, the shift to college means a shift to a new "culture" with its own set of norms. The shift is especially great for students from disadvantaged backgrounds. All students must find ways to relate to professors, classmates, coworkers, and other peers, but educationally disadvantaged students often feel that they have little in common with their university community (Tierney et al., 2005). Educationally disadvantaged students must also coordinate their college-going identities with other, older, identities that may be in opposition to the values, expectations, and behaviors associated with college success (see also Cooper et al., 1998; Orbe, 2004). Among students from privileged backgrounds, being a good student may go hand-in-hand with filial responsibility and loyalty to family; among disadvantaged students, to be a good student may sometimes put a student at risk of disloyalty to friends and family. Disadvantaged students may also feel that their educational success is distancing them from their friends and jeopardizing their close relationships.

María Elena,* a Latina participant, had an excellent transition to the university. She found her coursework exciting and challenging, obtained very good grades, made friends, and participated actively in dorm and college activities. In her fall interview, she remarked that things were going even better than she had expected. She also told us that her parents and close friends from home—none of whom had done well enough in high school to qualify for admission to UC—were very proud and supportive of her being at a UC. Indeed, her parents and friends had encouraged her to choose UC over a university closer to home, and had celebrated when she decided to follow their advice.

Yet, in the winter quarter María Elena applied to transfer to a less prestigious university closer to home. She told us that she did so because she felt her going far away from home was disloyal to her younger sisters, who were counting on her help with school work and their personal lives. She added, "I feel like I'm missing out on seeing them grow up and go on to college." She indicated that although she felt her decision to transfer was best for her and her younger sisters, she felt torn because she knew her parents would be disappointed with her decision.

In the spring interview, María Elena disclosed that it wasn't only her commitment to her younger sisters that had sparked her decision to transfer. Her boyfriend, who was back in her home community and had opted to go to work rather than attend college, had also encouraged her to transfer so they could be together. She said that he did not really understand the difference in prestige between UC and the local university, because to him, college was college, an educational goal to which he did not aspire.

Robert, an African-American participant from a very low-income and dangerous neighborhood, had a bumpier transition to college. Although he had accrued a high GPA at his high school, he was unprepared for the rigors of college work. In the fall quarter he failed one of his classes, and throughout the year he faced the threat of being

---

* All names have been changed to protect the anonymity of the participants.

put on academic probation. As one of the few African-American male students on the campus, he struggled to make friends and feel a sense of community. Particularly difficult for him was noticing the fear in European-heritage female college students' eyes when they encountered him on the paths late at night; he could understand their fear, but it added to his feelings that he was out of place at the university.

An additional challenge for Robert was that he was the only person in his circle of friends who went to college and one of the few who graduated from high school. Robert told us that his friends had not been very supportive of him going to college because they felt that once he was a "college man," he would no longer want to hang out with them. He explained that he came to the university because his loyalty to his mother—a single mother who worked three jobs but still managed to keep tabs on him and his brothers and keep them on positive educational pathways—superseded his loyalty to his friends. He dreamed of graduating and getting a job so he could buy his mother a house, "You know, in a quiet neighborhood with no 'drive-bys' [shootings] with a yard, trees, and all the things she deserves." In his spring interview, he told us that the dream to help his mother was the only thing that kept him going, and that he had avoided visiting his friends from home because he knew that given his feelings about the university, it would have been very easy for them to convince him to drop out.

Bridging the Distance   About 10% of the students in our study were required to participate in the Summer Bridge academic outreach program at the university because although their grades and test scores made them ineligible for admission to UC, their especially disadvantaged circumstances made them eligible through exception. This program involved students residing at the university for an extended period during the summer prior to their fall enrollment. The purposes of the summer program are to reinforce students' skills in English, writing, and math, to allow students to develop relationships with university staff, to learn about the university's "culture," and to connect new students with others from educationally disadvantaged families who were more advanced in standing.

The participants in our study who had taken part in Summer Bridge spoke highly of the program. Virtually all of those who had been Summer Bridge students stated that the program had facilitated their transition to college. Some tagged the experience as very important in allowing for a smooth adjustment to college life, and several spoke of how the experience had enhanced their sense of self-confidence and efficacy. In the words of one of the students, "The main thing that helped me adjust was that I came for Summer Bridge and I met a lot of people and counselors." Later in the interview, the same student identified the writing class as the most helpful aspect of the program, saying, "I'm not so used to writing that much and with that intensity. I just didn't realize it was going to be hard, but [because of Summer Bridge] I was prepared for it."

We found no evidence in our interviews that the participants in the Summer Bridge program felt diminished or otherwise hampered by the experience. Contrary to what one would expect from reading Shelby Steele (1990), the adolescents in our sample did not find their self-confidence eroded by being invited into a special program designed for students from educationally disadvantaged backgrounds. Indeed, rather than experiencing feelings of shame and inadequacy, the students we interviewed tended to express sentiments of solidarity and pride. In the sophomore year interview, when we asked them for suggestions for how the university could improve the experiences and success of future students, many of these students suggested that the university keep this important program in place, despite threats of cutting it out of the university's budget.*

The Summer Bridge program also tended to cement the students' relationship to the institution. Participants were aware that their high schools were not as high quality as those attended by other UC students. Typically being the first person in their family to attend college, they knew also that they could not rely on their families for information about college or strategies for college success. Thus, they saw the Summer Bridge invitation as not only an excellent aid to the transition, but also as a sign of the university's commitment to their success.

Invisible Disadvantages   Some of the students in our sample were European-heritage adolescents from educationally disadvantaged backgrounds. Such students tended to do well at the university, but they expressed feelings of discomfort, unease, and alienation. The alienation came in part from feeling "invisible" because their whiteness led their peers and teachers to assume, incorrectly, that they were from privileged backgrounds (see also Bettie, 2002; Ostrove, 2003). Many of the disadvantaged European-heritage students in our study recounted conversations during which wealthier peers planned extravagant vacations

---

* Given the state's and consequently, the university's budget woes, at the time of the interview the Summer Bridge program was in danger of being at best cut back drastically and at worst, eliminated.

or complained about having to work a few hours per week to pay for expensive purchases. The students added that these conversations made them feel frustrated and angry because they had to work long hours just to pay rent and buy food.

Additional feelings of alienation among disadvantaged European-heritage students stemmed from the belief that although UC had included them in their targets for diversity, the university was not investing the same level of resources in them as in their educationally disadvantaged ethnic minority peers. To support their point, some disadvantaged European-heritage participants mentioned several scholarships that were only available to ethnic minorities. They also complained that campus employers wanting to diversify their workforce privileged race, not class.

Other researchers investigating the alienation felt by educationally disadvantaged European-heritage university students have described similar findings and suggested that these experiences stem, at least in part, from the absence of a discourse about social class in the United States (Cole & Omari, 2003; Ostrove, 2003). Because the United States considers itself a democracy and a meritocracy, social class has not infused the discourse about discrimination and disadvantage as much as it has in nations where class hierarchies are more readily acknowledged (hooks, 2000). Yet, as Coleman (1988) and others concerned with the social reproduction of inequality have consistently shown, class matters because it confers social capital to adolescents.

By their sophomore year, several of our European-heritage first generation participants had worked through the anger and distress they felt about their experiences of alienation and invisibility. Some had recast their view of privilege by perceiving that they had better values and priorities of what was important in life than their wealthier peers. Others had developed a close friendship with another educationally disadvantaged European-heritage adolescent with whom they felt comfortable talking about how class and race affected their university experiences. Finally, a handful of these adolescents emphasized the pride they felt at having made it through their first two years of college so successfully. Susan told us that all the low-income European-heritage students from her community who had gone to college had dropped out and gone back home, and she was determined not to be one of them. Surviving her first year and doing even better her second year had made her realize that she would succeed at college and bring pride to her family and home community.

CONCLUDING OBSERVATIONS

Reflection on the issues at hand evokes a few observations about the nature of privilege and justice in an increasingly diverse nation.

College as a Visible Path to Prosperity

Our focus has been on affirmative action in education, and we have said virtually nothing about how affirmative action programs operate in the context of employment. Yet it is worth noting that affirmative action in employment touches the lives of many more Americans than does affirmative action in education (Downing et al., 2002). Nationwide, somewhere between three and seven million students are affected by affirmative action plans in schools, colleges, and universities (Crosby & Blake-Beard, 2004). In contrast, 25% of the adult workforce of the nation—or about 37 million people—are affected by E.O. 11246, because one in four workers is employed by a contractor or subcontractor of the federal government or by the federal government itself.

Given the disparities in numbers of Americans affected, it may seem paradoxical that affirmative action policies in education (and especially race-sensitive admissions policies) stir so much more controversy than affirmative action policies in employment. We believe several factors are at play. Chief among them, we think, is the symbolic aspect of a college education, serving simultaneously as a validation of one's worth and as a visible way station on the path to prosperity. Also important is the fear among those who are currently privileged, that their children or grandchildren might have to compete for their privileges rather than simply assume entitlement.

Outreach and Admissions

Outreach is vastly more popular than are race-sensitive admissions programs (Crosby, 2004). The question is: Why? One reason that Americans may find it acceptable for colleges and universities to devise special race-sensitive outreach programs is that such programs valorize the schools, or at least they do not explicitly or tacitly call into question anything about how the school functions. When one reaches out to the barrios to find the hidden talent and to bring that talent to Harvard or Yale or to the University of California, one does not question that there is such a thing as "talent" or that said talent is the coin of the realm at Harvard, Yale, or UC. Nor does one imply that the methods used by Harvard, Yale, or UC to assess talent are in any way flawed.

How different is the situation with race-sensitive admissions policies, justified as they are by a frank acknowledgment of the unfair nature of existing systems? Outreach programs also highlight the importance of developmentally appropriate interventions for educationally disadvantaged students. Outreach programs that have been especially successful target key transitions in educationally disadvantaged students' lives, incorporate family, and recognize that forming friendships is a key priority of adolescence. Increasingly, scholars have also recognized that it is important to continue outreach into college to ensure that disadvantaged students graduate (Gándara & Bial, 2001).

Social Class Issues

The interviews with adolescents participating in the UCSC transition to college study reveal the importance of social class. Educational disadvantage takes economic as well as color form. We propose that researchers, educators, and policy makers must acknowledge not only race, but also class and familial factors when discussing affirmative action policies. This recognition will make assessments of educational disadvantage more sensitive and help ensure that those who truly need institutional support can get it.

Help and Agency

The transition project at UC Santa Cruz and research elsewhere show that it is not enough just to push open the doors to those who have been excluded in the past. We must also bestir ourselves to make the newcomers feel as welcomed and to feel as entitled to a good education as those whose backgrounds never let them imagine otherwise. In the transformative process, the schools should not forget that students, even those who come newly to higher education, must be enlisted into the process in order for the enterprise to succeed. Sustaining students' sense of efficacy is of vital importance if students, faculty, staff, and administrators are to join together effectively in opening up higher education to all and for all.

Diversity and Fairness as Reinforcing Values

The emphasis on diversity in the defense of the University of Michigan left many public commentators wondering if diversity were being bought at the price of fairness (Crosby & Smith, in press; Smith & Crosby, in press). As is evident from our earlier discussion, we see all forms of affirmative action—race-sensitive admissions policies as well as outreach programs—as replacing systems that only appear to be fair with systems that actually are fair in practice.

When we move beyond a consideration of individuals in society and concentrate on groups, furthermore, we see how fairness and diversity, far from being in opposition, are intricately intertwined. In the words of Crosby, Iyer, Clayton, and Downing (2003, p. 109):

> Questions of affirmative action in both employment and education have illuminated an observation of fundamental importance: organizations need a variety of different talents. It is unlikely that any one person would be the most outstanding individual on all dimensions of talent. While it may be psychologically satisfying to recognize and reward outstanding achievements of individuals, groups, teams, organizations and societies may function best if they include and make use of many different types of talent. Thus, in the end, the merit of the group may depend on the diversity of talented individuals within it.

REFERENCES

Antonio, A. L., Chang, M. J., Hakuta, K., Kenny, D. A., Levin, S., & Milem, J. E. (2004). Effects of racial diversity on complex thinking in college students. *Psychological Science, 15*, 507–510.

Ayers, L. R. (1992). Perceptions of affirmative action among its beneficiaries. *Social Justice Research, 5*, 223–238.

Ayres, I., & Brooks, R. (2005). Does affirmative action reduce the number of Black lawyers? *Stanford Law Review, 57*, 1807–1854.

Azmitia, M., & Cooper, C. (2001). Good or bad? Peer influences on Latino and European American adolescents' pathways through school. *Journal of Education for Students Placed at Risk, 6*(1–2), 45–71.

Bettie, J. (2002). *Women without class: Girls, race, and identity.* Berkeley: University of California Press.

Bowen, W. G., & Bok, D. (1998). *The shape of the river: Long-term consequences of considering race in college and university admissions.* Princeton, NJ: Princeton University Press.

Brown, R. P., Charnsangavej, T., Keough, K. A., Newman, M. L., & Rentfrow, P. J. (2000). Putting the "affirm" into affirmative action: Preferential selection and academic performance. *Journal of Personality and Social Psychology, 79*, 736–747.

Cabrera, A. F., & La Nasa, S. M. (2000, May). *Using national databases to study the college choice of low-SES students.* Paper presented at the 40th Annual Forum of the Association for Institutional Research, Cincinnati, OH.

California Department of Education. (2005). *Advancement via individual determination.* Retrieved June 15, 2005 from http://www.cde.ca.gov/ci/gs/ps/avidgen.asp.

Carter, S. L. (1991). *Reflections of an affirmative action baby.* New York: Basic Books.

Chambers, D. L., Clydesdale, T. T., Kidder, W. C., & Lempert, R. O. (2005). The real impact of eliminating affirmative action in American law schools. *Stanford Law Review, 57*, 1855–1898.

Chang, M. J., Astin, A., & Kim, D. (2004). Cross-racial interaction among undergraduates: Some causes and consequences. *Research in Higher Education, 45*(5), 529–553.

Cole, E. R., & Omari, S. R. (2003). Race, class and the dilemmas of upward mobility for African-Americans. *Journal of Social Issues, 59*(4), 785–802.

Coleman, J. S. (1988). Social capital in the creation of human capital. *American Journal of Sociology, 94* Suppl., 95–120.

Cooper, C. R., Jackson, J. F., Azmitia, M., & Lopez, E. M. (1998). Multiple selves, multiple worlds: Three useful strategies for research with minority youth on identity, relationships, and opportunity structures. In V. C. McLoyd & L. Steinberg (Eds.), *Studying minority adolescents: Conceptual, methodological and theoretical issues* (pp. 111–126). Mawah, NJ: Lawrence Erlbaum.

Crosby, F. J. (2004). *Affirmative action is dead; long live affirmative action*. New Haven, CT: Yale University Press.

Crosby, F. J., & Blake-Beard, S. (2004). Affirmative action: Diversity, merit, and the benefit of white people. In M. Fine, L. Weis, L. C. Powell, & L. M. Wong (Eds.), *Off white: Readings on race, power, and society* (2nd ed., pp. 146–160). New York: Routledge.

Crosby, F. J., Iyer, A., Clayton, S., & Downing, R. (2003). Affirmative action: Psychological data and the policy debates. *American Psychologist, 58*, 93–115.

Crosby, F. J., & Smith, A. E. (in press). The University of Michigan cases: Social scientific studies of diversity and fairness. In R.L. Weiner, B. Bornstein, R. Schopp, & S. Willborn (Eds.), *Legal decision making in everyday life: Controversies in social consciousness*. New York: Springer.

Downing, R., Lubensky, M. E., Sincharoen, S., Gurin, P., Crosby, F. J., & Quierolo, S. (2002). Affirmative action in higher education. *The Diversity Factor, 10*, 15–20.

Eccles, J., Midgley, C., Wigfield, A., Buchanan, C., Reuman, D., Flanagan, C., et al. (1993). Development during adolescence: The impact of stage-environment fit on young adolescents' experiences in schools and families. *American Psychologist, 48*, 90–101.

Elizondo, E., & Crosby, F. J. (2004). Attitudes toward affirmative action as a function of the strength of ethnic identity among Latino college students. *Journal of Applied Social Psychology, 34*, 1773–1796.

Gándara, P. (1995). *Over the ivory walls: The educational mobility of low-income Chicanos*. New York: State University of New York Press.

Gándara, P., & Bial, D. (2001). *Paving the way to higher education: K–12 interventions for underrepresented youth.* Washington, DC: National Center for Educational Statistics.

Geiser, S., & Studley, R. (2001). *UC and the SAT: Predictive validity and differential impact of the SATI and SAT II at the University of California.* Retrieved November 11, 2003, from http://www.ucop.edu/sas/research/

Gratz v. Bollinger (2003). 539 U.S. 244.

Grutter v. Bollinger (2003). 539 U.S. 306.

Gurin, P. (2004). The educational value of diversity. In P. Gurin, J. S. Lehman, & E. Lewis (Eds.), *Defending diversity: Affirmative action at the University of Michigan* (pp. 97–188). Ann Arbor, MI: University of Michigan Press.

Gurin, P., Dey, E. L., Hurtado, S., & Gurin, G. (2002). Diversity and higher education: Theory and impact on educational outcomes. *Harvard Educational Review, 72,* 330–366.

Gurin, P., Nagda, B. R. A., & Lopez, G. E. (2004). The benefits of diversity in education for democratic citizenship. *Journal of Social Issues, 60,* 17–34.

Heilman, M. E., Block, C. J., & Lucas, J. A. (1992). Presumed incompetent? Stigmatization and affirmative action efforts. *Journal of Applied Psychology, 77,* 536–544.

Heilman, M. E., Block, C. J., & Stathatos, P. (1997). The affirmative action stigma of incompetence: Effects of performance information ambiguity. *Academy of Management Journal, 40,* 603–625.

hooks, B. (2000). *Where we stand: Class matters.* New York: Routledge.

Jencks, C. (1998). Racial bias in testing. In C. Jencks & M. Phillips (Eds.), *The black-white test score gap* (pp. 457–479). Washington, DC: Brookings Institution.

Johnson, J. (2004). *It ain't all good: Why black men should not date white women.* Chicago: African American Images.

Larson, K., & Rumberger, R. (1995). Doubling school success in highest-risk Latino youth: Results from a middle school intervention study. In R. F. Macías & R. G. García Ramos (Eds.), *Changing schools for changing students: An anthology of research language minorities* (pp. 157–180). Santa Barbara, CA: UC Linguistic Minority Research Institute.

Lehman, J. S. (2004). The evolving language of diversity and integration in discussions of affirmative action from *Bakke* to *Grutter.* In P. Gurin, J. S. Lehman, & E. Lewis (Eds.), *Defending diversity: Affirmative action at the University of Michigan* (pp. 61–96). Ann Arbor, MI: University of Michigan Press.

Lempert, R. O., Chambers, D. L., & Adams, T. K. (2000a). Michigan's minority graduates in practice: The river runs through law school. *Law and Social Inquiry, 25,* 395–505.

Lempert, R. O., Chambers, D. L., & Adams, T. K. (2000b). Law school affirmative action: An empirical study of Michigan's minority graduates in practice: Answers to methodological queries. *Law and Social Inquiry, 25,* 585–597.

Mehan, H., Hubbard, L., & Villanueva, I. (1994). Forming academic identities: Accommodation without assimilation among involuntary minorities. *Anthropology and Education Quarterly, 25*(2), 91–117.

National Center for Education Statistics. (2003). *Student effort and educational progress.* Retrieved June 7, 2005, from http://nces.ed.gov/programs/coe/2005/section3/table.asp?tableID=275

Oakes, J. (1985). *Keeping track: How schools structure inequality.* New York: Yale University Press.

O'Hare, W., & Pollard, K. M. (1998). Assessing the devolution revolution: How accurate are state-level estimates from the current population survey? *Population Research and Policy Review, 17*(1), 21–36.

Orbe, M. P. (2004). Negotiating multiple identities within multiple frames: An analysis of first-generation college students. *Communication Education, 53*(2), 131–149.

Orfield, G., & Whitla, D. (2001). Diversity and legal education: Student experiences in leading law schools. In G. Orfield & M. Kurlaender (Eds.), *Diversity challenged: Evidence on the impact of affirmative action* (pp. 143–174). Cambridge, MA: Harvard University Press.

Ostrove, J. M. (2003). Belonging and wanting: Meanings of social class background for women's constructions of their college experiences. *Journal of Social Issues, 59*(4), 771–784.

Policy Analysis for California Education (PACE). (1997, January). *Higher education outreach programs: A synthesis of evaluations.* A report commissioned by the Outreach Task Force Board of Regents of the University of California. Berkeley: University of California at Berkeley.

Regents of University of California v. Bakke (1979), 438 U.S. 912.

Rodriquez, R. (1982). *Hunger of memory: The education of Richard Rodriquez, an autobiography.* Boston, MA: Godine.

Rothman, S., Lipset, S. M., & Nevitte, N. (2003). Does enrollment diversity improve university education? *International Journal of Public Opinion Research, 15*, 8–26.

Sander, R. H. (2004). A systemic analysis of affirmative action in American law schools. *Stanford Law Review, 57*, 367–483.

Schmermund, A., Sellers, R., Mueller, B., & Crosby, F. (2001). Attitudes toward affirmative action as a function of racial identity among African American college students. *Political Psychology, 22*, 759–774.

Seidman, E., Allen, L. R., Mitchell, C., & Feinman, J. (1994). The impact of school transition in early adolescence on the self-system and perceived social context of poor urban youth. *Child Development, 65*(2), 507–522.

Simmons, R. G., & Blyth, D. A. (1987). *Moving into adolescence: The impact of pubertal change and school context.* New York: Hawthorne.

Smith, A. E., & Crosby, F. J. (in press). From Kansas to Michigan: The path from desegregation to diversity. In G. Adams, M. Biernat, N. Branscombe, C. Crandall, & L. Wrightsman (Eds.), *The social psychology of racism and discrimination, fifty years after Brown*. Washington, DC: APA Books.

Stanton-Salazar, R. D. (2004). Social capital among working-class minority students. In M. Gibson, P. Gándara, & J. Koyama (Eds.), *School connections: U.S. Mexican youth, peers, and school achievement*. New York: Teachers College Press.

Steele, S. (1990). *The content of our character: A new vision of race in America*. New York: Harper Perennial.

Stohr, G. (2004). *A black and white case*. Princeton, NJ: Bloomberg Press.

Thernstrom, S. A., & Thernstrom, A. M. (1997). *America in black and white: One nation indivisible*. New York: Simon & Schuster.

Tierney, W., Colyar, J. E., & Corwin, Z. B. (2005). *Preparing for college: Nine elements of effective outreach*. Albany: State University of New York Press.

Tierney, W. G. (1997). The parameters of affirmative action: Equity and excellence in the academy. *Review of Educational Research, 67*, 165–196.

Truax, K., Wood, A., Wright, E., Cordova, D. I., & Crosby, F. J. (1998). Undermined? Affirmative action from the targets' point of view. In J.K. Swim & C. Strangor (Eds.), *Prejudice: The target's perspective* (pp. 171–188). New York: Academic Press.

U.S. Department of Labor. (2004). *Education pays*. Retrieved June 7, 2005, from http://www.bls.gov/emp/emptab7.htm

van Laar, C., & Levin, S. (2000). Social and personal identity in stereotype threat: Is affirmative action stigmatizing? Paper presented at the biannual meeting of the Society for the Psychological Study of Social Issues, Minneapolis, MN.

Wilkins, D. B. (2005). A systematic response to systemic disadvantage: A response to Sander. *Stanford Law Review, 51*, 1915–1961.

Zuniga, X. B., Nagda, A., & Sevig, T. D. (2002). Intergroup dialogues: An educational model for cultivating student engagement across differences. *Equity and Excellence in Education, 35*, 7–17.

AUTHORS' NOTE

The transition to college project was funded by grants to the second author from UC-ACCORD, UC-LMRI, and the Academic Senate of the University of California. During the project, the first author was supported by a traineeship from the National Institute of Health (T32-MH20025). We thank Michelle Handy and the EOP office, the admissions office, the university registrar, and student services for their help with the project. Most important, we thank the adolescents who participated in the research and the many undergraduate students who helped collect and transcribe the data. Thanks to Emily Farrell-Keresey for help with preparation of the manuscript. Address correspondence to the authors at the Psychology Department, SS2, University of California, 1156 High St., Santa Cruz, CA 95064. The authors can also be reached through email, gills@gmail.com, azmitia@ucsc.edu, kschmukl@ucsc.edu, or fjcrosby@ucsc.edu.

5

THE BIOLOGY OF SOCIAL JUSTICE
Linking Social Inequalities and Health in Adolescence

Elizabeth Goodman and Nancy E. Adler

How the social world influences children's physical and psychological development has been the subject of decades of research, much of which is documented in this book. However, research into how the social world influences health (e.g., morbidity and mortality) is less well explored. Social inequalities in health are widely recognized and reducing health disparities is an important public health priority, yet the processes by which the social environment becomes translated into psychological and physiological processes that influence health remain unclear for any age group (Adler et al., 1994; Anderson & Armstead, 1995; Bradley & Corwyn, 2002; Wlliams, 1990).

Health inequalities occur at every age starting at birth. Babies born to mothers with fewer socioeconomic resources are more likely to be low birthweight, a risk factor for later development and for subsequent health conditions such as cardiovascular disease (Barker & Fall, 1993). Although children and adolescents as a group are relatively healthy, children from lower socioeconomic status (SES) families have a greater risk of death within the first year of life, higher rates of obesity, higher rates of upper respiratory infection and asthma and of serious attacks resulting in hospitalization, and more frequent school absence due to illness (Bradley & Corwyn, 2002; Chen, Matthews, & Boyce, 2002).

Health disparities during childhood and adolescence are of concern in and of themselves. In addition, physical, mental, and behavioral proclivities that develop during this period may contribute to diseases in adulthood and, ultimately, to premature mortality. As some other chapters in this volume discuss, the foundation of many psychological processes are laid down in adolescence. This chapter discusses how interactions between social and biological factors in adolescence are involved in the development of disease.

A particular focus of this chapter is the relationship of lower social status to increased risk for cardiovascular disease (CVD). The consistent inverse association between CVD as well as key cardiovascular risk factors, and SES is well established (Kaplan & Keil, 1993; Robbins, Vaccarine, Zhang, & Kasl, 2001; Sobal & Strunkard, 1989). CVD is the leading cause of morbidity and mortality in the United States, and cardiovascular risk factors are extremely prevalent in American society. Although CVD is rare in childhood and adolescence, obesity and Type 2 diabetes, two important public health problems for both children and adolescents that increase risk for CVD, are prevalent, and their rates are increasing. Currently, 31% of adolescents 12–19 years of age are considered overweight, and 16% are considered obese (Hedley et al., 2004).

These problems are not randomly distributed in society. Rates of both have increased more dramatically among children from lower SES families and children from some ethnic groups (Goodman, 1999). Over the past 30 years, as rates of diabetes and obesity have increased, the gap between rich and poor in this country has widened. Since 1980, growth in family income has increased among the two upper fifths of the U.S. population, whereas in the lower three fifths, family income has, in fact, decreased (Auerbach, Krimgold, & Lefkowitz, 2000). Although these trends do not establish causal links, they may hold clues to broader societal influences on regulatory systems and potential biologic mediators of social status' impact on health.

This chapter is organized in four sections. In the first, we detail why we focus on adolescence. The second provides an overview of the concept of social status. The third discusses the relationship between social status and health. In the fourth section, as a conclusion, we synthesize the preceding sections and focus on understanding how differences in social status may affect biological processes to create health disparities, in other words, how the biology of social justice is created.

WHY FOCUS ON ADOLESCENCE?

Major developmental changes in social and psychological functioning occur in the second decade of life. Of particular relevance here are changes in relation to social position. During adolescence, the transition between social standing of childhood, largely determined by familial social standing, and adult social status, which is more self-determined, occurs. Hand in hand with this are growth in cognitive abilities and the development of abstract thought. As these processes unfold, adolescents' perceptions of social stratification crystallize. This occurs against the backdrop of a maturing self-concept, decisions about educational attainment, and greater experience in the labor market. Together, these developmental changes make it likely that differences develop in the relationship of social status to health during the second decade of life. These transitions also highlight the need to move from a focus on family (parental-based) measures of social status to include self (adolescent-specific) measures of social position.

In addition to social and psychological changes, adolescence is a time of profound physiological change. For example, there is significant growth in the prefrontal cortex, an area of the brain used in planning and decision making during this developmental phase. Puberty brings with it a whole host of changes in major regulatory axes, such as the hypothalamic–pituitary–adrenal axis, which regulates hormonal responses to stress and influences multiple endocrine systems, including insulin regulation. These connections lead to changes in the interaction between psychological and physiological systems during adolescence. This has implications for a range of health problems. It may help explain, for example, why maintaining control over blood glucose in adolescent diabetics is a particular challenge. Thus, adolescence may be a critical developmental period with regard to the interactions between social and biological mediators of risk and resiliency independent of health behaviors.

Many young people are developing in environments marked by few socioeconomic resources and low social status. Both of these factors may influence psychological and physiological functioning. U.S. census data indicate that nearly one in six children under the age of 18 years lives in poverty. Data from The National Longitudinal Study of Adolescent Health revealed that 7 out of every 10 teens live in a home without a college-educated parent; for 1 in 10, no parent in the home completed high school or received a GED. As children move out into larger society through school and work experiences, they are likely to be increasingly aware of their social position and experience the material and social disadvantages associated with lower SES. Below we elaborate on the concept of social status and discuss how experiences of disadvantage may affect adolescents' health.

THE CONCEPT OF SOCIAL STATUS

Social Stratification

In 1927, Sorokin defined social stratification as

> The differentiation of a given population into hierarchically super-posed classes. It is manifested in the very existence of upper and lower social layers. Its basis and very existence consist of unequal distribution of rights and privileges, duties and responsibilities, social values and privations, social power and influence among members of a society. (Sorokin, 1927, p.11)

This definition lays out many of the factors theorists associate with the concept of social position to this very day.

Karl Marx and Max Weber are the two major theorists in this area. Their conceptualizations of social stratification have been widely applied in many disciplines ranging from history to sociology to public health and medicine. Marx's and Weber's views of social status differed. Marx's conception was founded in the relationship of an individual to work, material possessions, and members of different class groups. He saw social class as a fundamental characteristic that determined a person's cultural and community experiences, financial and environmental resources, and health-related behaviors (Johnson & Hall, 1995). The Marxian ideology reflects distinct, bounded social groups that are categorical (Vanneman & Pampel, 1968).

Weber's theories proposed more of a social status continuum characterized by differential access to social resources or prestige. His work gave rise to the concept of socioeconomic status commonly used in the scientific literature (Nam & Powers, 1983). Although objective and subjective elements are found in both theories, most of the work has focused on objective indicators of social status. Subjective perceptions of social status have been largely unexplored until recently.

Objective Measures of Social Status

Socioeconomic status, which reflects Weber's theoretical stance, is typically measured by income, education, and occupation. Together, these three factors make up the constellation of variables used to derive indices of socioeconomic status, such as the Hollingshead index (Hollingshead, 1975). Because research suggests these factors act through differing pathways and may not be comparable across cultural and ethnic groups, current recommendations are to use these indicators separately, not to create composite indices (Kaplan & Keil, 1993). Operationalization of each specific indicator of SES has varied widely among studies, making it difficult to compare studies and replicate findings. Wealth and assets are also growing areas of interest, as recognition of the importance of the intergenerational transfer of wealth grows (Shapiro, 2004). These new areas of inquiry reflect the burgeoning interest in capital, be that financial capital (wealth and assets), human capital (education), or social capital (social networks, reciprocity; Coleman, 1990). Each of these types of capital influences social position, and may affect health and well-being.

Subjective Measures of Social Status: Social Class Identification

Despite the vast literature on SES effects on health, little is known about peoples' perceptions of their placement in the social hierarchy, what determines these perceptions, or how these perceptions relate to health. Due to a lack of indicators of subjective social status (SSS), studies relied for many years on measures of social class identification such as that used by Centers (1949) in his seminal work, *The Psychology of Social Classes*. Centers asked respondents to identify membership in one of four social class groups: the lower, working, middle, or upper class. Over half of the white male adults he studied reported belonging to the working class and 43% to the middle class with very few identifying themselves as being lower or upper class. Most studies of social class identification since Centers' early work have focused on political and cultural attitudes and behavior associated with social class identification (e.g., Gurin, Miller, & Gurin, 1980; Jackman, 1979), but there has been little research on health effects.

Even less is known about adolescents' perceptions of placement within the social hierarchy than is known about adults. In 1947, Centers studied high school students and demonstrated that adolescents were more likely to place themselves in the middle or upper classes than did adults from the same social backgrounds. This tendency toward upward identification lessened with increasing age (Centers, 1950). From this, Centers concluded that the process of developing a social class identity was not completed during the high school years. He also concluded that socioeconomic position was the major component of social class identification in both adolescents and adults.

Research exploring the conceptualization of social standing and position among American youth since 1950 has been limited (Simmons & Rosenberg, 1971). Recently, Goodman et al. (2000) reported on the conceptualization of social structuring among a sample of 98 white youth. When asked to identify their social class, only 17% of working class subjects identified with their objectively defined social class, as compared to 74% of upper middle class youth. The working class youth felt that their parents had been treated unfairly in their life experiences, but believed that compared to their parents, they had more social mobility and equality of opportunity and that they would be better off financially than their parents. In contrast, although upper middle class youth believed they had a better than average chance to get ahead, they were more likely to feel that compared to their parents, they would be less well off at their parents' age and that they had decreasing social mobility.

Subjective Measures of Social Status

Use of a class-based tool assessing categories of class membership is subject to two major problems. One is that the categorical nature of the measures of social class identification does not adequately tap the full spectrum of socioeconomic stratification. The second is that the socially charged nature of the language used to describe the discrete classes may affect how people respond to these measures. Social desirability may influence an individual's choice of middle versus upper class, or working versus lower class.

To address these problems, Adler and colleagues developed the Subjective Social Status Scale to assess perceived placement within the social hierarchy among adults (Adler, Epel, Castellzazzo, & Ickovics, 2000). The Subjective Social Status Scale is a visual scale, a drawing of a ladder on which people place themselves. It is anchored at the top by those in U.S. society who are best off in terms of income, education, and occupation and at the bottom by those who are worst off. A second ladder assesses placement in the community, defined individually by each respondent anchored at the top by those with the highest standing and respect, and at the bottom by those with the least. This measure has been used in a number of studies with adults (Adler et al., 2000; Ostrove & Adler, 1998; Singh-Manoux, Adler, & Marmot, 2003).

Ladder rankings appear to be determined by multiple facets of social position, including traditional indicators of SES, as well as satisfaction with standard of living and financial security (Singh-Manoux et al., 2003). Negative affect and other potential psychological biases do not appear to confound the assessment of SSS (Adler et al., 2000; Singh-Manoux et al., 2003). Rather, it appears that individuals summate across the various dimensions of social status. The measure thus may function as self-rated health, a global evaluation that has been shown to predict mortality even when controlling for objective indicators of health status.

In 2001, a youth-specific version of the Subjective Social Status Scale was developed and validated (Goodman et al., 2001). One ladder assesses perception of the family placement within the social hierarchy in terms of family income and parental occupation and education. The second ladder assesses social standing within the youth's school community. This second ladder allows exploration of the relationship among social status, social development, and health in a community of peers. Such communities become increasingly important to adolescents' self-concept as youth mature.

Early work with the youth-specific measure supports the idea that there are developmental trajectories in perceptions of social stratification (Goodman et al., 2001). In analyses that looked at mother–child dyads, the adolescents tended toward higher perceived social status compared to their mothers; perceptions of SSS between mothers and their adolescent children were more strongly correlated among older teens than younger ones, suggesting a convergence of beliefs between parent and child as an adolescent matures. This may reflect a broader understanding of social positioning that accompanies the growth in cognitive abilities and experience during the adolescent years.

SOCIAL STATUS AND HEALTH

The SES–Health Gradient

The robust association between objective measures of SES and health has been the subject of intense research for several decades. Although much has been done to understand the effects of poverty on health, the relationship between social position and health is not confined to the lowest end of the social spectrum. Throughout, each increase in social position is associated with better health, although the steepness of the gradient is greatest at the very lowest end of the SES hierarchy. Classic studies showing this gradient effect include, in the United Kingdom, the Whitehall studies of mortality (Marmot, Shipley, & Rose, 1984; Marmot et al., 1991) and in the United States, the work of Kitagawa and Hauser (1973). The gap between the more- and less-advantaged has changed over time. Pappas, Hadden, and Fisher (1993) demonstrated that, despite an overall decrease in mortality since 1960, the decrease was greater for those with more education, thus increasing the differential mortality rate. This has serious implications for health today given the continued trends toward increasing economic inequalities.

The pervasive nature of the SES-health "gradient" does not mean that all diseases are more prevalent among lower status groups. The relationship between SES and cancer, for example, is not straightforward, but depends on the specific cancer under study and whether incidence or prevalence is assessed. Survivorship, which affects prevalence but not incidence, is influenced by SES, especially for cancers for which effective treatment exists and early detection and treatment can dramatically change prognosis. Demonstration of a gradient effect also does not explain the direction of the causal relationship between SES and health. The question of whether the gradient represents a "social drift" phenomenon, where those with poorer health migrate down the social hierarchy, or a "social causation" phenomenon, where lower social status creates the health differentials, remains. However, except for a few chronic debilitating conditions, such as schizophrenia, or severe childhood diseases that are relatively rare, the bulk of the evidence favors the social causation direction (Adler & Ostrove, 1999).

The inverse association between SES and poorer cardiovascular health among adults is well established (Kaplan & Keil, 1993; Winkleby, & Kraemer, Ahn and Varady, 1998). One study of particular importance is the Coronary Artery Risk Development in Young Adults (CARDIA) study. CARDIA is a prospective epidemiological study that investigates the distribution, antecedents, and etiology of risk factors for developing atherosclerotic CVD in a biracial cohort of over 4,000 non-Hispanic black and white adults who were between 18 and 30 years of age at baseline in 1985–1986 (Friedman et al., 1988).

CARDIA has yielded a number of important findings concerning the relationship between educational attainment and physiologic CV risks (Dyer et al., 1999; Greenlund et al., 1996; Van Horn et al., 1991). For example, CARDIA has demonstrated that lower parental education is associated with greater body mass index (BMI) in black men and white women, and with increase in BMI over seven years in white women (Greenlund et al., 1996).

The finding that socioeconomic position of one's family of origin is linked to risk factors in adulthood is consistent with data from the 1958 British birth cohort longitudinal study. This study has shown that the socioeconomic influences between birth and age seven years have significant impact on obesity in young adulthood (Power, Manor, & Matthews, 2003). CARDIA studies have also examined relationships between educational attainment and psychological factors that are known risks in CVD. Education has been shown to be inversely related to hostility levels (Allen, Markovitz, Jacobs, & Knox, 2001). This effect is moderated by both age and race of individuals (Allen et al., 2001). Educational attainment also showed an inverse association with risk of depressive symptoms (Whooley et al., 2002).

Although most studies have focused on the socioeconomic status gradient in adult health, infant mortality and childhood health problems have also been studied. Studies have consistently shown that the poorer the family, the more likely the children are to experience chronic illness, health problems, and inactivity (Chen, Matthews, & Boyce, 2002; Starfield, 1991). This is persuasive evidence of the pervasive nature of the gradient. However, the association between social status and health in adolescence is less well studied than in other developmental periods.

It is important in thinking about the cause of health disparities in childhood and adolescence to differentiate parental behaviors versus child-specific processes. For example, for a child to receive an immunization, an adult must bring the child to the health care provider. Similarly, asthma hospitalizations in a young child may measure the parents' ability to manage this chronic condition, rather than actual differences in asthma severity between SES groups.

Child-specific outcomes are more frequently found in the assessment of adolescent health, when the maturing child takes on more individual responsibility for health. Engaging in health-risk behaviors, such as smoking, poor diet, and physical inactivity, are increasingly determined by the young person's choices as they move into middle and later adolescence. However, although these are choices made by the young person, these choices are shaped by the socioeconomic environment (including the family environment) in which the adolescent is living. The resulting behaviors, in addition to the many physiological and psychological changes of puberty and development, may place the adolescent on trajectories that result in greater morbidity and mortality. Together these processes point to the importance of adolescence as a critical developmental period for health and well-being.

Much of the literature focusing on understanding the SES–adolescent health relationship comes from work done in Europe. In the United States, most studies dichotomized SES to focus on poverty and the most disadvantaged youth. Few studies of SES and adolescent health have assessed health outcomes along the full SES spectrum, but those that have suggest that the gradient occurs in relation to adolescent health. Data from National Health and Nutrition Examination Survey III and the 1992 National Health Interview Survey showed that both family income and parental education were associated with cardiovascular risk factors among youth along the entire SES spectrum (Lowry, Kann, Collins, & Kolbe, 1996; Winkleby et al., 1999).

In cross-sectional analyses from the National Longitudinal Study of Adolescent Health (Add Health), a nationally representative study of American adolescents who were in grades 7–12 at baseline in 1994 (Bearman, Jones, & Udry 1997), mother's education, father's education, and highest level of parent education were each significantly associated with fair to poor self-rated health, depression, and obesity (Goodman,

1999); all three indicators of parental education functioned identically in relation to these health outcomes. However, in this study of 15,483 parent–teen dyads, gradients were not found for asthma, suicide attempts, or sexually transmitted diseases (Goodman, 1999).

The relationships between SES (parental education and household income), depression, and health services utilization among girls in the Add Health study have also been assessed (Goodman & Huang, 2001). Access to health care is one possible explanatory factor in the SES/health gradient. However, the odds ratios for both income and education were unaffected by addition of indicators of health service utilization, showing that the effects of SES on depression among these adolescent girls at one year follow-up did not appear to be mediated by health service use.

One intriguing finding was that the main effect of household income on subsequent depression was much less than that of parental education. There was a significant income × baseline depression interaction, which suggests that, once depressed, the protective effect of increasing income is negated. It appears that income and education act through separate pathways. No significant baseline depression × education interaction was noted, which suggests that there are differences in the mechanisms underlying the protective effects of income and education on follow-up depression. Education may confer a greater ability to cope with life stressors and thereby provide resilience, whereas income may relate more to material goods, which may not provide buffering mechanisms for depressed adolescent women.

Subjective Social Status and Health

Perceptions of placement within the social hierarchy among adults are associated with health-related outcomes, independent of the influence of traditional objective measures of SES (Adler et al., 2000; Cohen, 1999; Ostrove, Adler, Kuppermann, & Washington, 2000; Singh-Manoux et al., 2003). For example, in a sample of healthy women with a high school degree or more, subjective SES showed stronger relationships to indicators of physical and mental health (self-rated health, sleep latency, negative affect, chronic stress, subjective stress, pessimism, and control) than did traditional SES indicators (education and household income) and remained significant when controlling for objective SES (Adler et al., 2000). The associations generally also remained significant even when controlling for negative affect, which could have influenced reporting style.

Although higher objective SES was related to lower baseline cortisol in these women, subjective status was linked to habituation to stress as assessed by cortisol response to a stress task repeated over several days. Nonhabituators who continued to show a cortisol increase placed themselves lower on the society ladder than habituators. These data suggest that lower subjective status may be associated with greater stress arousal and that chronic arousal may have implications for health.

Given the difficulties of identifying adolescents' socioeconomic position as they transition from their experiences and identity being framed primarily by their family's characteristics to establishing their own socioeconomic position, a global subjective measure may be particularly helpful in studying adolescents. The adult findings suggest that lower status adolescents will have increased vulnerability to depression, lower optimism, increased hostility, greater maladaptive coping, and morbidities such as obesity and insulin resistance than do higher status adolescents.

Some of these associations have been demonstrated in empirical studies. In a large, predominantly non-Hispanic white sample, lower perceived SES was associated with obesity (Goodman et al., 2001). Lower perceived SES has also been associated with increased stress (Goodman, McEwen, Dolan, Schafer-Kalkhoff, & Adler, 2005b), greater depressive symptoms (Goodman et al., 2001), and increased optimism (Finkelstein, Kubzansky, & Goodman, 2006). Because the ability to measure subjective perceptions of social status is relatively new, there are few studies to date that assess this domain.

Previously unpublished analyses using data from a subset of participants in the Princeton School District Study (Goodman, Dolan, Morrison, & Daniels, 2005a) indicate that subjective social status is associated with physiological risks in adolescents, although not consistently. Subjective SES was inversely associated with fasting glucose, and this relationship was maintained with adjustment for age, gender, race, and parental education throughout. However, subjective SES was not associated with the nine other measured cardiovascular risk factors.

Theoretical Frameworks for Social Inequalities in Health

The processes by which social hierarchies become embodied over time are complex and require careful conceptualization. Halfon and Hochstein (2002 p. 438) have created a synthetic developmental framework for understanding how social and biological factors interweave over the course of an individual's life to influence health outcomes, the Life Course Health Development Framework (LCHD, Figure 5.1). This framework is based on the multiple contexts, design and process of health development, the mechanisms that explain variations in health trajectories over time, and the time course inherent in the creation of trajectories of health development. The LCHD framework emphasizes the interplay between the macrocontexts created by the multiple environments in which individuals live, the microcontexts central to biological embedding, and developmental transitions as we move through the various life stages, including adolescence.

Halfon and Hochstein (2002) list three "Health Development Processes" related to the microcontext of the developing individual. These are behavioral, physiological, and psychological pathways and systems. Health-related behaviors are important contributors to the development of morbidity and mortality in any age group, and socioeconomic difference in health-related behaviors have been documented in adolescence (Goodman & Huang, 2002; Lowry et al., 1996; Winkleby et al., 1999).

However, the literature's focus on adolescent health risk behaviors fosters an assumption that adolescent health risks are individually determined by faulty lifestyle choices. These are often framed as behavioral choices, such as the choice to smoke, be physically inactive, engage

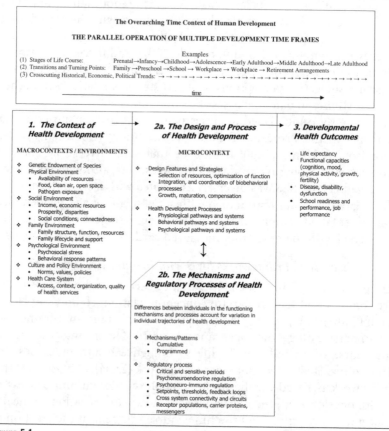

Figure 5.1

in unprotected sexual intercourse, or drop out of school. Yet behavioral choices are constrained and influenced by socially and biologically mediated processes. Environmental determinants of choice, such as socioeconomic status, are often ignored or viewed as confounders in an attempt to focus on proximal, more easily identifiable and malleable individual characteristics (Blum et al., 2000).

This focus does not give adequate attention to the other two processes highlighted by Halfon and Hochstein, psychological and physiological. Our purpose here is to highlight the distal, oft-ignored causes of developmental health disparities and outline some mechanisms for understanding their influence including psychological and physiological processes that may be active in the development of health disparities. Below, we explore a promising model for how these processes interact over time to create poorer health in lower status individuals.

Allostatic Load

In the past two decades there has also been substantial research on the biological processes that result in health disparities, for example, the processes by which social factors get "under the skin." The translation of external social forces into physiological and psychological processes that create health differentials has been termed "the sociobiologic translation" (Tarlov, 1996). The brain is a critical organ in this translation. McEwen and others have hypothesized that lower social status is a chronic environmental stressor, creating the link between lower social status, the brain, hypothalamic–pituitary–adrenal (HPA) axis dysfunction, the autonomic nervous system, and disease risk (Brunner, 1997; McEwen, 1998; Rosmond & Bjorntorp, 2000).

The HPA axis, which links the brain, especially the limbic system, to the body's periphery, is the key source of regulatory mechanisms for mounting and controlling the stress response. When there is dysregulation or dysfunction in limbic areas in the brain that help us process the external environment, such as the amygdala or hippocampus, this system, which sends signals to the hypothalamus, can go awry, leading to dysregulation of the HPA axis (see Schulkin, Gold and McEwen, 1998, for details). This dysregulation can have a cascade of effects. Although these responses are adaptive in the short term in dealing with immediate threat, over time and with repeated cycles of activation, they may result in longer-term damage (e.g., hypertension, central obesity, and dyslipidemia) which promotes development and progression of disease, such as cardiovascular disease. This chain of events, and the multisystem deregulation and development of disease that follows, has been termed "allostatic load" (McEwen, 1998).

Social status may shape how environmental cues are interpreted and whether a stress response is elicited. Chen et al. (2004) showed that compared to higher SES peers, older teens from lower SES families are more likely to interpret ambiguous situations to be negative, although no differences in interpretation occur with situations that are clearly negative. More frequent exposure of lower SES children to negative experiences that establishes expectancies or vigilance in attending to possibly threatening stimuli has been suggested as a possible explanation for these differences. In the ambiguous situations lower SES adolescents also showed greater physiological responses (increased diastolic blood pressure and increased heart rate). If lower SES children and adolescents experience more negative circumstances and, in addition, view ambiguous situations more negatively, they will experience more frequent stress response cycles.

Animal Models Supportive of Allostatic Load

Data from both animal models and humans support the allostatic load model explaining the link between social stratification and CV disease. The most extensive animal data come from cynomolgus monkeys. Social dominance hierarchies among these nonhuman primates are analogous to social status gradients among humans. These dominance hierarchies and kinship ties are central organizing features within macaque society (Shively et al., 1997). Females generally are ranked at the same level as their mothers at birth and maintain this rank throughout their lives unless group fission occurs. Male macaques have their mother's social status as juveniles, but then leave the group and live in all male bands or alone for a brief period. Their adult rank is obtained when they enter a new group and is correlated with time spent in the group.

Evidence from both male and female macaques supports the theory that lower social status contributes to development and progression of CV disease through stress exposure that results in dysregulation of major regulatory axes and increased allostatic load. Lower social status among male macaques is associated with lower body weight, higher adrenal weights, increased plasma glucose levels, and more pronounced cortisol response to social reorganization (Cohen et al., 1997; Shively & Kaplan, 1984).

Hypersecretion of cortisol has also been demonstrated among subordinate female macaques (Shively et al., 1997). Studies suggest that the adrenal glands of subordinate females are hypersensitive to HPA axis signals from the central nervous system (Shively et al., 1997). Social subordination also appears to influence the hypothalamus and lower fertility among subordinate females (Shively et al., 1997). Subordinate females also have lower bone density and higher rates of coronary artery disease, which may be due to their lower fertility (Shively & Clarkson, 1994). Interestingly, experimental manipulation of social status has a powerful effect on heart disease risk independent of baseline status. Both dominant and subordinate female macaques whose social status was manipulated had an increase in atherosclerosis, the hardening of the arteries, which increases risk of heart attacks, compared with animals whose social status did not change (Shively & Clarkson, 1994).

Dominant males placed in an unstable social grouping who were forced to reassert their dominance also showed increased CAA; the increased risk of CAA was partly due to increased sympathoadrenal activation. These studies suggest that, although dominant status is protective in stable environments, it may be a risk factor in unstable environments (Kaplan & Manuck, 1999).

Research in Humans Supportive of Allostatic Load

In humans, experiences of chronic stress have been linked to HPA axis dysregulation as well as disease risk. Hippocampal atrophy has been demonstrated using MRI in stress-related disorders, including recurrent depression, posttraumatic stress disorder, dementia, and Cushing's disease (McEwen & Magarinos, 1997). These diseases have also been associated with hypercortisolemia or an inappropriately exaggerated cortisol response to ACTH (for review, see Schulkin, Gold and McEwen, 1998). Both inborn temperament and environmental exposure can affect HPA axis functioning. Excessively fearful and shy children develop high levels of cortisol (Schmidt et al., 1997).

Environmental exposures also have an effect. For example, children who had lived eight or more months in a Romanian orphanage have higher cortisol throughout the day than those adopted within four months (Gunnar, Morison, Chisholm, & Schuder, 2001). One study of Canadian children aged 6, 8, and 10 years showed significantly higher cortisol levels among low SES children compared to high SES age-matched peers (Lupien, King, Meaney, & McEwen, 2000). However, this was not found in the older age group, and a U.S. study failed to replicate the SES gradient in cortisol in young children (Goodman et al., 2005c). Secondary outcomes in the allostatic load model include several cardiovascular risks.

Using data from high school students in Wave 1 of the Princeton School District study, Goodman et al. (2005c) explored associations between parent education and a range of traditional CV risk factors as well as a cumulative risk score (CRS) derived from these risks. This cumulative score provides a measure of the multiple metabolic pathways involved in the brain–body link, which controls physiological adaptation to the social environment. The lower the educational attainment of the adolescent's parent the higher his or her insulin, glucose, insulin resistance, waist circumference, body mass index (BMI), low density lipoprotein (LDL)-cholesterol, and lower high density lipoprotein (HDL)-cholesterol. The associations persisted in analyses adjusted for age, gender, and race.

The associations between parent education and insulin, insulin resistance, and waist circumference were mediated by BMI, whereas those between parent education and glucose, HDL-C, and LDL-C were independent of BMI. Lower parent education was associated with higher cumulative risk, even after adjustment for BMI. These data suggest that lower social status is associated with multiple metabolic risks and cumulative risk in adolescents, and that these relationships are not wholly explained by weight status. These findings support the allostatic load model, which posits that, over time, processes that were initially adaptive lead to cumulative dysregulation across multiple systems and suggest that the processes that lead to this dysregulation begin in childhood. They may harm health in childhood as well as set the stage for premature onset of CVD and other chronic diseases in adulthood.

CONCLUSION

This chapter has covered a wide range of material with the goal of showing how socioeconomic factors and social inequalities influence physiology and contribute to health disparities. There are a number of important contributors to such disparities that we have not discussed. These include parenting and intrafamilial processes, school-level contextual effects, and the role of health care, among others. Our focus has been on the biological embedding of social hierarchies and the developmental context in which that embedding occurs, particularly in relation to adolescence. This direct link between social structure and health adds a new perspective to the bulk of the research on adolescent health, which has focused primarily on individual behavior change or the provision of better health care.

For example, in relation to obesity, children and parents are urged to eat better and exercise more, but at the same time, physical education programs are being cut from schools, and fast food and foods of minimum nutritional value have invaded school cafeterias and many children's lives. Availability of healthy choices has decreased, especially in high-risk areas, food marketing to young children has increased, portion sizes have skyrocketed, and opportunities for children to play safely and even walk to school have been diminished. These factors are often differentially distributed by SES.

In addition, although it is acknowledged by many that growing up today is more "stressful" than it was in the past, there is less awareness that exposure to stress is exacerbated in lower SES environments. Moreover, how stress affects the body is often ignored. This chapter demonstrates that there are connections among social structure, the developing brain's processing of that social structure, and the physiological costs of that adaptation over time. The unequal allocation of these physiological costs creates a fundamental injustice that is made manifest by the differential distribution of disease in our society. Social justice, therefore, is not just a political or social phenomenon. It is a biological phenomenon as well.

REFERENCES

Adler, N. E., Boyce, T., Chesney, M. A., Cohen, S., Folkman, S., Kahn, R. L., & Syme, S. L. (1994). Socioeconomic status and health: The challenge of the gradient. *American Psychologist, 49,* 15–24.

Adler, N. E., Epel, E. S., Castellazzo, G., & Ickovics, J. R. (2000). Relationship of subjective and objective social status with psychological and physiological functioning: Preliminary data in healthy white women. *Health Psychology, 19,* 586–592.

Adler, N. E., & Ostrove, J. M. (1999). Socioeconomic status and health: What we know and what we don't. *Annals New York Academy Science, 896,* 3–15.

Allen, J., Markovitz, J., Jacobs, D. R., Jr., & Knox, S. S. (2001). Social support and health behavior in hostile black and white men and women in CARDIA. Coronary artery risk development in young adults. *Psychosomatic Medicine, 63,* 609–618.

Anderson, N. B., & Armstead, C. A. (1995). Toward understanding the association of socioeconomic status and health: A new challenge for the biopsychosocial approach. *Psychosomatic Medicine, 57,* 213–225.

Auerbach, J., Krimgold, B., & Lefkowitz, B. (2000). *Improving health; it doesn't take a revolution* (No. 298). Washington, DC: National Policy Association.

Barker, D. J., & Fall, C. H. (1993). Fetal and infant origins of cardiovascular disease. *Archives of Disease in Childhood, 68,* 797–799.

Bearman, P. S., Jones, J., & Udry, J. R. (1997). The national longitudinal study of adolescent health: Research design. Retrieved April 24, 1997, from http://www.cpc.unc.edu/projects/addhealth/design.html

Blum, R. W., Beuhring, T., Shew, M. L., Bearinger, L. H., Sieving, R. E., & Resnick, M. D. (2000). The effects of race/ethnicity, income, and family structure on adolescent risk behaviors. *American Journal of Public Health, 90,* 1879–1884.

Bradley, R. H., & Corwyn, R. F. (2002). Socioeconomic status and child development. *Annual Reviews in Psychology, 53,* 371–399.

Brunner, E. J. (1997). Stress and the biology of inequality. *British Medical Journal, 314,* 1472–1476.

Centers, R. (1949). *The psychology of social classes: A study of class consciousness.* Princeton: Princeton University Press.

Centers, R. (1950). Social class identifications of American youth. *Journal of Personality, 18,* 290–302.

Chen, E., Langer, D. A., Raphaelson, Y. E., & Matthews, K. A. (2004). Socioeconomic status and health in adolescents: The role of stress interpretations. *Child Development, 75,* 1039–1052.

Chen, E., Matthews, K. A., & Boyce, W. T. (2002). Socioeconomic differences in children's health: How and why do these relationships change with age? *Psychological Bulletin, 128,* 295–329.

Cohen, S., Line, S., Manuck, S. B., Rabin, B. S., Heise & Kaplan. (1997) Chronic social stress, social status, and susceptibility to upper respiratory infections in nonhuman primates. *Psychosomatic Medicine, 59,* 213–221.

Cohen, S. (1999). Social status and susceptibility to respiratory infections. *Annals of the New York Academy of Sciences, 896,* 246–253.

Coleman, J. S. (1990). *Foundations of social theory.* Cambridge, MA: Belknap Press of Harvard University Press.

Dyer, A. R., Liu, K., Walsh, M., Kiefe, C., Jacobs, D. R., Jr., & Bild, D. E. (1999). Ten-year incidence of elevated blood pressure and its predictors: The CARDIA study. Coronary artery risk development in (young) adults. *Journal of Human Hypertension, 13,* 13–21.

Finkelstein, D. M., Kubzansky, L., & Goodman, E. (2006). Socioeconomic differences in adolescent stress: The role of psychological resources. *Journal of Adolescent Health, 38,* 100.

Friedman, G. D., Cutter, G. R., Donahue, R. P., Hughes, G. H., Hulley, S. B., Jacobs, D. R., Jr., et al. (1988). Cardia: Study design, recruitment, and some characteristics of the examined subjects. *Journal of Clinical Epidemiology, 41,* 1105–1116.

Goodman, E. (1999). The role of socioeconomic status gradients in explaining differences in US adolescents' health. *American Journal of Public Health, 89,* 1522–1528.

Goodman, E., Adler, N. E., Kawachi, I., Frazier, A. L., Huang, B., & Colditz, G. A. (2001). Adolescents' perceptions of social status: Development and evaluation of a new indicator. *Pediatrics, 108,* http://www.pediatrics .org/cgi/content/abstract/108/102/e131.

Goodman, E., Amick, B. C., Rezendes, M. O., Levine, S., Kagan, J., Rogers, W. H., et al. (2000). Adolescents' understanding of social class: A comparison of white upper middle class and working class youth. *Journal of Adolescent Health, 27,* 80–83.

Goodman, E., Dolan, L. M., Morrison, J. A., & Daniels, S. R. (2005a). Factor analysis of clustered cardiovascular risks in adolescence: Obesity is the predominant correlate of risk among youth. *Circulation, 111,* 1970–1977.

Goodman, E., & Huang, B. (2001). Socioeconomic status, depression, and health service utilization among adolescent women. *Women's Health Issues, 11,* 416–426.

Goodman, E., & Huang, B. (2002). Socioeconomic status, depressive symptoms, and adolescent substance use. *Archives of Pediatrics & Adolescent Medicine, 156,* 448–453.

Goodman, E., McEwen, B. S., Dolan, L. M., Schafer-Kalkhoff, T., & Adler, N. E. (2005b). Social disadvantage and adolescent stress. *Journal of Adolescent Health, 37,* 484–492.

Goodman, E., McEwen, B. S., Huang, B., Dolan, L. M., & Adler, N. E. (2005c). Social inequalities in biomarkers of cardiovascular risk in adolescence. *Psychosomatic Medicine, 67,* 9–15.

Greenlund, K. J., Liu, K., Dyer, A. R., Kiefe, C. I., Burke, G. L., & Yunis, C. (1996). Body mass index in young adults: Associations with parental body size and education in the CARDIA study. *American Journal of Public Health, 86,* 480–485.

Gunnar, M. R., Morison, S. J., Chisholm, K., & Schuder, M. (2001). Salivary cortisol levels in children adopted from Romanian orphanages. *Developmental Psychopathology, 13,* 611–628.

Gurin, P., Miller, A., & Gurin, G. (1980). Stratum identification and consciousness. *Social Psychology Quarterly, 43,* 30–47.

Halfon, N., & Hochstein, M. (2002). Life course health development: An integrated framework for developing health, policy, and research. *Milbank Q, 80,* 433–479, iii.

Hedley, A. A., Ogden, C. L., Johnson, C. L., Carroll, M. D., Curtin, L. R., & Flegal, K. M. (2004). Prevalence of overweight and obesity among US children, adolescents, and adults, 1999–2002. *Journal of the American Medical Association, 291,* 2847–2850.

Herman, J. P., & Cullinan, W. E. (1997). Neurocircuitry of stress: Central control of the hypothalamo–pituitary–adrenocortical axis. *Trends in Neurosciences, 20,* 78–84.

Hollingshead, A. B. (1975). *Four factor index of social status* (Working Paper, Dept. of Sociology). New Haven, CT: Yale University.

Jackman, M. (1979). The subjective meaning of social class identification in the United States. *Public Opinion Quarterly, 43,* 443–462.

Johnson, J. V., & Hall, E. M. (1995). Class, work, and health. In B. J. Amick, S. Levine, A. R. Tarlov, & D. C. Walsh (Eds.), *Society and health* (pp. 247–271). New York: Oxford University Press.

Kaplan, G. A., & Keil, J. E. (1993). Socioeconomic factors and cardiovascular disease: A review of the literature. *Circulation, 88*, 1973–1988.

Kaplan, J. R., & Manuck, S. B. (1999). Status, stress, and atherosclerosis: The role of environment and individual behavior. *Annals of the New York Academy of Sciences, 896*, 145–161.

Kerr, D. S., Campbell, L. W., Applegate, M. D., Brodish, A., & Landfield, P. W. (1991). Chronic stress-induced acceleration of electrophysiologic and morphometric biomarkers of hippocampal aging. *Journal of Neuroscience, 11*, 1316–1324.

Kitagawa, E. M., & Hauser, P. M. (1973). *Differential mortality in the United States: A study in socioeconomic epidemiology.* Cambridge, MA: Harvard University Press.

Lowry, R., Kann, L., Collins, J. L., & Kolbe, L. J. (1996). The effect of socioeconomic status on chronic disease behaviors among US adolescents. *Journal of the American Medical Association, 276*, 792–797.

Lowy, M. T., Wittenberg, L., & Yamamoto, B. K. (1995). Effect of acute stress on hippocampal glutamate levels and spectrin proteolysis in young and aged rats. *Journal of Neurochemistry, 65*, 268–274.

Lupien, S. J., King, S., Meaney, M. J., & McEwen, B. S. (2000). Child's stress hormone levels correlate with mother's socioeconomic status and depressive state. *Biological Psychiatry, 48*, 976–980.

Marmot, M. G., Shipley, M. J., & Rose, G. (1984). Inequalities in death: Specific explanations or a general pattern? *Lancet, 1*, 1003–1006.

Marmot, M. G., Smith, G. D., Stansfeld, S., Patel, C., North, F., Head, J., et al. (1991). Health inequalities among British civil servants: The Whitehall II study. *Lancet, 337*, 1387–1393.

McEwen, B. S. (1998). Protective and damaging effects of stress mediators. *New England Journal of Medicine, 338*, 171–179.

McEwen, B. S., & Magarinos, A. M. (1997). Stress effects on morphology and function of the hippocampus. *Annals of the New York Academy of Science, 821*, 271–284.

Nam, C. B., & Powers, M. G. (1983). *The socioeconomic approach to status measurement: With a guide to occupational and socioeconomic status scores.* Houston: Cap and Gown Press.

Ostrove, J. M., & Adler, N. E. (1998). The relationship of socioeconomic status, labor force participation and health among men and women. *Journal of Health Psychology, 3*, 451–463.

Ostrove, J. M., Adler, N. E., Kuppermann, M., & Washington, A. E. (2000). Objective and subjective assessments of socioeconomic status and their relationship to self-rated health in an ethnically diverse sample of pregnant women. *Health Psychology, 19*, 613–618.

Pappas, G., Hadden, W., & Fisher, G. (1993). The increasing disparity in mortality between socioeconomic groups in the United States, 1960 and 1980. *New England Journal of Medicine, 329,* 103–109.

Power, C., Manor, O., & Matthews, S. (2003). Child to adult socioeconomic conditions and obesity in a national cohort. *International Journal of Obesity & Related Metabolic Disorders, 27,* 1081–1086.

Robbins, J., Vaccarine, V., Zhang, H., & Kasl, S. (2001). Socioeconomic status and type 2 diabetes in African American and non-Hispanic white women and men: Evidence from the Third National Health and Nutrition Examination Survey. *American Journal of Public Health, 91,* 76–83.

Rosmond, R., & Bjorntorp, P. (2000). The hypothalamic-pituitary-adrenal axis activity as a predictor of cardiovascular disease, type 2 diabetes and stroke. *Journal of Internal Medicine, 247,* 188–197.

Schmidt, L. A., Fox, N. A., Rubin, K. H., Sternberg, E. M., Gold, P. W., Smith, C. C., et al. (1997). Behavioral and neuroendocrine responses in shy children. *Developmental Psychobiology, 30,* 127–140.

Schulkin, J., Gold, P. W., & McEwen, B. S. (1998). Induction of corticotropin-releasing hormone gene expression by glucocorticoids: Implication for understanding the states of fear and anxiety and allostatic load. *Psychoneuroendocrinology, 23,* 219–243.

Shapiro, T. M. (2004). *The hidden cost of being African American.* New York: Oxford University Press.

Shively, C. A., & Clarkson, T. B. (1994). Social status and coronary artery atherosclerosis in female monkeys. *Arteriosclerosis & Thrombosis, 14,* 721–726.

Shively, C., & Kaplan, J. (1984). Effects of social factors on adrenal weight and related *Physiology and Behavior, 33,* 777–782.

Shively, C. A., Laber-Laird, K., & Anton, R. F. (1997). Behavior and physiology of social stress and depression in female cynomolgus monkeys. *Biological Psychiatry, 41,* 871–882.

Simmons, R., & Rosenberg, M. (1971). Functions of children's perceptions of the stratification system. *American Sociological Review, 36,* 235–249.

Singh-Manoux, A., Adler, N. E., & Marmot, M. G. (2003). Subjective social status: Its determinants and its association with measures of ill-health in the Whitehall II study. *Social Science and Medicine, 56,* 1321–1333.

Sobal, J., & Strunkard, A. J. (1989). Socioeconomic status and obesity: A review of the literature. *Psychological Bulletin, 105,* 260–275.

Sorokin, P. (1927). *Social mobility.* New York: Harper.

Starfield, B. (1991). Childhood morbidity: Comparisons, clusters, and trends. *Pediatrics, 88,* 519–526.

Tarlov, A. R. (1996). Social determinants of health: The sociobiological translation. In D. Blaine, E. J. Brunner, & R. G. Wilkinson (Eds.), *Health and social organizations* (pp. 71–93). London: Routledge.

Van Horn, L. V., Ballew, C., Liu, K., Ruth, K., McDonald, A., Hilner, J. E., et al. (1991). Diet, body size, and plasma lipids-lipoproteins in young adults: Differences by race and sex. The coronary artery risk development in young adults (CARDIA) study. *American Journal of Epidemiology, 133,* 9–23.

Vanneman, R., & Pampel, F. (1968). The American perception of social class and status. *American Sociological Review, 42,* 422–437.

Whooley, M. A., Kiefe, C. I., Chesney, M. A., Markovitz, J. H., Matthews, K., & Hulley, S. B. (2002). Depressive symptoms, unemployment, and loss of income: The CARDIA study. *Archive of Internal Medicine, 162,* 2614–2620.

Williams, D. R. (1990). Socioeconomic differentials in health: A review and a redirection. *Social Psychology Quarterly, 53,* 81–99.

Winkleby, M. A., Kraemer, H. C., Ahn, D. K., & Varady, A. N. (1998). Ethnic and socioeconomic differences in cardiovascular disease risk factors: Findings for women from The Third National Health and Nutrition Examination Survey, 1988–1994. *Journal of the American Medical Association, 280,* 356–362.

Winkleby, M. A., Robinson, T. N., Sundquist, J., & Kraemer, H. C. (1999). Ethnic variation in cardiovascular disease risk factors among children and young adults: Findings from The Third National Health and Nutrition Examination Survey, 1988–1994. *Journal of the American Medical Association, 281,* 1006–1013.

6

LEAVING LGBT (LESBIAN, GAY, BISEXUAL, AND TRANSGENDER) STUDENTS BEHIND
Schools, Sexuality, and Rights

Stacey S. Horn

In 1995, Derek Henkle was a 14-year old student in a Gifted and Talented program in a Reno, Nevada, high school. Despite the on-going harassment and abuse he had endured because he was openly gay, Derek had expectations of graduating with honors and attending a top college. In the fall of that year, two boys strung a lasso around Derek's neck and threatened to drag him from their pick-up truck. School officials responded to the incident by transferring Derek to an alternative high school for students with behavioral or academic problems, stating that they thought Derek would be "safer" there. His new principal demanded that Derek hide his sexual orientation and said to him, "I won't have you acting like a fag." After a semester Derek was transferred again for his own safety. Again Derek was told that he was not allowed to talk about his sexual orientation to other students or openly identify himself as gay. Despite the gag order, word got around. In the fall of 1996, two school police officers witnessed Derek being punched in the face six times by another student, doing nothing to break up the fight, and discouraging him from reporting the incident to school officials despite the fact that he had a ruptured eardrum and was bleeding severely. After this incident, at age 16, Derek quit school (Lambda Legal Defense and Education Fund, 2000).

In Arkansas in 2002, 13-year-old Thomas McLaughlin's science teacher overheard him being teased about being gay by a fellow classmate. When Thomas refused to deny that he was gay, the teacher told the assistant principal that Thomas was gay and that something should be done about it. Later that day Thomas was called out of class by the assistant principal who asked him if his parents knew that he was gay. When Thomas said no, the assistant principal told him that he had until the end of the day to tell his parents, or the school would. Unable to focus in class, Thomas went to his guidance counselor for help. The counselor called the mother and told her over the phone that her son was gay.

Even though Thomas' parents were accepting of his sexual orientation, Thomas continued to face abuse at school, not from his peers, but from the teachers and administration. Teachers told Thomas that they thought he was "sickening" and "disgusting," punished him for talking about being gay, and threatened that if he didn't keep quiet he would end up like Matthew Shepherd, a college student in Laramie, Wyoming, who was the victim of an anti-gay hate crime that ultimately led to his death. When one teacher publicly said that being gay was a sin and called Thomas "unnatural," Thomas, himself a Christian, argued with the teacher about what the Bible says about homosexuality. The teacher sent him to the assistant principal who punished him by having him read aloud passages from the Bible that allegedly condemn homosexuality. When Thomas told his friends about the punishment, he was suspended for two days and warned that he would be expelled if he told anyone about the reason for the suspension or the forced Bible reading (American Civil Liberties Union, 2003a, 2003b; Cianciotto & Cahill, 2003).

In 2002, George W. Bush signed into legislation the No Child Left Behind Act. One of the major premises of the act is

> ... the promotion of school safety, such that students and school personnel are free from violent and disruptive acts, including sexual harassment and abuse, and victimization associated with prejudice and intolerance, on school premises, going to and from school, and at school sponsored activities through the creation and maintenance of a school environment that...fosters individual responsibility and respect for the rights of others. (NCLBA, 2001)

Unfortunately, for many students in our schools, this has not been the case. Recent surveys on the experiences of lesbian, gay, bisexual, or transgender (LGBT) youth in schools provide evidence that many LGBT youth feel unsafe in school, frequently hear anti-gay language, and experience higher levels of physical and verbal assault than their non-LGBT identified peers (Gay, Lesbian, Straight Education Network, 2003). For many students who identify themselves or are perceived by others as lesbian, gay, bisexual, or transgender, school is a place where harassment and victimization are everyday occurrences. School is a place where they are subjected to prejudice and intolerance, not only from their peers but also from their teachers, counselors, school administrators, and other adults, the very people whose role it is to ensure that the learning environment is safe and supportive.

Although it is clear from the above examples and from recent surveys on the school climate for LGBT youth that LGBT students' rights are violated in schools, the question remains as to why this still so frequently happens. The data suggest that these are not isolated cases that resulted from ignorance and apathy of select individuals. Rather, these kinds of injustices are common in schools and result from larger systemic issues related to the purpose of education and how we think about adolescent development.

In this chapter, I argue that this type of injustice is pervasive within schools in the United States and has serious negative implications for the health and well-being of not only gay, lesbian, bisexual, and transgender students, but all students. I argue that part of the reason this injustice persists is due to the multifaceted nature of sexuality and the diversity of beliefs and attitudes about sexuality within society and discuss some recent research on heterosexual students' attitudes and beliefs about homosexuality and the treatment of lesbian, gay, and gender nonconforming peers. Next, I discuss how the multifaceted nature of sexuality relates to larger systemic issues embedded within the complexity and conflict inherent in educating students and our understanding of the role of the school in child and adolescent development. Finally, I discuss the implications that the research on adolescents' attitudes and beliefs about homosexuality has for creating safe schools for LGBT students within a pluralistic democracy.

INCIDENCE AND IMPACT OF VICTIMIZATION OF LGBT YOUTH IN SCHOOLS

Recent population-based studies on the school experiences of lesbian, gay, bisexual, and transgender students suggest that they are more likely to be injured with a weapon at school and to have their property damaged at school, and are subjected to higher rates of physical and verbal abuse than their heterosexual counterparts (Bontempo & D'Augelli, 2002; D'Augelli, 1998; Garofalo, Wolf, Kessel, Palfrey, & DuRand, 1998;

Gay, Lesbian, and Straight Education Network, 2001, 2003). As a result, LGBT youth are significantly less likely to feel safe in school than their heterosexual counterparts. These studies estimate that 33 to 95% of LGBT youth report being physically or verbally harassed on a regular basis (Rivers & D'Augelli, 2001; Russell, Franz, & Driscoll, 2001).

Although not all LGBT youth may be the victims of extreme forms of violence and harassment, almost all report that they experience some form of victimization in school (e.g., verbal harassment and teasing). For example, in a national study, 9 out of 10 students (LGBT-identified and straight) reported hearing homophobic comments in school frequently or often, and almost all youth surveyed said that they heard anti-gay language (e.g., the use of "gay" or "fag" in a derogatory manner) on a daily basis (Gay, Lesbian, & Straight Education Network, 2001, 2003). Surprisingly, almost half of the youth report that school staff rarely intervenes in these situations, and a number of youth report that this type of victimization is perpetrated not only by their peers but also by their teachers (Gay, Lesbian, and Straight Education Network, 2001).

For lesbian, gay, bisexual, and transgender students the impact of experiencing victimization in school is often exacerbated by the fact that they do not have the support structure within their families that other marginalized or victimized youth have. For LGBT students, family can also be a place where they have to hide their sexual orientation for fear of rejection or, in many cases, fear of harm. Youth who are not "out" to their families typically do not share their experiences of bias-related victimization and harassment with them due to the fear of their parents and families learning about their sexual orientation (D'Augelli, 1998; Savins-Williams, 1998). This environment of secrecy cuts off an important avenue of support for LGBT youth, leaving them to deal on their own with the harassment and victimization they face in school.

Unfortunately, these fears of rejection and victimization by family are not unfounded. For many LGBT youth, home is also a place where they are subjected to victimization and harassment (D'Augelli, 1996; Remafadi, 1987). Research on harassment and victimization within the family estimates that within the population of youth who have disclosed their sexual orientation to their families, 20–40% face verbal abuse from their parents and siblings, and 4–10% face physical violence and abuse (D'Augelli, 1996; Hunter, 1990). This type of family violence, harassment, and rejection often leads to homelessness for LGBT youth, placing them at increased risk for further victimization.

LGBT youth who experience this form of victimization in school or in the home are at greater risk for negative mental health outcomes such as depression, anxiety, and suicide (D'Augelli, 1998) as well as at greater risk for engaging in health-compromising behaviors such as abusing alcohol and drugs and engaging in unsafe sexual behaviors (D'Augelli, 1998; Russell, 2003; Russell & Joyner, 2001; Russell, Truong, & Driscoll, 2002). In addition to research documenting the negative mental and physical health outcomes for LGBT youth, more recent reports suggest that this type of victimization also leads to negative academic and career-related outcomes for these students. A recent national study estimates that LGBT youth are more likely than their heterosexual peers to miss school, and in some cases to drop out of school, because they feel unsafe (Gay, Lesbian, and Straight Education Network, 2003; Russell, Seif, & Truong, 2001). In addition, LGBT youth who experienced harassment reported lower levels of academic achievement and were less likely to report future plans to attend college (Gay, Lesbian, and Straight Education Network, 2003; Russell et al., 2001).

Although anti-gay harassment in schools clearly has negative effects for developmental outcomes for students who identify as LGBT, anti-gay teasing and harassment has also been found to have negative effects on the entire school population. Recent investigations into the school shootings that occurred in Colorado, California, and Kentucky report that one of the common precipitating factors to those shootings was that the perpetrators were taunted and teased about being gay (Kimmel & Mahler, 2003). Even though none of them identified as gay, their peers used this type of harassment to belittle and demean them. Additionally, a recent report by the AAUW (2001) on sexual harassment in schools revealed that students report that being called gay or lesbian is one of the worst forms of harassment they could imagine, and for boys it was ranked even worse than physical harassment. This suggests that the homophobic and heterosexist climate in many schools in the United States is damaging not only to students who are gay, lesbian, bisexual, or transgender but also to the entire school community.

This type of victimization and harassment is quite prevalent during early and middle adolescence as young people are beginning to construct an understanding of their own sexual identity and are becoming more aware of others' sexual development. In addition, young people today are coming out earlier in their developmental trajectory (D'Augelli, 1998), making issues of same-sex sexuality very prevalent during this developmental period. Thus, it seems to be the case that adolescents are using both social and verbal harassment targeted toward issues of sexuality to communicate within the peer social structure the acceptable and normative expressions of sexuality and gender, as well as to sanction peers whose developing sexual and gender identities do not conform to these norms (Horn, 2005a).

With development, as adolescents become more comfortable with their own and others' sexual identities, tolerance toward individuals with nonnormative sexual and gender identities seems to increase (Horn, in press), suggesting that this type of harassment may be most prevalent in middle and high school contexts. Interestingly, despite this general trend toward increased tolerance, research suggests that most perpetrators of severe anti-LGBT hate crimes are youth between the ages of 17 and 20 (Franklin, 2000). This suggests that prejudice, discrimination, and intolerance toward LGBT people are multifaceted social issues that are related to developmental, as well as contextual, institutional, and cultural factors.

A recent report by the Human Rights Watch, an organization devoted to investigating and documenting human rights violations around the world, exposed the failure of school officials and the federal and state governments to fulfill their "obligation to ensure that all youth enjoy their right to education in an environment where they are protected from discrimination, harassment, and violence" (Bochenek & Brown, 2001, p. 5). The report documents case after case in which school officials turned a blind eye to, and in some cases participated in, serious human rights violations of gay, lesbian, bisexual, or transgender students, in clear violation of the intention of the No Child Left Behind Act.

Given the strong language of the No Child Left Behind Act regarding school safety and tolerance for differences, why is so little done at the school, state, or federal level to ensure that all students can exercise their right to an education free from harassment and violence? Despite the fact that we can document the rights violations of LGBT youth across the United States and despite the fact that we have straightforward evidence of the negative developmental outcomes for students who are subjected to this kind of abuse, the situation is complex. It is complex because of the multifaceted nature of sex and sexuality and the impact this has on how people understand the purpose of education in a pluralistic society.

THE MULTIFACETED NATURE OF SEXUALITY

Sexuality is a complex and controversial subject. Sexuality is an inherent part of what it means to be human and for most is an integral part of one's individual identity (Brooks-Gunn & Graber, 1999). As such, sexuality is defined as something that is personal and private. On the other hand, throughout history, for various reasons, individuals' sexuality, and in particular their sexual behavior, has been subjected to societal control and regulation. Furthermore, beliefs about sex and sexuality and how individuals come to understand their own and others' sexuality are often influenced by the societal conventions and norms that have developed to regulate and control the expression or manifestation of sexuality.

Thus, there is a tension between viewing sexuality as a private and personal issue that is under the control of the individual and viewing sexuality (or some parts of sexuality) as a public and societal issue that is under societal control through cultural norms and societal conventions. When it comes to children and adolescents' sexuality, this tension between individual control and societal control comes to the fore (Levesque, 2000).

The process of coming to understand oneself as a sexual being is a primary developmental task of adolescence (Brooks-Gunn & Graber, 1999). As with other types of identity development processes, one of the ways in which youth come to understand their sexual identities is through experimentation and exploration, that is, through engaging in intimate relationships and sexual behavior. This aspect of adolescents' lives, however, is subject to extreme regulation (Levesque, 2000) in efforts to help protect adolescents (and to some extent society) from the potential risks and consequences that could result from engaging in sexual behavior before an individual has reached adult status.

Regardless of the fact that during adolescence most individuals reach their biological adult reproductive status, many adults assume that adolescents are not yet ready to handle the risks and responsibilities that go along with this status. The socialization of adolescents into healthy and responsible sexual behavior and relationships, then, is viewed as a societal responsibility and obligation. Thus, it appears that sexuality, and in particular adolescent sexuality, is a multifaceted issue that involves multiple dimensions of social knowledge. Thus, understanding how individuals apply these different dimensions of their social knowledge to questions of sexuality and sexual prejudice is one way of better understanding the complex questions surrounding the rights and treatment of LGBT students in schools addressed in this chapter.

SOCIAL COGNITIVE DOMAIN THEORY AND REASONING ABOUT SEXUALITY AND SEXUAL PREJUDICE

Social cognitive domain theory, as a theoretical paradigm, is inherently suited to studying reasoning and judgments regarding multifaceted and complex social issues such as sexuality and sexual prejudice, as well as individual and contextual variation in judgments about these issues (Smetana, 1995, 2006; Tisak, 1995; Turiel et al., 1987, Turiel, Hildebrandt, & Wainryb, 1991). The central premise of social cognitive domain theory is that evaluative social judgments are multifaceted and draw from several conceptual domains rather than a single structure of socio-moral reasoning (Nucci, 2001; Smetana, 2006; Turiel, 1983, 1998).

Within domain theory, concepts of morality (issues of human welfare, rights, and fairness) are distinguished from concepts of social conventions, which are the consensually determined standards of conduct particular to a given social group that promote group functioning and group identity. Although morality and convention deal with aspects of interpersonal regulation, a third domain of personal issues refers to actions that comprise the private aspects of one's life (e.g., contents of a diary) and matters of preference and choice (e.g., friends, music, hairstyle) rather than right or wrong (Horn & Nucci, 2006; Nucci, 2001).

A final element included within the domain theory account of sociomoral cognition is the role of informational assumptions in the generation of social judgments (Smetana, 2006; Turiel et al., 1991; Wainryb, 1991). That is, unlike prototypical moral judgments in which the judgments are predicated upon information regarding the effects that actions have upon the welfare of others, other situations involve the use of culturally mediated information (e.g., concepts of the afterlife) as the basis for an individual's judgments of right and wrong. Thus, in the case of homosexuality, for example, individuals' judgments about whether homosexuality is right or wrong are going to be based on their concepts regarding homosexuality as a natural or normal expression of human sexuality that may be informed, in part, through individuals' adherence to particular religious or cultural ideologies (Turiel et al., 1991).

In fact, research on older adolescents' and young adults' reasoning about homosexuality provides evidence that conceptions of sexuality, and in particular homosexuality, are indeed multifaceted and involve conventions and social norms, concerns with personal choice, as well as issues of individual rights and fairness (Horn & Nucci, 2003; Turiel et al, 1991). Additionally, this research provides evidence that individuals' reasoning about issues of homosexuality is also influenced by their assumptions about the natural order of the world, assumptions that are mediated, in part, by religious or cultural ideologies.

For example, in a study utilizing social cognitive domain theory, Turiel et al. (1991) found that some adolescents and young adults viewed homosexuality as psychologically deviant and unnatural, whereas others viewed it as a natural form of sexual expression. They also found, however, that individuals' evaluations of the psychological "normalcy" of same-sex sexuality were not perfectly correlated with their judgments about whether homosexuality was wrong or whether it should be regulated by laws. It appears, then, that adolescents' and young adults' concepts of sexuality involve their understanding of people as psychological systems, of social conventions and laws, as well as their beliefs about the natural order of the world based on biological or religious assumptions. That is, although most adolescents and young adults viewed sexuality as inherent to the individual, they differed in their beliefs about what constitutes "normal" or "healthy" forms of sexuality.

In the next section of this chapter, I describe the results of a series of studies that have utilized social cognitive domain theory to not only further understand adolescents' and young adults' beliefs about homosexuality, but also how these beliefs are related to their social judgments regarding exclusion, teasing, and harassment based on sexual orientation and gender identity.

BELIEFS ABOUT HOMOSEXUALITY AND THE TREATMENT OF OTHERS BASED ON SEXUAL ORIENTATION AND GENDER IDENTITY

Decisions in everyday contexts often involve coordination among personal, conventional, and moral issues; individuals bring their knowledge about these issues to bear on the situation (Horn & Nucci, 2006; Turiel, 1983, 1998). Thus, understanding sexuality and sexual prejudice involves moral elements of fairness, the welfare of another, and individual rights and conventional elements related to societal and legal prescriptions regarding homosexuality and gay and lesbian persons, as well as personal elements of understanding sex and sexuality as a private and personal aspect of one's identity.

How individuals coordinate and apply these domains of knowledge in specific contexts will likely vary and will be influenced by the nature of the context (i.e., questions about whether homosexuality is wrong versus questions about the treatment of others based on their sexuality) and their informational assumptions about the normalness or naturalness of sexuality, as well as other factors such as religion, ethnicity, contact with gay and lesbian persons, and age. For example, when asked to evaluate homosexuality (is it wrong?), individuals may be more likely to draw upon beliefs that may be informed by religion or culture rather than their knowledge regarding the fairness and welfare of others. When asked to evaluate whether it is acceptable to exclude, tease, or harass gay or lesbian people, however, it is likely that individuals' responses will be informed by their knowledge about the fair treatment of people and the welfare of others (that are inherent to the situation) rather than their culturally mediated beliefs.

To explore these issues, we investigated high school–aged adolescents' beliefs and attitudes about homosexuality and the treatment of gay, lesbian, and gender nonconforming peers utilizing a social cognitive domain theory framework (Horn, 2007, 2006; Horn & Nucci, 2003, 2004). Using self-report surveys, adolescents rated whether they believed homosexuality to be wrong or right. We also asked them to choose from a list of 19 reasons why they believed the way they did. The reasons were generated from the theoretical paradigm as well as from previous literature on adults' attitudes and beliefs about homosexuality and included statements regarding religious prescription, the individuals' right to be or do what they wanted, as well as statements regarding the naturalness of homosexuality. We also asked participants to evaluate whether they thought it was wrong to exclude, tease, or harass someone based on his or her sexual orientation or conformity to gender conventions regarding appearance and behaviors and to provide reasons for their judgments.

The data presented in these studies are drawn from two samples. The first sample included 350 10th-grade, 12th-grade, and college-aged students. The high school students were from a large, economically and racially heterogeneous, suburban school outside a large Midwestern city. The college students attended a medium-sized economically and racially heterogeneous university within a large Midwestern city. Slightly over half of the participants were female (60%) and European American (56%). The remaining students identified as African American (20%), Asian American (6%), Latino/a (9%), and other (9%). The second sample included 337 ninth-graders from a large racially and economically diverse school in a somewhat more politically conservative suburban area. In this sample, students were slightly more likely to be female (57%) and were predominantly European American/European immigrants (40%) and Asian/Asian American (34%) with other students identifying as African American (7%), Latino/a (9%), and other (10%).

The results of this research provide compelling evidence that the majority of adolescents distinguish between their beliefs and attitudes about homosexuality and their understanding of the fair treatment of persons. In the first sample almost half of the participants held the belief that homosexuality was wrong or that it was neither right nor wrong. In spite of this, only 10% of the participants evaluated excluding a gay or lesbian peer as acceptable, and less than 1% of the students evaluated it as acceptable to tease or harass someone because they were gay or lesbian (Horn & Nucci, 2003, 2004).

In the second sample, 50% of the students believed that homosexuality was wrong, and another 32% of the students believed that homosexuality was neither right nor wrong. Despite the fact that over 80% of the students from this sample evaluated homosexuality as not acceptable, only 9% of the students evaluated excluding a gay or lesbian peer as permissible, and only 4% of the students evaluated teasing a gay or lesbian peer as permissible. Furthermore, of the 50% of the students who evaluated homosexuality as wrong, only 13% evaluated excluding a gay or lesbian peer as acceptable and only 8% evaluated teasing a gay or lesbian peer as acceptable. Conversely, 42% of these students evaluated excluding a gay or lesbian peer as completely wrong, and 62% evaluated teasing a gay or lesbian peer as completely wrong (Horn, in press).

Interestingly, assessments of the reasons students gave for their judgments showed that a majority rated excluding, teasing, or harassing someone because of his or her sexual orientation as wrong because it was unfair or hurtful to the person or because they felt everyone had the right to be treated with respect. On the other hand, most of the students who evaluated homosexuality as wrong justified their judgments on societal or religious conventions, rules, or norms (Horn & Nucci, 2003, 2004). These results suggest that adolescents and young adults can and do distinguish between their own personal and religious beliefs and attitudes about homosexuality and the rights of individuals to be free from harm regardless of their sexual orientation. In fact, these results suggest that adolescents' beliefs about whether homosexuality is wrong are conceptually distinct from their understanding of the fair and just treatment of others.

Overall, adolescents and young adults viewed excluding, teasing, or harassing a gay, lesbian, or gender nonconforming peer as wrong; however, the study did provide some evidence that adolescents were less likely to evaluate as wrong excluding (but not teasing, harassing, or assaulting) a gay or lesbian individual than a heterosexual individual (Horn, 2007a, 2006b; Horn & Nucci, 2003). It is important to note that the data also provide evidence that adolescents view individuals who are nonconventional in regard to their gender as less acceptable than individuals who are gender conforming, regardless of their sexual orientation (Horn, 2007a). In fact, boys evaluated a straight individual who was nonconforming in gender appearance as significantly less acceptable than a gay or lesbian individual who was conforming in gender appearance (Horn, 2007a). When asked why it was all right to exclude the straight boy who wore make-up and fingernail polish but not the gay boy who was gender conforming, one individual remarked, "Well if you know they are gay then it is not all right to tease them because that is who they are and they can't change it, but if they aren't gay and they just look gay by how they dress then it is O.K. to tease them because they are just being weird" (Horn & Nucci, 2005).

These results are critical, because they suggest that much anti-lesbian and gay harassment in schools may be based on individuals' understanding of conventional issues regarding gender norms and stereotypes rather than on their beliefs and attitudes about homosexuality, suggesting that preventing anti-lesbian, gay, bisexual, and transgender harassment and violence in schools is and should be quite distinct from advocating a particular set of beliefs or attitudes regarding homosexuality.

In fact, these results suggest that in order to reduce anti-lesbian, gay, bisexual, and transgender harassment, schools should be doing much more work around adolescents' understanding of gender, gender conventions, and gender roles rather than adolescents' beliefs and attitudes about sexual identity or sexual orientation. Furthermore, these results suggest that harassment of this type affects not just gay and lesbian students, but any student who does not fit into a traditional construction or stereotype of what it means to be male or female. Thus, the findings underscore the notion that reducing anti-gay and lesbian harassment and victimization in schools benefits the entire school population, not just those who identify as gay or lesbian.

Finally, this research also provides some evidence for age-related differences in adolescents' attitudes toward exclusion, teasing, and harassment of gay, lesbian, and gender nonconforming peers, but not in their beliefs about the acceptability of homosexuality (Horn, 2006b). Although younger adolescents were less likely than older adolescents to evaluate exclusion, teasing, and harassment of gay and lesbian peers as wrong, they were not more likely than older adolescents to evaluate homosexuality as wrong (Horn, 2006).

These results provide further evidence for the argument that adolescents' beliefs about homosexuality are conceptually distinct from their reasoning regarding the treatment of gay, lesbian, and gender nonconforming peers and that educating students toward respect and acceptance of gay, lesbian, and gender nonconforming peers is not synonymous with changing adolescents' personal beliefs about the acceptability of homosexuality. This finding has important implications for understanding the conflict and controversy surrounding the role of schools in protecting the rights of LGBT students. In the next section of this chapter, I outline this controversy as well as address the implications that the above research has regarding this controversy.

EDUCATION AND ADOLESCENT SEXUALITY

One of the defining and most enduring purposes of public education in the United States has been to prepare youth for future involvement as productive and contributing citizens in a democratic society (Dewey, 1916/1944; Levesque, 2000). To that end, one of the goals of school is to socialize youth to the norms, values, and traditions of adult membership in society. Because the United States is a pluralistic society, however, the specific norms, values, and traditions discussed in and espoused by schools are complicated and are the focus of heated debate and conflict. Nowhere is this more apparent than issues dealing with adolescent sexuality.

Due to the multiplicity of beliefs about sex and sexuality in the United States, people hold varying definitions of healthy and responsible sexual behavior and relationships (Turiel et al., 1991). Thus, socializing adolescents into their mature roles as sexual adults and the role that schools should play in this process varies in accord with beliefs and assumptions about sex and sexuality individuals within a particular context hold. As such, adolescent sexuality in general and issues relating to same-sex sexuality in particular have become one of the central and defining issues in the "culture wars" between traditional/conservative and progressive/liberal camps in the United States, and schools have become one of the primary arenas in which this conflict is being played out (Levesque, 2000).

At the crux of this debate are fundamental beliefs about how children and adolescents develop and the role of adults and society in this process. On one side is a set of beliefs that the role of society and adults is to transmit a particular set of cultural values and norms to children and adolescents by protecting them from negative influences and risks, providing clear definitions of right and wrong, and cultivating in children and adolescents attachment and obedience to the social group, its norms, and traditions (Ellison & Sherkat, 1993; Killen & Horn, 2000; Levesque, 2000). From this point of view, adolescents are passive recipients of culture that is passed down to them by adults.

On the other side is a set of beliefs that adolescents are active participants in their own development and as such, should be given access to information and resources, should be provided with opportunities to make decisions about their own lives, and should be supported and guided in debating and exploring issues of right or wrong in their own lives and in society (Killen & Horn, 2000; Nucci, 2001). The different sides of this argument have alternately been more or less popular throughout history. When it comes to adolescent sexuality and the role that schools should play in socializing adolescents toward healthy and responsible sexual behaviors and relationships, however, the traditional/conservative side seems to prevail in the United States (Donovan, 1998; Levesque, 2000; Smith, 1994).

This can be seen in current federal legislation that prohibits federal funding to schools that utilize comprehensive sexuality education curricula, yet provides millions of dollars of funding to schools, faith-based institutions, and other not-for-profits that utilize Abstinence Only Until Marriage curricula, despite the fact that these programs have not been proven effective in reducing sexual behavior or sexual health risks in adolescence (SIECUS, 2005). Further evidence of this trend within the United States can be seen in the language and programming around adolescent sexuality put forth by agencies within the Federal Government such as the Department of Health and Human Service. For example, a Web site aimed at helping parents talk to their teens about healthy choices regarding sexuality, "4parents.gov," provides the following advice to parents.

> Abstinence is the healthiest choice for teens because they are not ready for the adult emotions of sex and the adult choices that sex entails... . This is the best choice emotionally and physically for all teens. The values that come from abstinence, such as respect, responsibility, and self-control, will benefit their future relationships. By choosing abstinence, your teen will learn to recognize that the joys and benefits of experiencing sex as part of a healthy, trusting, committed adult relationship far outweigh any of the fleeting perceived benefits of early sexual activity. You owe it to your teen to provide guidance about abstinence that will benefit him or her for a lifetime. (Department of Health and Human Services, undated, pp. 1–2)

These statements come after a long list of points regarding the inherent dangers of early sexual behavior on adolescents' health and development. Absent from the document is advice for parents on how to talk with their children about responsible and healthy sexual decision making and behaviors if their teen is or is going to be sexually active, or information on safe sex practices or contraceptives. In fact, the only discussion of contraceptives is in terms of their ineffectiveness in preventing sexually transmitted diseases and pregnancy.

Because a central premise of the traditional/conservative argument regarding sexuality is that homosexuality is wrong, unnatural, or a sin (Burdette, Ellison, & Hill, 2005; Levesque, 2000), it has affected every aspect of schooling for students questioning their sexual orientation or those who identify as lesbian, gay, bisexual, or transgender. That is, if the schools' obligation is to prepare adolescents for responsible and productive citizenship, it is then the schools' obligation to socialize students toward heterosexual identities, behaviors, and relationships, and away from homosexual identities, behaviors, and relationships.

The implications of this approach for school policy and practice are numerous and range from the kinds of messages students receive about sexuality and their access to information regarding sexualities other than heterosexuality to their very right to exist in the school at all. For example, a number of states, such as Arizona, Georgia, and South Carolina, have passed laws or statutes that prohibit teachers from mentioning the word "homosexual" in class. They have mandated that if it is to be discussed at all, it should be discussed exclusively in a negative manner (in relation to HIV/AIDS and sexually transmitted diseases), and that it is permissible to prohibit any discussion of same-sex sexuality that could be construed as advocating or promoting homosexuality or homosexual behavior (Cianciotto & Cahill, 2003). Most recently, schools in many states have been under pressure to provide students who identify as LGBT or are questioning their sexuality with information and resources on reparative therapy and other ways to "cure" them of being gay (Focus on the Family, 2005).

Even in states where these kinds of laws do not exist, teachers and administrators are likely to avoid dealing with issues related to same-sex sexuality altogether in efforts to avoid controversy and backlash from parents or other community members. The fear of controversy surrounding these issues is not unfounded. Even in states or school districts where there are clear legal or policy mandates concerning the role of schools in creating a safe environment for LGBT students and families, controversies surrounding these issues continue and often lead to negative situations for schools and for teachers and students within those schools.

In 2004 in California, for example, despite a state law requiring that schools that receive state funding develop and implement safe schools policy and programs for LGBT youth, the school board of Westminster school district (in Orange County, CA) refused to comply with state law regarding language around the definition of gender and gender expression in its nondiscrimination policy. The language provides specific protection to transgender students and staff or those whose gender expressions do not conform to societal gender norms. The three-person majority on the school board stated that this type of language would promote immoral behavior and transsexuality and cited religious reasons for their opposition.

This action of the school board, which was not endorsed by a majority of the students or staff within the school district, delayed the district from receiving a $15 million construction loan and put in jeopardy another $40 million of state funding, almost two thirds of the district's funding (American Civil Liberties Union, 2005). In 2002 in West Virginia, the attorney general's office pulled from schools a state-funded anti-bullying campaign that included gay students as a protected class when some parents and community members protested that it "indoctrinated students into accepting the homosexual lifestyle" (Smith, 2003, p. 1).

In a Chicago suburb in 2003, after a heated and very public debate at a school board meeting, teachers and school personnel throughout the district were ordered by the school board to remove "safe zone" stickers (the stickers indicate that those classrooms and those teachers are safe zones for LGBT students) from classroom doors. The opponents of the "safe zone" program, a small minority of community members, many without any personal connection to the schools, cited that the schools were recruiting students to be gay or lesbian and that the program discriminated against students and families from religions that believe homosexuality is wrong (Neumann, 2000).

As can be seen from these examples, one of the reasons that anti-gay harassment continues to be so prevalent in our schools is the multifaceted nature of sexuality and the conflation between protecting LGBT students from harm and advocating that homosexuality is permissible. That is, if schools acknowledge that LGBT students exist and have rights to protection, then they (the schools) are endorsing homosexuality as acceptable and indoctrinating other students into this belief. In the extreme case, people have argued that if schools are teaching students that harassment and discrimination of LGBT adolescents is wrong, then they are essentially telling the students that they have to believe homosexuality is acceptable and this, in turn, infringes on parents' rights to raise their children into their own traditions and beliefs.

The research presented earlier in this chapter, however, provides evidence that this is not necessarily the case. Adolescents' and young adults' beliefs about homosexuality were conceptually distinct from their understanding of the fair treatment of persons, suggesting that schools can engage in work to reduce anti-gay, lesbian, bisexual, and transgender harassment without impinging on other students' or families' beliefs regarding homosexuality.

Interestingly, the results of the research presented earlier in the chapter, that most students found harassment of gay, lesbian, and gender nonconforming peers as wrong, seem inconsistent with the extreme negative school environments experienced by LGBT students presented at the beginning of the chapter. If most heterosexual adolescents evaluate exclusion, teasing, and harassment of lesbian, gay, and gender nonconforming students as wrong, why is it that schools continue to be negative and hostile places for many LGBT youth?

First, it is likely that a small number of individuals are actually perpetrating the extreme forms of harassment outlined in the beginning of this chapter. In fact, a small number of students (less than 10) wrote comments on their surveys such as "All the fxxxing fags should die!" and "Kill all the butt-fxxxing fags!" suggesting that the sample did include students holding these extremely negative views. It could be the case that these perpetrators are not being sanctioned or stopped by the peers or adults in their environments from engaging in these harmful behaviors due to the conflict and controversy surrounding these issues in schools. It is quite possible that in negotiating their everyday experiences adolescents are faced with additional factors that add to the complexity of these kinds of judgments. For example, although adolescents may evaluate anti-gay harassment as wrong, they may be afraid of intervening when witnessing this type of harassment for fear of being labeled gay or lesbian themselves.

Second, it could also be that this type of harassment is more common in particular kinds of contexts that were not directly assessed in the studies described above. The messages that students receive about homosexuality in our society are extremely complex. Lesbian and gay individuals are granted some legal rights and not others, religious leaders can be seen on TV saying that gay people deserve to die, and hate messages and language regarding homosexuality are quite prevalent. Thus, peer groups, schools, or communities with high levels of heterosexism or anti-lesbian, gay, bisexual, and transgender discourse and actions may provide adolescents with tacit social sanctions or approval for engaging in behaviors that they would otherwise judge as morally wrong.

Finally, the research described in this chapter did not investigate adolescents' judgments about the acceptability of such things as using anti-gay language (e.g., calling someone a "fag" to mean stupid). Adolescents may find these lower-level kinds of harassment as acceptable, even though this type of harassment still creates a negative or hostile climate for students who identify as lesbian, gay, bisexual, or transgender.

Future research needs to investigate adolescents' reasoning about their own experiences of perpetrating or witnessing anti-LGBT harassment, about intervening in these types of harassment situations, as well as about other types of situations that may make schools unsafe or inhospitable for LGBT students (e.g., anti-LGBT language, lack of positive images and portrayals of LGBT people in the curriculum, high levels of heterosexism).

CONCLUSIONS

We live in an increasingly diverse society in which individuals hold extremely divergent viewpoints, values, and beliefs. Recent national events have made it abundantly clear that this diversity of views, upon which our democracy was founded, can lead to extreme conflict, controversy, and divisiveness. Unfortunately, far too often, schools become the sites in which these conflicts and controversies get played out, and research suggests that this has serious developmental implications for young people (D'Augelli, 1998). In such a pluralistic and diverse society, the role of public education should not be to endorse a particular set of conventional or religious norms or beliefs, but rather to provide students with the skills and resources they need to negotiate the increasingly diverse and global world and to respect and affirm every individual's right to freedom from harm, intolerance, and bigotry.

Furthermore, schools in a pluralistic country such as the United States have a moral obligation to both protect all students from harassment and discrimination regardless of their identities and to protect students' rights to construct their own beliefs about social issues and the world around them. The role of public education should be to ensure the right of all students to an education free from harassment, persecution, discrimination, and violence, regardless of religious background, national origin, race, ethnicity, culture, gender, and sexual orientation and gender expression.

We cannot continue to make LGBT students invisible and pretend that they do not exist, because they do. We know they exist because they are coming out at younger ages and are refusing to be silenced or closeted. We know they exist because they are demanding to be seen and heard and are fighting for their rights. For example, in 2002, Derek Henkel won a $451,000 settlement against the Reno, Nevada, school district for failing to protect him from violence and harassment and for denying him his right to free speech. In June 2003, Thomas McLaughlin and his family won a $25,000 settlement against the Pulaski County school board because they violated Thomas' rights to free speech, equal protection, privacy, and religious liberty.

On being asked about the settlement, Thomas said, "All I want out of this is for me and other gay students to be able to go to school without being preached to and without being expected to lie about who we are. I'm not ever going to forget about it. My rights were violated and it was wrong for the school to do that" (First Amendment Center, 2003, p. 1). As scholars, educators, and citizens it is our responsibility and our obligation to ensure that their rights are upheld regardless of the conflict and controversy this entails.

REFERENCES

American Association of University Women. (2001). *Hostile hallways: Bullying, teasing, and sexual harassment in school.* Washington, DC: American Association of University Women Educational Foundation.

American Civil Liberties Union. (2003, April). ACLU sues Arkansas school district to guarantee gay student's rights to be "out" at school. Retrieved May 11, 2004, http://www.aclu.org/LesbianGayRights/LesbianGay-Rights.cfm?ID=12298&c=106

American Civil Liberties Union. (2003, July). ACLU secures sweeping changes in Arkansas school district. Retrieved May 11, 2004, http://www.aclu .org/LesbianGayRights/LesbianGayRights.cfm?ID=12298&c=106

American Civil Liberties Union. (2005). Rogue school district challenges nondiscrimination law, then backs down. Retrieved July 20, 2005, http:// www.aclu-sc.org/News/OpenForum/1009/100666/

Bochenek, M., & Brown, A. (2001). *Hatred in the hallways: Violence and discrimination against lesbian, gay, bisexual, and transgender students in U.S. schools.* New York: Human Rights Watch.

Bontempo, D. E., & D'Augelli, A. R. (2002). Effects of at-school victimization and sexual orientation on lesbian, gay, or bisexual youths' health risk behavior. *Journal of Adolescent Health, 30,* 364–374.

Brooks-Gunn, J., & Graber, J. A. (1999). What's sex got to do with it? The development of sexual identities in adolescence. In R. Contrada & R. Ashmore (Eds.), *Self, social identity, and physical health: Interdisciplinary explorations* (pp. 155–183). New York: Oxford University Press.

Burdette, A., Ellison, C., & Hill, T. (2005). Conservative Protestantism and tolerance toward homosexuals. An examination of potential mechanisms. *Sociological Inquiry, 75,* 177–196.

Cianciotto, J., & Cahill, S. (2003). *Education policy: Issues affecting lesbian, gay, bisexual, and transgender youth.* New York: National Gay and Lesbian Task Force Policy Institute.

D'Augelli, A. (1998). Developmental implications of victimization of lesbian, gay and bisexual youths. In G. Herek (Ed.), *Stigma and sexual orientation: Understanding prejudice against lesbians, gay men, and bisexuals* (pp. 187–210). Thousand Oaks: Sage.

D'Augelli, A. R. (1996). Enhancing the development of lesbian, gay and bisexual youths. In E. Rothblum & L. Bonds (Eds.), *Prevention of heterosexism and homophobia* (pp. 124–150). Thousand Oaks, CA: Sage.

Department of Health and Human Services (undated). Parents, speak up! A guide for discussing abstinence, sex, and relationships. Retrieved December 15, 2005, http://www.4parents.gov

Dewey, J. (1916/1944). *Democracy and education*. New York: Macmillan.

Donovan, P. (1998). School-based sexuality education: The issues and challenges. *Family Planning Perspectives, 30*, 188–194.

Ellison, C. & Sherkat, D. (1993). Obedience and autonomy: Religion and parental values reconsidered. *Journal for the Scientific Study of Religion, 32*, 313–329.

First Amendment Center. (April, 2003). Suit filed after boy punished for talking about homosexuality. Retrieved May 11, 2004, http://www.firstamendmentcenter.org/news.aspx?id=11321

Focus on the Family. (2005). Homosexuality in children and teens. Retrieved July 20, 2005, http://www.focusonyourchild.com/hottopics/A0001284.cfm

Franklin, K. (2000). Antigay behaviors by young adults: Prevalence, patterns and motivators in a noncriminal population. *Journal of Interpersonal Violence, 15*, 339–362

Garofalo, R., Wolf, R. C., Kessel, S., Palfrey, J., & DuRant, R. H. (1998). The association between health risk behaviors and sexual orientation among a school-based sample of adolescents. *Pediatrics, 101*, 895–902.

Gay, Lesbian, and Straight Education Network. (2001). *National School Climate Survey*. New York: Gay, Lesbian, and Straight Education Network.

Gay, Lesbian, and Straight Education Network. (2003). *National School Climate Survey*. New York: Gay, Lesbian, and Straight Education Network.

Horn, S. S. (2005a). Adolescents' peer interactions: Conflict and coordination between personal expression, social norms, and moral reasoning. L. Nucci (Ed.), *Conflict, contradiction and contrarian elements in moral development and education* (pp. 113–128). New York: Erlbaum.

Horn, S. S. (2005b). [Adolescents' judgments about the treatment of gay, lesbian, and gender non-conforming peers]. Unpublished data.

Horn, S. S. (2007a). Adolescents' acceptance of same-sex peers based on sexual orientation and gender expression. *Journal of Youth and Adolescence, 26*, 363–371.

Horn, S. S. (2006). Age-related differences in heterosexual adolescents' and young adults' beliefs and attitudes about homosexuality and the treatment of gay and lesbian peers in school. *Cognitive Development, 21*, 420–440.

Horn, S. S. (in press). The multifaceted nature of sexual prejudice: What can we learn from studying how adolescents reason about sexual orientation and sexual prejudice. In S. Levy & M. (Eds.) Intergroup relations: An integrative development and social psychological perspective. Oxford: Oxford University Press.

Horn, S. S., & Nucci, L. P. (2003). The multidimensionality of adolescents' beliefs about and attitudes toward gay and lesbian peers in school. *Equity and Excellence in Education, 36*, 1–12.

Horn, S. S., & Nucci, L. P. (2004). Relationships between adolescents' beliefs about homosexuality and their evaluations of anti-gay harassment. Unpublished manuscript, University of Illinois at Chicago, Chicago, Illinois.

Horn, S. S., & Nucci, L. P. (2006). Harassment of gay and lesbian youth and school violence in America: An analysis and directions for intervention. In C. Daiute, L. P. Nucci, Z. Beykont, & C. Higson-Smith (Eds.), *Global perspectives on youth conflict* (pp. 139–155). Oxford, UK: Oxford University Press.

Hunter, J. (1990). Violence against lesbian and gay male youths. *Journal of Interpersonal Violence, 5*, 295–300.

Killen, M., & Horn, S. S. (2000). Facilitating children's development about morality, community, and autonomy: A case for service-learning experiences. In W. Van Haaften, T. Wren, & A. Tellings (Eds.), *Moral sensibilities and the education, Volume II: The schoolchild* (pp. 89–113). Bemmel, Netherlands: Concorde.

Kimmel, M., & Mahler, M. (2003). Adolescent masculinity, homophobia, and violence: Random school shootings, 1982–2001. *American Behavioral Scientist, 46*, 1439–1458.

Lambda Legal Defense and Education Fund (2000). *Derek Henkle: Survivor of school violence in Reno, Nevada.* Retrieved July 20, 2005, from http://www.lambdalegal.org/cgi-bin/iowa/news/resources.html?record=561

Levesque, R. (2000). *Adolescents, sex and the law: Preparing adolescents for responsible citizenship.* Washington, DC: American Psychological Association.

Neumann, J. (2000, January 14). School bans gay-safe-zone signs. *Chicago Tribune.*

No Child Left Behind Act of 2001 (2002). 115 U.S.C. Article 1425.

Nucci, L. P. (2001). Education in the Moral Domain. Cambridge, UK: Cambridge University Press.

Remafedi, G. (1987). Male homosexuality: The adolescent perspective. *Pediatrics, 79*, 326–330.

Rivers, I., & D'Augelli, A. (2001). The victimization of lesbian, gay and bisexual youths. In A. D'Augelli & C. Patterson (Eds.), *Lesbian, gay, and bisexual identities and youth* (pp. 199–223). New York: Oxford University Press.

Russell, S. T. (2003). Sexual minority youth and suicide risk. *American Behavioral Scientist, 46*, 1241–1257.

Russell, S. T., Franz, B. T., & Driscoll, A. K. (2001). Same-sex romantic attraction and experiences of violence in adolescence. *American Journal of Public Health, 91,* 903–906.

Russell, S. T., & Joyner, K. (2001). Adolescent sexual orientation and suicide risk: Evidence from a national study. *American Journal of Public Health, 9,* 1276–1281.

Russell, S. T., Seif, H., & Truong, N. L. (2001). School outcomes of sexual minority youth in the United States: Evidence from a national study. *Journal of Adolescence, 24,* 111–127.

Russell, S. T., Truong, N. L., & Driscoll, A. K. (2002). Adolescent same-sex romantic attractions and relationships: Implications for substance use and abuse. *American Journal of Public Health, 92,* 198–202.

Savins-Williams, R. C. (1998). *"And then I became gay:" Young men's stories.* New York: Routledge.

Sexuality Information and Education Council of the United States (2005, May). Siecus Fact Sheet on Sexuality Education. Retrieved December 15, 2005, http://www.siecus.org/policy/research_says.pdf

Smetana, J. G. (1995). Morality in context: Abstractions, applications, and ambiguities. In R. Vasta (Ed.), *Annals of child development, Vol. 10* (pp. 83–130). London: Jessica Kingsley.

Smetana, J. G. (2006). Social-cognitive domain theory: Consistencies and variations in children's moral and social judgments. In M. Killen & J. G. Smetana (Eds.), *Handbook of Moral Development* (pp. 119–154). Mahwah, NJ: Lawrence Erlbaum.

Smith, C. (2003, January 23). Attorney general's office scraps anti-bullying effort. *Charleston Daily Mail on-line,* Charleston, WV, retrieved January 24, 2003, http://www.dailymail.com/news/News/2003012323/

Smith, T. W. (1994). Attitudes toward sexual permissiveness: Trends, correlates, and behavioral connections. In A. S. Rossi (Ed.), *Sexuality across the life course* (pp. 63–97). Chicago: Chicago University Press.

Tisak, M. (1995). Domains of social reasoning and beyond. *Annals of Child Development, 11,* 95–130.

Turiel, E. (1983). *The development of social knowledge: Morality and convention.* Cambridge, UK: Cambridge University Press.

Turiel, E. (1998). The development of morality. In W. Damon (Series Ed.) & N. Eisenberg (Vol. Ed.), *Handbook of child psychology: Vol. 3. Social, emotional, and personality development* (5th ed., pp. 863–932). New York: Wiley.

Turiel, E., Hildebrandt, C., & Wainryb, C. (1991). Judging social issues: Difficulties, inconsistencies, and consistencies. *Monographs of the Society for Research in Child Development, 56* (Serial No. 224).

Turiel, E., Killen, M., & Helwig, C. (1987). Morality: Its structure, functions, and vagaries. In J. Kagan & S. Lamb (Eds.), *The emergence of morality in young children* (pp. 155–243). Chicago: University of Chicago Press.

Wainryb, C. (1991). Understanding differences in moral judgments: The role of informational assumptions. *Child Development, 62*, 840–851.

7

THE DEVELOPMENT OF STEREOTYPE THREAT
Consequences for Educational and Social Equality

Catherine Good and Joshua Aronson

Social and educational equality requires all members of a society to be able to envision a career path that enables them to fulfill their intellectual potential and thus participate fully in that society. Unfortunately, however, this may not be the case for many females in the United States. As a recent report by The National Academy of Sciences (2006) argues, women in math-based fields such as science and engineering face many barriers to their success and participation in these domains, a situation that leads to potential educational inequalities for nearly half of the nation's population.

For example, although women earn nearly half of all science and engineering doctoral degrees, they are vastly underrepresented in the so-called hard sciences. Specifically, in 2003 women earned over half of the doctoral degrees in the social and behavioral sciences, yet they earned only 29% of doctoral degrees in the physical sciences, 24% of doctoral degrees in mathematics, and 19% of doctoral degrees in engineering (National Science Foundation, 2006). The composition of the doctoral science and engineering workforce mirrors these numbers: White women represent only 22.1% of this important workforce.

The disparities in men's and women's career aspirations and pursuits may have their roots in early performance differences in mathematics. For example, a higher percentage of males than females performs at or above proficiency in mathematics in the 4th (35% versus 30%), 8th (30% versus 27%), and 12th (19% versus 14%) grades. Moreover, although the gap between males and females on the SAT has shrunk over the years, males still outperform females by 34 points on this high-stakes test (College Board, 2005). These early differences in mathematics achievement and subsequent differences in career participation rates represent a troubling and important area of social inequality.

What explains these sex-based performance and participation differences? Although some have argued for the role of innate biological differences (see Halpern, 1992, for a review of sex-based differences; Summers, 2005), the role of social forces, such as ability-impugning stereotypes, has been well established (see Aronson & Steele, 2005; Steele, Spencer, & Aronson, 2002, for reviews). One extensive line of research suggests that females (or any individual who faces negative stereotypes about their academic abilities) often suffer negative performance outcomes, not necessarily because they lack ability, but because of their vulnerability to the effects of ability-impugning stereotypes. Indeed, the research shows that when stereotypes are not activated, negatively stereotyped individuals often perform as well on intellectual tasks as do nonstereotyped individuals. However, when negative stereotypes are activated, they trigger psychological processes that undermine the performance of stereotyped individuals, such as females in math (Inzlicht & Ben-Zeev, 2000; Spencer, Steele, & Quinn, 1999) and African Americans in academics more generally (Steele & Aronson, 1995).

In this chapter we discuss what research suggests is a significant contributor to educational and social inequalities for females and minority students: contending with stereotypes that allege some sort of intellectual or academic inferiority. This phenomenon is called "stereotype threat" (Steele & Aronson, 1995). First, we document the inequality between males and females in math and science and between minority and White students in academics more generally. Second, we review the risk factors for and the situations that are most likely to increase students' vulnerability to stereotype threat. Third, we identify the developmental precursors and trends in students' vulnerability to stereotype threat. Finally, we report research that has yielded beneficial remedies to stereotype threat.

ACADEMIC ACHIEVEMENT OF MINORITIES AND FEMALES

The underrepresentation of girls and women in math and science domains and the academic underperformance of Blacks and Latinos are long-standing concerns among anyone concerned with educational and social inequalities. Each year, fresh statistics from statewide and national tests and national surveys replicate the troubling pattern of underachievement noted for as long as records have been kept. For example, girls and young women have long been underrepresented in the areas of math and science. Although most studies find no gender gap in math performance until about the eighth grade (NCES, 2001), girls' enjoyment and confidence in math tends to be measurably lower than boys' as early as elementary school, despite performance equal to that of boys.

But over time in school, the gender gap in confidence increasingly is accompanied by actual performance differences. For example, scores on the Third International Mathematics and Science Study (TIMMS), an achievement test given to half a million 4th-, 8th-, and 12th-grade students in 41 nations, reveals a gender gap that widens with age; by the 12th grade, boys significantly outscore girls. Behavioral changes also become more pronounced over time, with girls significantly less likely than boys to enroll in the more advanced courses in math and science (AAUW, 1992). Furthermore, girls who do pursue an advanced math course are more likely to drop out before finishing the course (Hanson, 1996; Stumpf & Stanley, 1996). The results of this trend are quite clear at the graduate and professional level, as discussed previously.

A more general trend of underperformance by African American and Hispanic students on nearly every measure of achievement from grade school through college also persists, despite efforts to remedy this educational inequality. Compared to White and Asian students, they receive lower grades, obtain lower scores on tests of reading, math, and science, and have higher dropout rates from school (NCES, 2001). Although the Black–White gap has narrowed, the average African American student still scores below 75% of White students on most standardized tests (Jencks & Phillips, 1998). Hispanic students fare somewhat better than Blacks, but their test and school performance tends also to lag substantially behind that of Whites and Asians (e.g., College Board, 2005; Romo & Falbo, 1995). What is more troubling is that these disparities persist even after differences in socioeconomic factors are taken into account (Warren, 1996). And as with females, underrepresented minorities make up a paltry 5.9% of the academic doctoral workforce in science and engineering (National Science Foundation, 2006).

Much psychological and educational research has examined the various factors presumed to underlie these educational inequalities. For example, researchers have identified specific sociological processes that impede the achievement of Blacks (e.g., Jencks & Phillips, 1998), of

Hispanics (e.g., Romo & Falbo, 1995; Valencia, 1997), and that of girls and women in math and science domains (e.g., Congressional Hearing, 1994; Eccles & Jacobs, 1992; Sadker & Sadker, 1994).

Recent research in social psychology has suggested the operation of a more general process that may systematically contribute to the underachievement of all these groups (see Aronson & Steele, 2005; Steele, Spencer, & Aronson, 2002, for reviews). This research suggests that individuals suffer negative performance outcomes—lower test scores, and less engagement with and less enjoyment of academics—because they are burdened by an uncomfortable awareness of cultural stereotypes impugning their intellectual and academic abilities. Steele and Aronson (1995) called this burden "stereotype threat," and established in their experiments with Black college freshmen and sophomores a link to substantial decrements in standardized test performance.

Subsequent experimental work has established that stereotype threat also undermines the academic performance of Hispanics (Aronson & Salinas, 1998), students from low socioeconomic backgrounds (Croizet & Claire, 1998), and females in math (Good, Aronson, & Harder, in press; Inzlicht & Ben-Zeev, 2000; Spencer, Steele, & Quinn, 1999). The view emerging from this research is that underperformance occurs because stereotypes facilitate pejorative interpretations of failure or academic difficulty, suggesting low ability rather than surmountable challenges. This adds stress and self-doubt to the educational experience and uneasiness about not belonging in the academic arena (Good, Dweck, & Rattan, 2006a, 2006b). Ultimately, stereotype threat can undermine the degree to which students value academic achievement in the stereotyped domain, an effect that appears to accumulate for students over time (Aronson et al., 2002; Osborne, 1995; Steele, 1997). It can also lead students to choose not to pursue the domain of study, a choice that limits the range of professions that are open to them, thus contributing to educational and social inequality (Good et al., 2006a).

RISK FACTORS AND SITUATIONS THAT LEAD TO STEREOTYPE THREAT

Since the publication of Steele and Aronson's 1995 study, researchers have identified individual risk factors that increase one's vulnerability to stereotype threat, their "stereotype vulnerability" (Aronson, 2002). One clear factor—at least in laboratory research—is "domain identification," the degree to which one values achievement in a given academic domain as a personally defining construct. The higher the domain identification, the more one is bothered by implications of inferiority in that domain. And thus, underperformance due to stereotype-related stress is most pronounced for those who value and care about doing well in the stereotyped domain (Aronson et al., 1999). Other personal factors that influence stereotype vulnerability include racial or gender identification (Schmader, 2002), expectations for being discriminated against, and beliefs about the nature of intelligence (see Aronson, 2002, for a review). These vulnerability factors, however, may be less influential than the situational factors that have been shown to induce stereotype threat: the evaluative scrutiny and racial or gender salience that arise in many academic situations.

Evaluative Scrutiny

Perhaps the most fundamental factor associated with vulnerability to stereotype threat is the predicament of having one's ability evaluated. Tests that purportedly measure intelligence create a situation in which low performance could indicate limited ability and thus verify the stereotype (Aronson et al., 1998; Steele & Aronson, 1995). Research has shown that under such "diagnostic" conditions, stereotyped individuals' performance suffers; under "nondiagnostic" conditions, when ability evaluation is downplayed, their performance improves.

The classic example of how evaluative scrutiny undermines performance involves African American students solving verbal problems on a standardized test (Steele & Aronson, 1995). In these studies, African American and White college students took a difficult verbal test resembling the GRE under one of two conditions. Participants were told either that the test measured their intellectual abilities, or alternatively, that the test measured psychological processes involved in problem solving. Results showed that in the "diagnostic" condition, the White participants outscored African Americans, a performance pattern resembling the SAT racial gap. However, in the "nondiagnostic" condition, the racial gap disappeared. In other words, African Americans performed far better when the threat of evaluation was lifted.

Steele and Aronson (1995) argued that African Americans' underperformance occurred because stereotypes change the meaning and consequences of failure. All students face the risk of shame or discouragement if they perform poorly on a task. For stereotyped individuals, however, the normal risks of low performance that anyone feels taking a test escalate. A single failure on an evaluative task can raise the troubling possibility that the stereotype is true of one's self, or that it may accurately characterize one's self in the eyes of others. Thus, although most people strive to do well on a diagnostic test, stereotyped individuals may become hypermotivated to perform well in order to disprove the stereotype (Aronson, 2002). This hypermotivated state appears to create an added level of stress and anxiety that inhibits the relaxed concentration optimal for high performance on complex cognitive tasks (Aronson, 2002; Osborne, 2000).

Steele and Aronson (1995) also found evidence to suggest that the diagnosticity of the exam aroused race-related thoughts among African Americans, presumably compounding their distraction and anxiety. In a study similar to the one previously described, Steele and Aronson manipulated test-diagnosticity and then measured the cognitive activation of race-related constructs. African Americans in the diagnostic condition—that is, participants who thought they would have their abilities measured by an upcoming test—were more likely to think about race. The specter of ability evaluation thus appears to be cognitively linked to racial stereotypes.

Yet stereotype threat is not inevitable, even for students in highly evaluative situations. For example, in a study conducted by Good, Aronson, and Harder (in press), advanced calculus students took a difficult test presented as a reliable measure of their calculus aptitude, an achievement situation that typically produces a sizable gender gap (see AAUW, 1998). In this study, however, the experimenters led half the test-takers to believe that the diagnostic calculus test had never shown any gender differences. In other words, the participants in this condition believed that males and females had an equal chance of performing well on the test and thus, that the stereotype of males' superiority in math did not apply to this particular testing situation. Females in this condition not only performed better than females who did not receive the "no gender differences" manipulation, but also performed better than the males in either condition. Thus, even though the females believed that the experimenter was evaluating their calculus abilities, they apparently trusted the test to be an unbiased measure of their abilities and that they would not be judged stereotypically (see also Spencer et al., 1999).

Taken together with the experiments on race, these findings offer hope that the stubborn race and gender gaps in test performance can be overcome with wise attention to situational details that shape people's psychological experiences and performance (Steele, 1997).

Group Identity Salience and Identification

Another significant situational precursor to stereotype threat is group identity salience: when one's stereotyped group status is made relevant or conspicuous by features of the situation. Such would be the case if a Black student were taking a test in the presence of a group of White students, or if a female were asked to solve math problems in a male-dominated classroom. Steele and Aronson (1995) examined the effects of racial salience by having African American college students in one study indicate their race on a test booklet prior to taking a test. They found that merely asking participants to indicate their race on the test booklet (as is required by many official standardized tests) caused Black students' anxiety to increase and their test scores to drop, even though the test, in this study, was presented as a nondiagnostic exercise.

Evaluative situations in which someone judges another person's competencies and abilities are understandably threatening for stereo-typed individuals. And, as indicated by the study described above, any performance situation, explicitly evaluative or not, can disrupt performance if a person's stereotyped group membership is expressly brought to mind (Steele & Aronson, 1995). There is mounting evidence that identity salience can disrupt performance even when it is very subtly activated (Ambady, Shih, Kim, & Pittinsky, 2001; Shih, Pittinsky, & Ambady, 1999; Wheeler & Petty, 2001). For example, Shih and her colleagues found that Asian females underperformed on a math test (relative to a control group) when their female identity had been subtly primed by a previously completed questionnaire.

Interestingly, in a parallel condition in which the questionnaire primed their Asian identity, females performed better than the control group, presumably because the Asian stereotype facilitates math performance. Thus, making one's stereotyped group membership salient (as in the Steele and Aronson study) can turn a nonevaluative performance situation into a threatening experience for stereotyped group members. But subtle activation of a stereotype can either impair or boost performance—without any detectable emotional reaction—depending on whether the stereotype predicts strength (e.g., Asians and math) or weakness (women in math) in a domain.

These subtle stereotype effects, sometimes referred to as "stereotype susceptibility" effects (e.g., Ambady et al., 2001), are distinct from stereotype threat effects first identified by Steele and Aronson (1995) in that they appear not to involve anxiety. Rather, they appear to be mediated by a simpler process, wherein one behaves automatically in line with a cognitively activated image (e.g., Bargh, Chen, & Burroughs, 1996; Wheeler & Petty, 2001). As such, the performance deficits associated with susceptibility effects tend to be substantially smaller and occur significantly earlier in a child's development than stereotype threat effects, most likely because their operation seems to require little more than knowledge of stereotype content.

It is important to note that the role of identity salience means that stereotype threat can arise in situations just by dint of a group's composition. Inzlicht and Ben-Zeev (2000) demonstrated that females taking a math test could experience stereotype threat due to the presence of a single male in a testing situation. In their study, the experimenters manipulated the gender composition of the groups taking a diagnostic math test. The three-person groups included three females, two females and one male, or one female and two males.

The results showed that when females took an evaluative test without the presence of a male, their performance remained high. But when even one male was introduced into the group, females' performance was impaired. And, with every additional male, females' performance deteriorated proportionately. Inzlicht and Ben-Zeev argued that the male presence increased the salience of females' gender identities and that the salient gender identities, in turn, evoked the negative stereotype about females' math competencies. Thus, situations that increase the salience of one's racial or gender identity—either subtly or blatantly—can influence performance.

Some individuals appear to be more chronically vulnerable to stereotype threat, for one of two reasons. For some, gender or ethnic identity remains highly salient in almost any situation. These are people who feel deeply attached to their racial or gender group and highly identify with that aspect of their self. Research has found that the more investment in one's gender identity, the more one will be burdened by negative stereotypes suggesting limited ability (Schmader, 2002). A related vulnerability factor appears to be what Pinel (1999) calls "stigma consciousness," the chronic expectation that one will be discriminated against. For some individuals, past experience with parental warnings about prejudice can breed a persistent vigilance, a cross-situational tendency to be on the lookout for bias (e.g., Hughes & Chen, 1999). Such individuals appear more likely to underperform in stereotype threat situations, that is, when their stigmatized status is activated (Brown & Pinel, 2003). Both of these differences, either separately or in conjunction, can intensify the experience of stereotype threat.

To summarize, any person contending with negative stereotypes could potentially experience the debilitating effects of stereotype threat. And as research shows, vulnerability to stereotype threat is most pronounced in situations that are evaluative or that direct conscious attention to one's stereotyped status. It is important to note that these two conditions—evaluative scrutiny and identity salience—are characteristic of most testing environments in which adolescents find themselves, especially in high stakes situations such as Advanced Placement examinations, the SAT, the GRE, and so on.

One's performance on these tests can have important implications for one's future in terms of college credit, scholarships, and school admissions. Furthermore, group salience is endemic to the testing situation, not only because students often indicate their race and gender prior to taking the test, but also because minority and female students take the tests in the presence of White students and males. It is these tests—those that hold the key to future opportunity—that not only show the greatest gaps in achievement between stereotyped and nonstereotyped students, but also contain the very variables so strongly related to stereotype threat, evaluative scrutiny, and identity salience.

STEREOTYPE THREAT AND SOCIAL INEQUALITY

Research has clearly documented how stereotype threat can contribute to educational inequalities for stereotyped students. But another extremely serious consequence of stereotype threat is the social inequality that is often born from previous educational inequities. For example, recent research has shown that stereotype threat can alter stereotyped students' professional identities by redirecting the career paths that they pursue (Good, Dweck, & Rattan, 2006a). For example, women who perceived that their college calculus classes conveyed negative stereotypes about women's math abilities reported a lower sense of belonging to the math community—that is, they felt less like accepted members of the math community whose presence was valued—than those who did not perceive a stereotypical climate (Good et al., 2006a).

Moreover, this threat to their identity as a future mathematician (or scientist) had real consequences for their achievement and career aspirations: When women's sense of belonging was reduced by their perceptions of a stereotypical environment, they earned lower grades in the course and were less likely to intend to take any more math classes in the future.

Thus, stereotypes can cause individuals enough discomfort to lead them to drop out of the domain and redefine their professional identities. When the domain is something as fundamental as mathematics, domain avoidance essentially shuts the door to potentially lucrative careers in science, engineering, and technology. Moreover, the effects of stereotypes on professional identity has roots early in schooling, for it has been found that stereotypes can undermine a sense of belonging for girls in math as early as middle school (Good et al., 2006b). This has important consequences for girls' identities as future mathematicians and scientists, because it is precisely the middle school years when girls' confidence in and liking of mathematics begins to wane.

THE DEVELOPMENT OF STEREOTYPE THREAT

We have learned much about the stereotype threat process as it affects college students (see Aronson, 2002; Steele, Spencer, & Aronson, 2002, for reviews). Yet relatively little is known about the development of vulnerability to stereotypes: when and under what conditions children and young adolescents become meaningfully affected by ability-relevant stereotypes about the groups to which they belong. Although even young children are aware of and use stereotypes, the age at which negative ability stereotypes influence performance has received little attention.

Are children susceptible to negative stereotypes about their intellectual abilities? If so, at what age and under what circumstances does their awareness of negative ability stereotypes disrupt their achievement? Does the stereotype threat process work in the same way for children and early adolescents as it does for older adolescents and young adults? Because stereotype threat may contribute to the educational and social inequalities described above, it is important to better understand its development in young adolescents, especially because it is at these ages that identities and professional aspirations begin to take root.

That stereotype threat can affect academic achievement in late adolescence is clear. As we continue to study the phenomenon, we have gained greater understanding of the personal and situational factors that moderate stereotype threat, the processes that mediate it, and some useful tactics for reducing its impact on performance and engagement (see Aronson, 2002). This knowledge can serve as a useful guide in thinking about the development of stereotype vulnerability in younger adolescents, which, admittedly, researchers have only begun to examine. When and under what conditions will young adolescents experience extra anxiety on evaluative tasks as a function of their stereotyped-group membership? It seems reasonable to assume that children must achieve a certain level of developmental maturity to be meaningfully affected by stereotypes about their group.

Current knowledge suggests the following as necessary conditions: awareness of ethnic and gender stereotyping, a sufficiently developed ethnic or gender identity, a well-formed conception of academic ability, and the cognitive skills necessary to consider and fully comprehend the implications that negative stereotypes have. And the developmental literature devoted to these constructs suggest the age of 11 or 12 as a reasonable period to expect to see stereotype vulnerability in children, that is, to see explicit evaluation of ability result in extra stress and appre-hension among members of groups alleged to lack some intellectual ability (see Aronson & Good, 2003, for a discussion of these factors).

The confluence of these developmental factors maps quite consis-tently onto the achievement literature. Early adolescence is precisely when girls begin to lose ground in math performance and when ethnic minorities notoriously experience increased decrements in academic achievement (e.g., Eccles et al., 1993; Eccles, Lord, & Midgley, 1991; Harter, Whitesell, & Kowalski, 1992; Simmons & Blyth, 1987).

Our own recent research suggests that stereotype threat may play a role in this pattern of underperformance. For example, employing the evaluative scrutiny paradigm pioneered by Steele and Aronson (1995), we administered math and reading tests to 10-, 11-, and 12-year-old students in elementary school. The results were remarkably clear. On a test comparing girls and boys' standardized test performance, evalu-ative scrutiny had no discernable effect on the math performance of 10- and 11-year-olds, but did affect 12-year-olds and resulted in signifi-cantly lower math performance among the girls relative to boys (Good & Aronson, 2006a).

On the reading test, however, there were no corresponding differ-ences in performance. Because no differences were found on girls' read-ing test performance under evaluative versus nonevaluative conditions, the differences found on the math test very likely resulted from stereo-type threat, not a general evaluation threat. Interestingly, this corre-sponded precisely to girls' questionnaire ratings indicating worry about their future math performance; they indicated no such worries before they were 12 years old. These performance effects were replicated in a similar study with 10-, 11-, and 12-year-old students taking a math test (Good & Aronson, 2006b) and with Latinos taking a verbal test (Aron-son & Good, 2006).

An additional study revealed another dimension to this vulnerabil-ity. Ten-, 11-, and 12-year-old boys and girls took grade-appropriate math and reading tests under stereotype threat or nonthreat con-ditions. Before they took the tests, however, they were told that they would be taking a second test of both math and reading, but on this sec-ond test, they would get to choose the difficulty level of the problems. We then offered them a choice of five different problem difficulty levels for reading and math ranging from very easy to very hard. The results showed an effect of the stereotype threat manipulation for 12-year-old girls: Under the stereotype threat condition, they selected easier prob-lems than boys. Under nonevaluative (no stereotype threat) conditions, girls chose more difficult problems than boys. And as with the previous study, there were no differences between boys and girls on the verbal problems prior to this age.

This last study suggests that one strategy used by students to cope with stereotype threat may be to arrange things so as to avoid or reduce the risk of confirming the stereotype. When there is a clear choice between easy tasks with a high probability of success and more difficult tasks with a greater chance of failure, stereotype threat may lead people to play it safe and avoid the challenge. Because challenge is required for intellectual growth and for developing the skills and abilities needed for future success, evaluative settings may actually impede learning—not just the performances—of stereotyped individuals. The accumulated effect of years of reduced opportunities to strengthen and grow one's capabilities may eventually lead to the very differences in performance to which the stereotype refers. We replicated this study with Latino students taking a verbal test and choosing the difficulty level of verbal tasks under threat or nonthreat conditions (Aronson & Good, 2006). The results paralleled those found for girls in math: Under evaluative scrutiny, Latinos selected easier tasks. As with the girls, this pattern emerged only among the sixth-grade students.

Other researchers, it should be noted, have found what appear to be stereotype threat effects in children younger than sixth grade, although in substantially different paradigms. For example, McKown and Weinstein (2003) investigated stereotype threat in minority children (African Americans and Latinos) between the ages of 6 and 11. They found that the most important predictor of a child's vulnerability to stereotype threat was not the child's age, but rather, the child's ability to report stereotypes operating in the real world.

To measure this ability, McKown and Weinstein told the children a story about an imaginary land comprised of two groups of people, Greens and Blues. In this land, they were told, Greens think Blues are not smart. Next, the experimenter asked the children to describe any similarities between the imaginary land and the real world. The children's responses—the number of similarities each reported—comprised the measure of their ability to report stereotypes. After this measure, the children participated in a stereotype threat experiment in which they wrote the alphabet backward in 45 seconds under either diagnostic or nondiagnostic conditions. In the diagnostic condition, they were told that the task would show how good they were at different types of school problems. Thus the task purportedly measured general academic ability.

The results of the study indicated that among students who were developmentally advanced enough to draw parallels between the stereotypes in the story and those in real life, evaluative scrutiny undermined minority students' performance. In the diagnostic condition, the White students outperformed the minority students; however, in the nondiagnostic condition, the performance pattern reversed and the minority students did slightly better than the White students, even when controlling for prior ability. Students who could not report stereotypes did not exhibit evidence of stereotype threat.

Because the researchers did not analyze the data by age, no conclusions can be drawn about the age at which stereotype threat undermines performance. The researchers argue, however, and we agree, that the ability to understand how intelligence stereotypes can be used against people in the world is a more valid predictor of stereotype threat than age alone. They further argue that children who report stereotypes are vulnerable to stereotype threat because they are developmentally advanced enough not only to be aware of stereotypes—which occurs very early on in childhood (Aboud, 1988)—but also to attend to and care about the meaning of stereotypes about their group.

Despite these studies (Aronson & Good, 2006; Good & Aronson, 2006a, 2006b; McKown & Weinstein, 2003), it is still unclear how early in a child's development stereotypes influence cognitive performance. A study by Ambady and colleagues (2001) suggests that stereotypes can influence cognitive performance even earlier than our discussion so far suggests. In their experiments, Asian American girls between kindergarten (5 years old) and eighth grade (14 years old) completed a stereotype activation task designed to evoke either their gender identity or their ethnic identity. A control group also participated but did not respond to any manipulations making their gender or ethnic identity salient. The younger participants (kindergarten through second grade) either colored a picture of a girl holding a doll or of two Chinese people eating with chopsticks. The older participants (grades three through eight) either answered gender-related questions or ethnicity-related questions. Participants then took a difficult math test appropriate for their grade level.

The results showed an interesting pattern of stereotype susceptibility that depended on grade level. Girls in the early elementary grades (kindergarten through second grade) and middle school grades (sixth through eighth grade) had the highest accuracy on the math test when their ethnic identity was made salient and the lowest accuracy when their gender identity was made salient. Interestingly, girls in the upper elementary grades (third through fifth grade) showed the reverse pattern: Girls were more accurate when their gender identity was made salient than when their ethnic identity was made salient.

It is instructive to note that these experiments find very small differences in actual test performance, presumably because the subtle activation of stereotypes tends not to arouse anxiety. Thus, although they demonstrate that increasing the salience of a stereotyped identity can influence performance—either positively or negatively—the process is quite distinct from the typical stereotype threat finding, which involves measurable apprehensiveness and a desire to disprove the stereotype rather than an "automaticity" effect (see Wheeler & Petty, 2001, for a discussion).

Indeed, as a recent study with college students demonstrates (Cheryan & Bodenhausen, 2000), if one makes the connection between the identity and the performance explicit rather than implicit, the process changes: Either identity (Asian or female) induces performance pressure and undermines performance. Thus, the Ambady et al. research may involve some other process than stereotype threat. In our own research (Aronson & Good, 2006; Good & Aronson, 2006a, 2006b), explicitly making gender or ethnicity salient shows no evidence of affecting performance until the sixth grade. We believe that some critical factors, such as those we have discussed, need to develop in order for ability evaluation or identity salience to induce anxiety among girls and minorities. For most children, these do not develop before early adolescence.

Interestingly, although identification with the stereotyped domain is an important predictor of older adolescents' vulnerability to stereotype threat (see Aronson et al., 1999), there is no research yet that demonstrates a clear relationship between academic identification and vulnerability to stereotype threat in younger children. Because of the importance of this variable in older adolescents' vulnerability to stereotype threat, there is clearly a need for more research investigating the relationship between domain identification and stereotype vulnerability in children and young adolescents.

The Changing Academic Context

By the time that children reach early adolescence, they may be developmentally ready to experience stereotype threat. The transition to middle and junior high school capitalizes on this readiness, producing what we think are significant manifestations of stereotype threat: a significant decline for many students, particularly girls in math and minorities more generally. Several studies report significantly more problems—suspensions, low academic performance, conflicts with parents, and the like—among Black and Latino students than among White students making the transition to junior high, or from one school to another (e.g., Felner, Primavera, & Cauce, 1981; Simmons, Black, & Zhou, 1991). Why might this be?

We think one reason is the "stereotype climate" that we hypothe-size is engendered and reinforced by the middle school setting and the developmental stage in question. The transition confronts many stu-dents who attend public schools with the most intensive, if not the first, contact with youngsters from diverse ethnic backgrounds. In most cases, this will not be the "equal status" contact considered essential to minimizing prejudice. Rather, Black and Latino children, because they tend to come from poorer school districts, are likely to be academi-cally behind their White counterparts by as much as two grade levels (Gerard, 1983).

Such pre-existing differences may be underscored by "ability group-ing" (i.e., "tracking"), prevalent in many middle and junior high schools (Eccles et al., 1993), which tends to racially stratify the classrooms (Romo & Falbo, 1995). Furthermore, the middle school or junior high setting is likely to be more competitive than grade school (Harter et al., 1992), which may further encourage overt and covert racial stereo-typing (Aronson & Patnoe, 1997). Thus, the existing stereotypes (e.g., "Blacks are not as smart as Whites") may be confirmed and intensi-fied by the type of contact afforded by the middle school or junior high structure.

Students' vulnerability to the stereotype climate may be magnified by the fact that, relative to those of grade school, middle and junior high school contexts tend to place a higher premium on social comparison. Peers and peer evaluations become powerful influences, making "fit-ting in" a high priority (e.g., Harter, 1990; Spencer & Dornbusch, 1990). Because stereotype threat stems to a great extent from concern about how one is viewed by others (e.g., peers, teachers), it seems reasonable to assume that the threat may be particularly acute, and, at this stage of development, particularly damaging to the formation of a healthy academic self-image.

Eccles and her colleagues (see Eccles et al., 1991, 1993) have argued that the classroom environment in junior high school is different from that of elementary school and that this change in environment may cause difficulty for some students. Middle school and junior high class-rooms are often larger and more impersonal than elementary school classrooms. Furthermore, Midgley, Anderman, and Hicks (1995) argue that junior high teachers hold different beliefs about students than do elementary school teachers. For example, junior high teachers are less likely to trust their students and more likely to emphasize control and discipline in their classrooms. More important, junior high teachers are more likely to believe that their students' abilities are fixed and are less likely to believe that students can increase their abilities through instruction. And as research is beginning to show, teachers who believe in fixed versus acquirable ability differ in their pedagogical theories and practices. For example, teachers who see abilities as fixed tend to judge students' abilities by comparing them to other students rather than observing personal improvement (Butler, 2000; Lee, 1996; Plaks, Stroessner, Dweck, & Sherman, 2001).

These different methods of evaluation have important implications, for it has been found that students of math teachers who emphasize normative evaluation rather than individual progress over time (in line with fixed ability perspective) come to value math less over time (Anderman et al., 2001). Moreover, as discussed in the next section, stereotype threat is exacerbated for students performing in a fixed-ability context, that is, when they believe that the abilities that are being evaluated are thought not to be expandable (e.g., Aronson, 2002). Because adolescence is the period in which students become more sophisticated in their understanding of societal stereotypes, the fixed-ability beliefs held by junior high school teachers may be particularly disruptive for minority students and for females in math and science.

This confluence of developmental and structural factors suggests that even if Black, Latino, and female students graduate from elementary school feeling competent and enjoying school as much as their counterparts, they may become demoralized not long after entering middle school.

Reducing Stereotype Threat: The Role of Implicit Theories of Intelligence

How can we help reduce the impact of stereotype threat? In addition to studying factors involved in evoking a stereotype threat response, researchers have been investigating factors that protect people from stereotype threat's debilitating effects. One obvious approach would be to change the existing stereotypes themselves, or to construct educational or testing situations that minimize evaluation or the salience of race or gender.

Unfortunately, such approaches are rarely feasible. First, as much research has shown, stereotypes doggedly resist change. And reducing evaluation and racial salience are, almost by definition, impossible in integrated testing centers or classrooms. Instead, recent stereotype threat research has focused on more realistic approaches, capitalizing on lessons learned from research in achievement motivation. In particular, Dweck and her colleagues (e.g., Dweck, 1986, 1999; Dweck & Leggett, 1988; Hong, Chiu, & Dweck, 1995) have shown that students' beliefs about intelligence strongly affect their achievement motivation.

This research suggests that people's implicit theories about the nature of intelligence—as a fixed stable trait (entity theory), or as something that increases with effort (incremental theory)—have important consequences for their academic achievement. And what the research consistently shows is that students with an incremental view of intelligence fare better than their entity-view counterparts, especially in the face of difficulty. For example, research has found that students with an entity view of intelligence persist less in the face of challenge, view failures as indicative of future abilities, avoid challenging tasks, and believe effort to be an ineffective strategy for success. Their goal is to perform at a level that marks them as smart, capable students; thus, they prefer unchallenging tasks, those that ensure high performance.

In contrast, incremental theorists persist longer when challenged, view failure as a signal to increase effort, and recognize challenging tasks as the route to increased knowledge. Their goal is to learn and increase their intelligence; thus, they prefer challenging tasks that increase their current understanding.

How do implicit theories of intelligence relate to stereotype threat? We have reasoned that stereotyped individuals may find themselves in the same mindset as people who hold an entity view of intelligence, especially when faced with academic difficulty or the possibility of low performance (Aronson, Fried, & Good, 2002). The very nature of the stereotype itself suggests that individuals, by virtue of their group membership, are inherently limited in their abilities. Thus, stereotyped individuals not only must contend with the expectation of low performance but also the suggestion that their abilities are fixed. The stereotype, with its implication of inborn and fixed traits, imposes an entity framework upon achievement situations. Consequently, stereotyped individuals may, at least temporarily, adopt an entity mindset, complete with all the trademark responses of entity thinking. If, however, stereotyped individuals can maintain an incremental mindset when faced with challenging academic tasks, perhaps they will be less vulnerable to the threat of ability-impugning stereotypes.

Adolescents' Theories of Intelligence and Vulnerability to Stereotype Threat

To test this reasoning, we (Aronson & Good, 2006; Good & Aronson, 2006a, 2006b) measured fourth-, fifth-, and sixth-grade students' theories of reading intelligence and math intelligence and then administered reading and math tests under stereotype threat and nonthreat conditions (as described previously). For the Latino students, a clear benefit of holding an incremental theory emerged for all students by the fourth grade (Aronson & Good, 2006). Specifically, in the fourth and fifth grades, students who endorsed an incremental theory of reading ability performed better on the test than those who endorsed an entity theory, regardless of threat condition.

By the sixth grade, however, incremental and entity theorists did not differ when taking the reading test under nondiagnostic conditions. When stereotype threat was activated by describing the test as a measure of underlying verbal ability, those endorsing an entity view did worse on the test than those endorsing an incremental view. That is, Latino students' previously held incremental theories of intelligence seemed to protect them against the negative effects of stereotype threat. What is more, when they were asked to choose the difficulty level of the second set of reading problems (as described previously), incremental theorists chose more difficult problems than entity theorists did when they thought their performance on the problems would measure their reading ability.

For females, holding an incremental theory of math intelligence had no discernable effect on their vulnerability to stereotype threat, in terms of their math test performance or math task choice. Although these students believed in incrementalism, their prior beliefs, without active reflection about those beliefs, may have been ineffective when confronted with the possibility of fulfilling a negative stereotype about one's limited ability. Perhaps, however, actively and deliberately encouraging students to contemplate their beliefs about the nature of intelligence would provide more powerful protection against stereotype threat. Indeed, this is exactly what both laboratory and field research has found.

The Benefits of Encouraging an Incremental Theory of Intelligence

In one laboratory study (see Aronson, 2002, for a review) students' conceptions of ability as fixed versus expandable were manipulated to investigate the effects on subsequent test anxiety and performance. In this study, participants (African American and White college students) took a challenging verbal test. One-third were told that the abilities being tested were highly expandable, one-third were told that the ability was fixed, and one-third were told that the test measured verbal ability. In the fixed ability condition, participants solved fewer items and reported more anxiety than participants in the control condition. When participants were led to believe that the ability being tested was malleable, they solved more items and reported less anxiety. These effects held for both the White and Black participants. In the control group, performance correlated to the test-takers' own views of intellectual ability measured prior to the test; the more malleable they thought it was, the better their performance on the test.

In a recent field study, researchers wanted to see if encouraging an incremental theory of intelligence would affect students' academic engagement and achievement outside the laboratory (Aronson et al., 2002). Three groups of African American and Caucasian undergraduates participated in the study. One group participated in an intervention that used various attitude-change techniques designed to teach them, help them internalize, and make cognitively available the notion that intelligence is expandable (malleable condition). The attitudes and achievement outcomes for this group were compared to those of two control groups: one that participated in the same intervention with a different intelligence orientation, and a third group that did not participate in the intervention. The results of the intervention showed that teaching African American students that intelligence is malleable created an enduring and beneficial change in their own attitudes about intelligence. Furthermore, they reported enjoying and valuing academics more and they received higher grades than did African Americans in the other conditions.

Reducing Early Adolescents' Vulnerability

As with college students, we wondered if we could reduce children's vulnerability to stereotype threat by encouraging them to view intelligence as something that could increase and expand with effort rather than as a fixed stable trait (Good, Aronson, & Inzlicht, 2003). To test this hypothesis we designed an in-depth intervention in which we taught seventh graders messages that we hypothesized would help them navigate the difficult transition year from elementary school to junior high school.

In this program, college students from The University of Texas mentored Latino and Caucasian junior high students. Seventh-grade students were randomly assigned to either the malleability of intelligence condition or the anti-drug condition and were also randomly assigned a mentor. The mentors met with their students in person for 90 minutes toward the beginning of the school year and then again for another 90 minutes at the beginning of the second semester. All remaining communication occurred via the Internet through an e-mail program we created.

The mentors served three purposes. First, they provided useful advice for the students regarding study skills and any adjustment problems the students may have experienced during the difficult transition to junior high school. Second, they explicitly taught the students the experimental message: the expandability of intelligence or the perils of drug use.

Finally, the mentors helped the students design and create a Web page in which the students advocated, in their own words and pictures, the experimental message conveyed by the mentor throughout the year.

To further help students internalize the message and to give them ideas about what to put on their own Web page, we designed a mini-Web space for each of the experimental conditions. In these closed Web spaces, students could "surf" the mini-Web and learn in more detail the experimental message. For example, students in the malleability of intelligence condition could view numerous pages that explained how the brain forms new connections under effortful problem solving. They also could read various testimonies and slogans regarding the expandability of intelligence, such as "The mind is a muscle; the more you use it, the stronger it grows." A similar mini-Web space was created for the anti-drug participants.

At year's end, we analyzed students' math and reading achievement as measured by the statewide standardized achievement test. Results showed that girls performed worse on the math test if they had been mentored in the harmful consequences of drug use. Moreover, the boys in the anti-drug condition performed better on the math test than the girls. However, when students learned about the expandability of intelligence the gender gap in math performance disappeared. The malleability of intelligence condition increased both boys' and girls' math performance, but this increase in math scores was particularly pronounced for the female students.

As with math performance, a similar pattern of increased achievement was found on the reading test. Students who were mentored in the malleability of intelligence performed better on the reading test than did students who were mentored in the perils of drug use, regardless of race. Consequently, encouraging children to think of intelligence as expandable rather than fixed goes a long way toward increasing student achievement, especially for those students who face negative stereotypes about their abilities.

In these studies (Aronson et al., 2002; Good et al., 2003) the researchers went to great lengths to explicitly teach students that intellectual skills are attainable. Yet, this is unlikely to be the way that fixed and malleable views are typically communicated in the real world. Indeed many educators may espouse the view that skills are expandable and that all students can learn, but they may contradict these views with their day-to-day actions. For example, teachers may unwittingly convey fixed-ability messages to their students through their classroom discourse and pedagogical practices, especially in math. This often may occur inadvertently through statements or practices that are actually meant to motivate students, perhaps specifically girls.

For example, teachers may attempt to make a math lesson more engaging and human by discussing the life of prominent mathematicians such as Pythagoras in a way that stresses their mathematical genius, or that implies that great discoveries came to these mathematicians naturally and without great effort. However, extolling the genius or talent of great mathematicians may operate in a similar fashion as praising individual students' ability (see Kamins & Dweck, 1999; Mueller & Dweck, 1998). That is, it may convey an entity theory to students, which in turn can make them vulnerable to impaired motivation and performance when they later encounter difficulty. Indeed, the day-to-day entity (or incremental) messages embedded in the environment may be just as powerful as explicit messages in conveying the idea that intellectual skills are relatively fixed (or acquirable).

Furthermore, although the effect of such (direct) messages on achievement is well known, how messages embedded in the environment affect other academic outcomes is less well known. For example, can implicit messages in the learning environment affect students' sense of belonging—their feelings that they are respected members of the academic community—and their desire to pursue that field of study (Good et al., 2006a)? Specifically, do environments focused on fixed ability exacerbate the negative effects of stereotype threat on both achievement and sense of belonging? Alternatively, can academic contexts focused on malleable ability protect against the threat of negative stereotypes?

To answer these questions, Good and her colleagues (Good et al., 2006a) conducted a longitudinal study of college calculus students in which participants completed the Sense of Belonging to Math Scale (Good et al., 2006a) during their calculus classes at three times during the course of the semester: at the beginning of the semester, after midterms, and just before finals. The questionnaires also included a measure of the extent to which students perceived their math classes as sending messages of a fixed view of math intelligence and of gender stereotyping about math ability.

Results showed that at the beginning of the semester, the most important determinant of whether females felt a sense of belonging to math was their prior math ability. Specifically, females with higher SAT scores reported a greater sense of belonging to math than did females with lower SAT scores. Over time, however, the educational environment in which the students were immersed began to influence the degree to which they felt that they belonged to the math domain. By the end of the semester, females' perceptions of both the amount of stereotyping in their environment and the extent to which the environment was focused on fixed ability each undermined their sense of belonging to math.

Furthermore, an interaction effect emerged, suggesting that high perceptions of gender stereotyping combined with high perceptions of a fixed-ability learning environment constituted a particular threat to females' sense of belonging to math: females who perceived both fixed-ability messages and gender stereotyping in their learning environment were the most vulnerable to a lowered sense of belonging to math, regardless of their prior ability. Moreover, when women's sense of belonging was undermined by their perceptions of their learning environment, they were also less likely to indicate an intention to pursue math in the future and they earned lower grades in the course.

Alternatively, evaluative contexts that portrayed skills as acquirable created resiliency to the negative stereotypes' debilitating message of fixed ability: Females with these perceptions maintained a sense of belonging to math even when they perceived their environment to be highly gender-stereotypical. And when their sense of belonging was high, they were also more likely to indicate a desire to pursue math in the future.

Thus, stereotypes, especially when coupled with an entity-oriented learning environment, can cause individuals enough discomfort to lead them to drop out of the domain and redefine their professional identities. When the domain is something as fundamental as mathematics, domain avoidance essentially shuts the door to potentially lucrative careers in science, engineering, and technology. Moreover, the effects of stereotypes on professional identity has roots early in schooling, for it has been found that stereotypes can undermine the sense of belonging for girls in math as early as middle school (Good et al., 2006b). This has important consequences for girls' identities as future mathematicians and scientists, because it is precisely the middle school years when girls' confidence in and liking of mathematics begins to wane.

These results suggest that one method of alleviating the negative effects of stereotypes, and thus reducing educational and social inequality, is to create learning environments that emphasize the incremental, rather than the entity, nature of intelligence. To test this hypothesis more carefully, Good and her colleagues (Good, Dweck, & Rattan, 2006c) designed an experiment in which they manipulated the entity and incremental flavor of a classroom mathematics lesson.

Specifically, sixth- through ninth-grade students watched one of two instructional videos designed to highlight the differences between Euclidean and spherical geometries. The math content in both videos was exactly the same, and both videos contained historical perspectives about the mathematicians who are credited with discoveries in these fields. What differed, however, was the content of the historical perspective. In one condition, the mathematicians were described as math geniuses for whom mathematical achievement came with little effort. In the other condition, the achievement of the mathematicians was attributed to their love of math and their desire to develop and cultivate their math skills. Thus, the first video endorsed an entity view of math intelligence, and the second video endorsed an incremental view of math intelligence. After the video, students in both video conditions were randomly assigned to either a stereotype threat or a nonthreat condition and took a grade-appropriate math test modeled after the statewide standardized tests.

Results indicated that for both male and female students, watching the incremental video increased their accuracy on the math test. Moreover, the incremental video protected female students against the negative effects of stereotype threat. Specifically, females who took the math test under stereotype threat conditions were more accurate when they had previously watched the incremental video than the entity video.

In addition, when we looked at overall performance on the test, the typical gender gap in achievement between males and females emerged when students took the test under diagnostic conditions (stereotype threat) after watching the entity video; this gap did not appear in the nonthreat conditions (regardless of which video students watched) or in the threat condition after watching the incremental video. These findings suggest that teaching from an incremental perspective not only can reduce females' vulnerability to stereotype threat, but can also go a long way toward reducing the gender gap in math achievement that begins to emerge in middle school and high school.

Taken together, these studies provide clear evidence of the benefits of holding an incremental theory of intelligence, especially when faced with a stereotype suggesting limited ability. Thus, although stereotype threat undermines performance, "incrementalism" appears to provide an effective defense against its negative effects, both in terms of achievement and sense of belonging. Using this model, stereotyped individuals may protect themselves from the negative effects of stereotype threat by rejecting an entity view of intelligence and adopting an incremental view.

CONCLUSIONS

Stereotype threat is a predicament that can undermine the achievement of a wide range of stereotyped groups and consequently lead to educational and social inequalities for members of these groups. Recently, researchers have investigated the age at which stereotypes become meaningfully disruptive to students' academic pursuits, that is, when stereotype vulnerability develops. What we have learned from this research is that students are aware of and to some degree influenced by ability-impugning stereotypes throughout their academic lives.

However, it is not until early adolescence that children develop the cognitive abilities necessary for stereotypes to be meaningfully disruptive, that is, to arouse extra performance anxiety when abilities are under scrutiny. We believe this is the case because it is during adolescence that children begin to think about and pay greater attention to others' perceptions, because they have developed complex ways of thinking about cognitive abilities, and because of an increasing awareness and application of stereotypes (Aronson & Good, 2003). Finally, these advances in cognitive ability and coherence of self-perceptions occur in the context of junior high or middle schools, environments that appear to be breeding grounds for sensitivity to stereotype-based judgments of ability. The effects of this stereotype vulnerability appear to be compromised performance, learning, engagement with academics, and sense of belonging to the stereotyped domain.

The good news is that the more we learn about these processes, the more optimistic we are that, with wise, research-based interventions, we can help students cope with stereotype threats during this critical period in life. Remedying the negative effects of stereotypes on academic outcomes is just one step toward remedying the educational and social inequalities that continue to plague stereotyped individuals.

REFERENCES

Aboud, F. (1988). *Children and prejudice*. New York: Blackwell.

Ambady, N., Shih, M., Kim, A., & Pittinsky, T. L. (2001). Stereotype susceptibility in children: Effects of identity activation on quantitative performance. *Psychological Science, 12*(5), 385–390.

American Association of University Women. (1992). *How schools shortchange girls*. Washington, DC: American Association of University Women Educational Foundation.

American Association of University Women. (1998). *Gendergaps: Where schools still fail our children. Executive Summary*. Washington, DC: American Association of University Women Educational Foundation.

Anderman, E. M., Eccles, J. S., Yoon, K. S., Roeser, R., Wigfield, A., & Blumenfeld, P. (2001). Learning to value mathematics and reading: Relations to mastery and performance-oriented instructional practices. *Contemporary Educational Psychology, 26,* 76–95.

Aronson, E., & Patnoe, S. (1997). *The jigsaw classroom: Building cooperation in the classroom (2nd edition).* New York: Addison Wesley Longman.

Aronson, J. (2002). Stereotype threat: Contending and coping with unnerving expectations. In J. Aronson (Ed.), *Improving academic achievement: Impact of psychological factors on education.* San Diego: Academic Press.

Aronson, J. (2006). The effects of conceiving ability as fixed or improvable on responses to stereotype threat. Manuscript submitted for publication.

Aronson, J., Fried, C., & Good, C. (2002). Reducing the effects of stereotype threat on African American college students by shaping theories of intelligence. *Journal of Experimental Social Psychology, 38*(2), 113–125.

Aronson, J., & Good, C. (2003). The development and consequences of stereotype vulnerability in adolescents. In F. Pajares & T. Urdan (Eds.), *Adolescence and education* (pp. 229–330). New York: Information Age.

Aronson, J., & Good, C. (2006). The development of stereotype threat in Latino adolescents. Unpublished manuscript, University of Texas, Austin.

Aronson, J., Lustina, M. J., Good, C., Keough, K., Steele, C. M., & Brown, J. (1999). When White men can't do math: Necessary and sufficient factors in stereotype threat. *Journal of Experimental Social Psychology, 35*(1), 29–46.

Aronson J., Quinn, D., & Spencer, S. (1998). Stereotype threat and the academic performance of minorities and women. In J. Swim & C. Stangor (Eds.), *Prejudice: The target's perspective* (pp. 83–103). San Diego: Academic Press.

Aronson, J., & Salinas, M. (1998). Stereotype threat: The role of effort withdrawal and apprehension on the intellectual underperformance of Mexican-Americans. Unpublished manuscript.

Aronson, J., & Steele, C. M. (2005). Stereotypes and the fragility of human competence, motivation, and self-concept. In C. Dweck & E. Elliot (Eds.), *Handbook of competence & motivation* (pp. 436–456). New York, Guilford.

Bargh, J. A., Chen, M., & Burrows, L. (1996). Automaticity of social behavior: Direct effects of trait construct and stereotype priming on action. *Journal of Personality and Social Psychology, 71,* 230–244.

Brown, R. P., & Pinel, E. C. (2003). Stigma on my mind: Individual differences in the experience of stereotype threat. *Journal of Experimental Social Psychology, 39,* 626–633.

Butler, R. (2000). Making judgments about ability: The role of implicit theories of ability in moderating inferences from temporal and social comparison information. *Journal of Personality and Social Psychology, 78,* 965–978.

Cheryan, S., & Bodenhausen, G. V. (2000). When positive stereotypes threaten intellectual performance: The psychological hazards of "model minority" status. *Psychological Science, 11,* 399–402.

College Board (2005). College-bound seniors: Total group profile report. (www.collegeboard.com).

Congressional Hearing. (1994). *Women and K-12 mathematics education.* Hearing before the Subcommittee on Energy of the Committee on Science, Space, and Technology, United States House of Representatives, One Hundred Third Congress, second session. June 1994.

Croizet, J., & Claire, T. (1998). Extending the concept of stereotype and threat to social class: The intellectual underperformance of students from low socioeconomic backgrounds. *Personality & Social Psychology Bulletin, 24*(6), 588–594.

Davies, P. G., Spencer, S. J., Quinn, D. M., & Gerhardstein, R. (2002). Consuming images: How television commercials that elicit stereotype threat can restrain women academically and professionally. *Personality & Social Psychology Bulletin, 28,* 1615–1628.

Dweck, C. (1999). *Self-theories: Their role in motivation, personality, and development.* Philadelphia: Psychology Press.

Dweck, C. S. (1986). Motivational processes affecting learning. *American Psychologist, 41*(10), 1040–1048.

Dweck, C. S., & Leggett, E. L. (1988). A social-cognitive approach to motivation and personality. *Psychological Review, 95,* 256–273.

Eccles, J. S. (1984). Sex differences in achievement patterns. *Nebraska Symposium on Motivation, 32,* 97–132.

Eccles, J. S., & Jacobs, J. E. (1992). The impact of mothers' gender-role stereotypic beliefs on mothers' and children's ability perceptions. *Journal of Personality and Social Psychology, 63*(6), 932–944.

Eccles, J. S., Jacobs, J. E., & Harold, R. D. (1990). Gender role stereotypes, expectancy effects, and parents' socialization of gender differences. *Journal of Social Issues, 46*(2), 183–201.

Eccles, J. S., Lord, S., & Midgley, C. (1991). What are we doing to early adolescents? The impact of educational contexts on early adolescents. *American Journal of Education, 99,* 521–542.

Eccles, J., Midgley, C., Wigfield, A., Buchanan, C., Reuman, D., Flanagan, C., & MacIver, D. (1993). Development during adolescence: The impact of stage-environment fit on young adolescents' experiences in schools and families. *American Psychologist, 48,* 90–101.

Felner, R. D., Primavera, J., & Cauce, A. M. (1981). The impact of school transitions: A focus for preventive efforts. *American Journal of Community Psychology, 9,* 449–459.

Fennema, E., & Sherman, J. (1977). Sex-related differences in mathematics achievement, spatial visualization and affective factors. *American Educational Research Journal, 14*(1), 51–71.

Gerard, H. (1983). School desegregation: The social science role. *American Psychologist, 38*, 869–878.

Good, C., & Aronson, J. (2006a). The development of stereotype threat in girls. Unpublished manuscript. Barnard College, New York.

Good, C., & Aronson, J. (2006b). The effects of stereotype threat on girls' math performance. Unpublished manuscript. Barnard College, New York.

Good, C., Aronson, J., & Harder, J. A. (in press). Problems in the pipeline: Women's achievement in high-level math courses. *Journal of Applied Developmental Psychology.*

Good, C., Aronson, J., & Inzlicht, M. (2003). Improving adolescents' standardized test performance: An intervention to reduce the effects of stereotype threat. *Journal of Applied Developmental Psychology, 24*, 645–662.

Good, C., Dweck, C. S., & Rattan, A. (2006a). The effects of perceiving fixed-ability environments and stereotyping on women's sense of belonging to math. Unpublished manuscript. Barnard College, New York.

Good, C., Dweck, C. S., & Rattan, A. (2006b). Do I belong here? Middle school girls' sense of belonging to math. Unpublished manuscript. Barnard College, New York.

Good, C., Dweck, C. S., & Rattan, A. (2006c). The effects of the learning context on females' vulnerability to stereotype threat. Unpublished manuscript. Barnard College, New York.

Halpern, D. F. (1992). *Sex differences in cognitive abilities.* Hillsdale, NJ: Lawrence Erlbaum.

Hanson, S. (1996). Gender, family resources, and success in science. *Journal of Family Issues, 17*, 83–113.

Harter, S. (1990). Self and identity development. In S. S. Feldman & G. R. Elliot (Eds.), *At the Threshold: The developing adolescent* (pp. 352–387). Cambridge, MA: Harvard University Press.

Harter, S., Whitesell, N. R., & Kowalski, P. (1992). Individual differences in the effects of educational transitions on young adolescent's perceptions of competence and motivational orientation. *American Educational Research Journal, 29*(4), 777–807.

Hong, Y., Chiu, C., & Dweck, C. S. (1995). Implicit theories of intelligence: Reconsidering the role of confidence in achievement motivation. In M. H. Kerns (Ed.), *Efficacy, agency, and self-esteem* (pp. 197–216). New York: Plenum Press.

Hughes, D., & Chen, L. (1999). The nature of parents' race-related communications to children: A developmental perspective. In L.Balter & C. S. Tamis-LeMonda (Eds.), *Child psychology: A handbook of contemporary issues* (pp. 467–490). Philadelphia: Psychology Press.

Inzlicht, M., & Ben-Zeev, T. (2000). A threatening intellectual environment: Why females are susceptible to experiencing problem-solving deficits in the presence of males. *Psychological Science, 11*, 365–371.

Jencks, C., & Phillips, M. (1998). *The Black–White test score gap.* Washington, DC: Brookings Institution Press.

Kamins, M., & Dweck, C. S. (1999). Person versus process praise and criticism: Implications for contingent self-worth and coping. *Developmental Psychology, 35,* 835–847.

Lee, K. (1996). A study of teacher responses based on their conceptions of intelligence. *Journal of Classroom Interaction, 31,* 1–12.

McKown, C., & Weinstein, R. S. (2003). The development and consequences of stereotype-consciousness in middle childhood. *Child Development, 74,* 498–515.

Midgley, C., Anderman, E., & Hicks, L. (1995). Differences between elementary and middle school teachers and students: A goal theory approach. *The Journal of Early Adolescence, 15,* 90–113.

Mueller, C. M., & Dweck, C. S. (1998). Intelligence praise can undermine motivation and performance. *Journal of Personality and Social Psychology, 75,* 33–52.

National Academy of Sciences (2006). Beyond bias and barriers: Fulfilling the potential of women in academic science and engineering. (http://www.nap.edu/catalog/11741.html).

National Center for Education Statistics (July 2001). Mathematics and science in the eighth grade: Findings from the Third International Mathematics and Science Study.

National Science Foundation (2006). Science and engineering indicators 2006. (http://www.nsf.gov/sbe/srs/seind06).

Osborne, J. W. (1995). Academics, self-esteem, and race: A look at the underlying assumptions of the disidentification hypothesis. *Personality and Social Psychology Bulletin, 21,* 449–455.

Pinel, E. (1999). Stigma consciousness: The psychological legacy of social stereotypes. *Journal of Personality and Social Psychology, 76*(1), 114–128.

Plaks, J., Stroessner, S., Dweck, C. S., & Sherman, J. (2001). Person theories and attention allocation: Preference for stereotypic vs. counterstereotypic information. *Journal of Personality and Social Psychology, 80,* 876–893.

Romo, H., & Falbo, T. (1995). *Latino high school graduation: Defying the odds.* Austin: University of Texas Press.

Sadker, M., & Sadker, D. (1994). *Failing at fairness: How our schools cheat girls.* New York: Touchstone.

Schmader, T. (2002). Gender identification moderates stereotype threat effects on women's math performance. *Journal of Experimental Social Psychology, 38*(2), 194–201.

Shih, M., Pittinsky, T., & Ambady, N. (1999). Stereotype susceptibility: Identity salience and shifts in quantitative performance. *Psychological Science, 10*(1), 80–83.

Simmons, R. G., Black, A., & Zhou, Y. (1991). African-American versus White children and the transition to junior high school. *American Journal of Education, 99,* 481–520.

Simmons, R. G., & Blyth, D. A. (1987). *Moving into adolescence: The impact of pubertal change and school context.* Hawthorne, NY: Aldine de Gruyter.

Spencer, M. B., & Dornbusch, S. M. (1990). Challenges in studying minority youth. In S. S. Feldman & G. R. Elliott (Eds.), *At the threshold: The developing adolescent* (pp. 352–387). Cambridge, MA: Harvard University Press.

Spencer, S., Steele, C. M., & Quinn, D. M. (1999). Stereotype threat and women's math performance. *Journal of Experimental Social Psychology, 35,* 4–28.

Steele, C. M. (1997). A threat in the air: How stereotypes shape intellectual identity and performance. *American Psychologist, 52*(6), 613–629.

Steele, C. M., & Aronson, J. (1995). Stereotype threat and the intellectual test performance of African-Americans. *Journal of Personality and Social Psychology, 69*(5), 797–811.

Steele, C. M., Spencer, S., & Aronson, J. (2002) Contending with images of one's group: The psychology of stereotype and social identity threat. In M. Zanna (Ed.), *Advances in experimental social psychology* (pp. 379–440). San Diego: Academic Press.

Stumpf, H., & Stanley, J. (1996). Gender-related differences on the College Board's Advanced Placement and Achievement tests, 1982–1992. *Journal of Educational Psychology, 88,* 353–364.

Summers, L. (2005). (http://www.president.harvard.edu/speeches/2005/nber.html).

Valencia, R. R. (1997). Latinos and education: An overview of sociodemographic characteristics and schooling conditions and outcomes. In M. Barrera-Yepes (Ed.), *Latino education issues: Conference proceedings* (pp. 13–37). Princeton, NJ: Educational Testing Service.

Warren, J. (1996). Educational inequality among White and Mexican-origin adolescents in the American Southwest: 1990. *Sociology of Education, 69,* 142–158.

Wheeler, S. C., & Petty, R. E. (2001). The effects of stereotype activation on behavior: A review of possible mechanisms. *Psychological Bulletin, 127,* 797–826.

8

HONOR, TRUTH, AND JUSTICE

Unni Wikan

Traditions are not monoliths. Any living culture contains plurality and argument; it contains relatively powerful voices, relatively silent voices, and voices that cannot speak at all in the public space.

Martha Nussbaum

Nebile is a 13-year-old girl whose story bears mention for the light it sheds on a child's trying to come to grips with the judgments and acts of her elders. She was caught in a conundrum that no one would want to experience: one where a family was ravaged by rage, shame, and despair, and where the protagonists, all of them dear to her, were bitterly, and in the end, deadly, opposed.

This is putting the matter prettily. What came to pass is that her father killed her sister, Fadime, as the two, Nebile and Fadime, were on their way out of another sister's flat.* Here the three had convened secretly with their mother in defiance of orders from the menfolk not to meet. Fadime had been ostracized for three years by then. She had been expelled and threatened to be killed if she ever ventured back to Uppsala, the family's hometown in Sweden.

---

* Nebile is pronounced Neble; Fadime is pronounced Fadeemeh.

185

On January 21, 2002, the execution took place. Execution is the word the United Nations special rapporteur on extrajudicial, summary, and arbitrary crimes, Dr. Philip Alston, uses in regard to honor killings;* and it was also how the father's crime was described in the verdict passed by the appeals court in Stockholm on June 3, 2002. Rahmi Sahindal was sentenced to life imprisonment, as he had also been in the lower court.

Fadime lived to be 26 years old.

She had been a public figure in Sweden for four years, ever since she told the media in 1998: "I know I must live with death threats till their breath expires; it is the only way they can regain their pride, their honor."**

Her deadly offense was of having chosen her own love in life, Patrik Lindesjö. Patrik died in a car crash on June 3, 1998, the day that he and Fadime were to have moved in together. Fadime gathered together the shreds of her life, and devoted herself to her studies in social work. She was about to finish her MA when her life was cut short. Three bullets fired by her father put the death sentence into effect.

VOICES OF SILENCE

Nebile attended both court cases. She was dressed in a red jacket and red pants, and looked like an ordinary Swedish girl with dark hair. (One in every five Swedes now has an immigrant background.) She had been born and raised in Sweden as the youngest of six children (five girls and one boy) of Kurdish immigrants from Turkey who had settled in Uppsala in the early 1980s. Her father was a steady worker in a dry-cleaning company, proud that he had never relied on social welfare; her mother was a housewife. They had many relatives in Sweden: The Sahindal clan counted some 300 members in Sweden by 2002. Some 30 of them attended the court case, complaining loudly that the family had been allotted far too few seats.

I happened to be seated right next to Nebile and her mother in the municipal court. Both burst into tears as the father and husband entered the court. The names of both mother and child appeared on the list of witnesses to be called, but only the mother was asked to testify.

---

* I am referring to his statement made at the international conference on "Patriarchal Violence – Focusing on Violence in the Name of Honour" in Stockholm on December 3, 2004.

** All translations from Swedish are mine. All appear in their original in *En fråga om heder* (2004a), the Swedish edition of my book, *For ærens skyld*, which was first published in Norwegian in 2003.

She declined, saying she had told it all to the police. It was explained to her, through a translator, that her testimony to the police could not be heeded by the court, which needed her to testify in person.

She persisted in her refusal, and Nebile was not called. Whether it was in consideration for the child, or for other reasons, I do not know.

A DISCORDANT VOICE

Up front on the side of the defense sat Songül in whose flat Fadime had been killed. She stared the mother to the ground when she refused to testify. Songül had defied pleas by the mother to keep silent and now appeared as the key witness for the prosecutor. The 21-year-old girl who had been in on the conspiracy between the mother and three of her (four) daughters to keep up relations with Fadime—knowing well that if detected, it might spell Fadime's death—now appeared as the foe of the whole family. She had a police escort; there was fear that she too might be killed.

"It has happened; tell nothing to the police," the mother warned Nebile and Songül shortly after the murder, this according to Songül. Indeed, Songül was the only one in the whole (extended) family who would testify in court. A cousin and best friend of the father claimed complete memory lapse. "But that Fadime was killed was a special event, you must remember," protested the prosecutor. "In my life there are no special days," replied the man who was later convicted of contempt of court. Other potential witnesses excused themselves with reference to their close kinship connection.

DENIAL, BETRAYAL, LOYALTY

The second day in the municipal court the mother stayed away, but Nebile was there in the company of the family members. Nebile followed the trial until the end, and also sat through the case at the appeals court in Stockholm. At this point she was faced with her mother testifying for her father and denying all that she and Nebile had told the police about the murder that they had witnessed first-hand.

It was not her husband, Elif Sahindal said, who had murdered Fadime but a man from the woods who had threatened him to take on responsibility or the whole family would be murdered, even the grandchildren. Her story was in conformity with what her husband had told the appeals court, an entirely new version of the atrocities that spelled Fadime's death.

The mother's testimony appeared as an act of betrayal of Fadime. The mother also appeared to betray Songül by casting her as a liar.

Songül spoke truth to justice so that "Fadime would not have lived in vain." She also said that she wanted her father to be convicted and suffer the punishment for what he had done, although she was explicit that she did not believe him to be singly responsible for the crime.

"My father fired the shots, but others were behind," said Songül and told of family encounters where people higher up on the echelon, especially her mother's brother, head of the Sahindal clan in Sweden, had said, "That whore must die."

GOING PUBLIC

Songül corroborated the story that Fadime had told on several occasions during the four years that she had been a public figure in Sweden. It began on February 4, 1998, when she went to the media with her story of threats on her life because she had a boyfriend. Going public was a last resort after an appeal to the police for help had failed: "My story was like a saga to them," she said and lay bare how humiliated she had felt that the police did not believe her. "Perhaps if I become known to the public, my family will not dare to kill me," she said in explanation of why she had gone to the media.

Fadime also wanted to give voice and face to the many silent others who suffered similar fates of being denied the right to choose their own love or spouse. It pertained to hundreds of girls in Sweden, she said. Posterity has proved her right.*

The family was enraged at this public scandalization of their name, as they saw it. Death threats kept pouring in to Fadime over the phone; she had left Uppsala and begun studies in social work in Östersund. Again she went to the police, and this time she was believed. A court case followed in which her father and brother were convicted of violence and death threats. Just after the court case, on May 6, 1998, a documentary on her life was featured on Swedish TV.** The Sahindal family, Nebile's family, was exposed as one likely to commit an honor killing.

Fadime also spoke of her intense longing for her mother and of her grief that she could never again expect to be in her embrace. Reconciliation

---

* In 2004–2005 the Swedish government granted SEK 100 million (c. $15 million) for shelters for persons whose lives are threatened. The majority are females of immigrant background, but increasingly boys are also seeking help and support, in Sweden as well as in many other European countries.

** SVT1: "Striptease." Samhällsmagasin, first featured May 6, 1998.

seemed impossible after the hurt and pain she had caused her family. "But a mother's love cannot just die?" protested the journalist. "You don't understand," said Fadime, "I have destroyed everything they had. I have trampled on their honor.... Now no one will want to marry girls of the family (clan). All are whores" (SVT1).

Her mother would carry the chief blame, said Fadime, and she would also blame herself, as it is a mother's duty to bring up the girls in conformity with the rules. Fadime consistently spoke of rules rather than culture, although she also used words such as *lifeways, worldview,* and *customs.* The point about rules was that they are precise and backed by sheer harsh sanctions. The aim of the upbringing was compliance with rules, not policing of people's thoughts and emotions.

Fadime's mother had produced a monster, from a certain point of view. "Fucking whore, why did you come into my family!" the father screamed as he shot Fadime dead, close up.

CULTURE: A PLURALITY OF VOICES

"Traditions are not monoliths," writes Nussbaum (1999, p. 8). "Any living culture contains plurality and argument; it contains relatively powerful voices, relatively silent voices, and voices that cannot speak at all in the public space." My brief exposé of Fadime Sahindal's nuclear family epitomizes the point. Here is a mother, a father, and six children: all of them part of what one might call Kurdish culture or Turkish–Kurdish culture or Swedish–Turkish–Kurdish culture. Whatever phrasing you choose, the point is that these eight individuals "belonged" in different measures and different degrees to one or more living cultures that had elements of Kurdish–Turkish and Swedish traditions. And they argue; there is no uniformity of viewpoint or moral position here. This little family—which distinguishes itself by the fact that more members than usual for people of their kind have spoken, or left records of speech and action in the public sphere—illuminates a general point about traditions eloquently expressed by Nussbaum (1999).

But power and perceptions of privacy might collude to give a semblance of unity or uniformity to the public. The killing of Fadime also illustrates that the idea of culture is often used selectively. Nasim Karim, a Norwegian writer and activist, stated to a group of some members of Parliament, "When a man is subject to violence it is called torture; when a woman is subject to violence, it is called culture."

"The situation is closed/hidden"—*mastur ilhal*—is an Arabic formulation of the way things should be in an ordinary respectful family. You do not expose family matters to outsiders, especially not things regarding the women. Fadime committed a deadly sin when she did not just choose her own love in life, and walk with him in public, but she also went to the media with her story, aggravating the family's disgrace.

Nebile's family is an ordinary family with an unordinary family history. "We're a normal family," said Fidan, the eldest sister, to the media after the murder. And she is right, they were, until a catastrophic event overtook them and put them up front in the media as a family ready to kill for honor's sake, and eventually—after the fact—as a family defying the rule of law in apparent support of a man who had killed his own daughter.

"It was the final solution; the problem is over now," Fadime's father told the police.

"He had no choice, no alternative," said some Kurds who condemned the murder, but sympathized with the father.

"He made a mistake," said some immigrant boys. "He had five bullets, and only used three."

"What Fadime did was seen by some as an offense towards the whole Kurdish minority in Sweden," a Kurdish–Swedish teacher explained.

"If you had a daughter like this Fadime, you would have wanted to kill her too," said the father to the prosecutor in Uppsala municipal court. But he also said, "I must be sick, no man would kill his own daughter if he wasn't sick.... This daughter who is dead now" had made him sick, he said, by exposing the family to world opinion, making them a laughing-stock. "World opinion"—*världsopinionen*—is key to understanding their plight.

HONOR, CULTURE, POWER

Honor is part of culture. Honor is above the law (Pitt-Rivers, 1965; Stewart, 1994; Welchman & Hossein, 2005). The honor code that was acted on in Fadime's case requires all members of the honor group (see Stewart, 1994), a collective, to keep quiet to the public in family matters. Privacy should be protected by all means. Honor is a matter of protecting the reputation of the honor group. Reputation is all, more important than fact or truth. Esteem lies in the eyes of the beholder more than in self-worth or personal esteem.* The two are linked, of course. But reputation carries weight as the arbiter of esteem.

---

* For a discussion of the relationship between self-regard and social esteem, see Pitt-Rivers (1965); Stewart (1994); Wikan (1984).

Women's sexual and social demeanors are crucial to honor. What is said or reputed thereof can make or unmake honor.* What Fadime did was disastrous from the point of view of her honor group, the Sahindals, with members in many countries, not just Sweden. What she did was even regarded by some as dishonorable to the whole ethnic minority of Kurds in Sweden. In other words, the honor group is no fixed entity. Depending on viewpoint, it can detract or expand, to the state, church, or nation (Das, 1995; Kertzer, 1993). But a woman's natal family is always strongly affected (Ginat, 1997).

Fadime's case offers a rare glimpse into a microculture: a family that, to the best of my judgment, is a microcosm of a larger tradition, but a nonmonolithic one. What is special about this case is not the code of honor that framed the lives and destinies of people, but the fact that things got to extremes. An honor killing is a final solution, a last resort. But its frightening specter haunts thousands of youngsters around the globe. It is meant to frighten, and it does. Compliance with norms—rules, as Fadime would say—is more easily enforced precisely because people know all too well what the price of disobedience or defiance might be.

Fadime's case is compelling also because it allows a rare view of persons as individuals, each with their character and history, who make their own judgments, based on their experience and interests (see Wikan, in press, for more extensive discussion). Every family is a nucleus of diverse, nonmonolithic viewpoints and preferences. Sometimes they converge, but they do not overlap as patterns to be patched one atop another. Also, so-called collectivist traditions comprise a mosaic of individuals who must grapple with their own world (Mernissi, 1994; Turiel, 2002; Wikan, 1991, 1996).

Fadime's five siblings all took distinct positions in regard to her. The eldest sister, Fidan, came to sympathize with Fadime and talked with her on the phone several times during Fadime's last year. The next one, Elmas, could not forgive Fadime for besmirching the family and causing her parents endless suffering. Mesuut, the brother, three years younger than Fadime, actually tried to kill her and was jailed in

---

* Examples of social demeanors that can affect family honor are, in some groups, a female's smoking or "staying out late." There are two distinct concepts of honor in languages such as Arabic, Turkish, Kurdish, Persian, Pashto, and Urdu that in English are rendered as honor (or Swedish *heder* or Norwegian *ære*). Only one of these relates to women's sexual/social conduct and is the critical one that can lead to honor killings. For my purposes here, it is not necessary to expatiate on the difference, but see Stewart (1994) and Wikan (in press).

August 1998, after having been convicted for threats on her life earlier that year. Songül, we know, stands by Fadime in thick and thin, also after her death, and "betrays" the family by testifying against the father. Nebile, 13 years old, is the little one caught in all this turmoil. Hers is a silent voice, a voice that cannot speak at all in public. But a particularity of the Swedish law allows us some insight into the mindset of this little girl whose thoughts and feelings were conveyed to the police investigator a few days after Fadime's death.

Police investigation reports are public in Sweden and accessible to anyone. They cannot be used in court as evidence, but they can be consulted and read by a researcher such as myself. I had access to some 350 pages on the Fadime case. Twenty-five of those were from an interview that a policewoman had with Nebile one week after the murder, and that lasted some five hours, with a break.

This document is unique in the history of anthropology (to my knowledge). Therefore, I give a lengthy rendition here to convey the pain and sorrow experienced by persons caught in the grip of a cultural tradition. It provides a revealing anthropological record that is usually missing in monolithic portrayals of "traditions" or cultures.

A SWEDISH TRAGEDY

Nebile's testimony to the police affected me deeply when I read it. Here was a child telling what it was like to be an innocent victim of an ordeal that could be labeled a Swedish tragedy. "Kurdish woman killed" announced the media in the morning after the murder. But Fadime's family had lived in Sweden for 20 years. They were no newcomers to the scene, nor were they marginalized in the sense of dispossessed. The father had been working all through the years in a Swedish company, and the family was moderately well-off; they lived in a middle-class neighborhood. Nebile went to a Swedish public school. None of the women in the family wore the veil or headscarf (hijab); "Muslim, but nonpracticing," is how they described themselves. And yet the international media featured them as Muslim, as if the tragedy that had come to pass had any reference to Islam.

"Islam" did not feature in any of the testimonies that Fadime gave to the public, and they were many, after she went public with her story in February 1998, hoping that would help save her life and draw attention to a neglected and ignored problem in Sweden: the rights and liberties of girls of immigrant background and the integration of people like her parents. What she referred to time and time again were the rules and lifeways of traditions that sacrificed the individual on the altar of the collective. The supreme evil, in this point of view, was placing one's individual happiness before the welfare of the group. The collectivist ethos that she described did violence not just to what we are wont to think of as victims: women and children. It also "claimed" men who were compelled to comply with an honor code, honor here referring not to personal integrity but to conformity with rules conferring respect linked with fear.

Fadime was not the first, nor the last, victim of an honor killing in Sweden.* There had been several before: murders committed to cleanse the dishonor of a collective. The best-known cases were Sara and Pela; Sara (15 years old) was murdered by her brother and cousin in 1996 (see Eldén, 2004; Wikan, 2002); Pela (19 years old) was murdered by two of her father's brothers in 1999 (see Begikhani, 2005; Swanberg, 2002; Wikan, 2003). The Swedish police estimate that there have been one or two honor killings yearly since 1980 (Älgamo, 2004).

Honor killings are premeditated, planned. Because honor is collective, anyone in the family can do "the job." Because a minor receives a mild sentence (not just in Sweden, but in many countries), the duty to kill is often imposed on a young man (Connors, 2005). Fadime believed her brother had been targeted, and he did assault her just before he turned 18. Fadime's father may have taken it on himself to carry out the deed so as to spare his one and only son. Be that as it may, Fadime's death had the impact of forcing Swedes to see that honor killings were not some foreign phenomena, but a part of Swedish reality. The one person who had done more than anyone else to draw attention to such atrocities had herself become a victim. Denial was no longer possible.

Sweden honored Fadime by giving her a state funeral, although it could not be labeled such, as her family was Muslim. She was buried from the ancient Cathedral in Uppsala in accordance with her own wishes. She wanted to lie next to Patrik in the old graveyard adjacent to the Cathedral. The Swedish crown princess, the head of Parliament, Cabinet ministers, and other dignitaries attended the funeral, which was broadcast live on TV. The day of Fadime's death, January 21, is being commemorated annually in Sweden in semi-official and other ways.

---

* There is much discussion, and much disagreement among experts, researchers, activists, politicians, and people regarding the use of the concept of honor killing. For an extended discussion, see Welchman and Hossein (2005), and several of the papers in that volume (see also Akkoc, 2004, and Mojab, 2004). I stick to the term, and without brackets as in "honor killing" or "so-called honor killing" for reasons that I expound on elsewhere (Wikan, in press). A useful definition of the term is provided by Hjärpe (2003). What sets honor killings apart is that they are premeditated, planned in order to cleanse collective dishonor, and that the murder confers honor or glory. The murderer becomes a hero; his honor group redeems honor.

When Nebile spoke to the police, on January 28, 2002, she could not know that she would remain the little sister of a girl who would become an icon in Sweden after her death.

A CHILD'S VOICE

It was January 21, 2002. Nebile went to the gym as usual around seven in the evening. She was part of a conspiracy this day. After the session she would go to her sister Songül to join her mother and Fadime for a happy encounter. Fadime had come on a secret visit, the third or fourth this year, but it would be a long time before the next, as Fadime was due to travel the next week to Kenya for half a year to do the fieldwork for her MA in social work.

Thirteen years her elder, Fadime had been like a mother to Nebile until she left home when Nebile was nine. It was not a voluntary departure but a choice between two impossible alternatives. Fadime wanted to keep both her family and her sweetheart, Swedish–Iranian Patrik. She has described her panic at having to make the choice. Exit Fadime with two policemen who accompanied her as she came home the last time to fetch her passport and belongings in September 1997.

Now they were reunited, mother and three daughters. But in utter secrecy. Fadime's brother was especially feared. He had vowed to kill her and had failed in an attempt in June 1998. He and the father had sworn that if she ever came to Uppsala, she would be killed. Here she was, the third or fourth time running this year. The mother had baked pirogs, Fadime's favorite food. Fadime had gifts for all of them, and Nebile had some for her. But their happiness was disturbed when the father came banging on the door, screaming to be let in. "Poor Daddy," said Fadime and suggested that she hide under the couch so they could let him in. The mother thought it better if she locked herself into the bathroom and they would say they had lost the key. Songül feared both alternatives. The father kept banging and screaming for a while. When they thought he had given up and left, Nebile and Fadime prepared to leave, Nebile to walk home, and Fadime to be picked up by a cousin at whose place she would spend the night. The mother who had pain in her knees would sleep over at Songül's place.

Nebile gives this account to the police of what then happened. She speaks in a Swedish–Kurdish idiomatic dialect that is poorly rendered in English here, but it is hoped that the essence of her messages comes through. Nebile tells:

Fadime put on her jacket; it was new; it was a beige jacket; she had just bought it. She said, "Isn't it nice?" and chatted a little about it, then she looked at herself in the mirror and said, "It's nice," and then she went and kissed Mama and said, "Good bye!" and then she took my present in her hand, and then I peeped in the keyhole; had he sat in the staircase, I think I would have seen him, but he wasn't there, so I opened the door, and there he stood right in front of me.... It was like a ghost ... and I was shocked.... His hair was disheveled, and he was yellow, and he had red eyes.

The father was shocked to see her.

He was supershocked; he was flabbergasted that I should be there, and then I screamed like, I don't remember if I grabbed him and pushed him or what I did; then I caught sight of the pistol, and I thought, I believed it looked like a toy pistol ... he was completely pale, and I didn't recognize him at all. I thought, "This is not my daddy; it is someone else," and then I thought quickly, like, "What shall I do now," and then, you know, when he grabbed Fadime by the hair, then my mother came rushing and pulled his arm, his pistol, and pulled it towards herself saying, "Don't kill my ...", she meant like, "Don't kill her; you can kill me; kill me instead of her," and then I thought, "I'm dreaming," I said to myself, I pulled my hair and I was not dreaming. I thought, what shall I do now? And I didn't know what to do. I went and pushed him, and all of us pushed him and ... then it fired, and I thought there are balloons, like I thought it was balloons that had exploded, I mean like when one takes a needle, you know, and do like this, you know, and then, I don't know if he shot her in the head, but for me it was three shots, but in the news they say it was two shots he fired, but for me it was three, and then, I don't know if she fell, but according to Mama, she fell at once.... I don't think she suffered or such, I don't think so; I think she died immediately, and then ... when he stood there, and I didn't know what to do, but I went and pushed against him and I thought he was to fire more or shoot more, and then I held him and said, "Fadime, run!" I said, "Fadime, go now!" She didn't go, she laid there, and I thought, I thought, perhaps she is afraid, she is perhaps in shock; she doesn't stand up. I didn't mean to kick, but I touched her a little with my foot, I said, "Fadime, Fadime!" She didn't rise, and then, then Mama ran out, I don't know why she ran ... I thought, where's she going now? I thought she was going to call on help or something,

I thought.... I thought she had been shocked, I thought perhaps she will commit suicide....

Nebile runs after her father, who has run down the stairway, and stands outside the apartment block. She catches him and grabs hold of him:

There were so many thoughts, and so much I wanted to say, but it wasn't the right time and not the right place. I held him, I looked him in the eyes, he looked at me; no, I felt, no, this is not my Daddy; it is an other ... he didn't look like himself at all ... he had tears in his eyes.

She was not afraid of him:

Deep inside I knew that he would never do me or anyone else any harm; he would have preferred, I think, that I wasn't there, and he was very surprised that I was there ... I have heard that he has phoned Fatma (an aunt) and said like, "I'm sorry that Nebile was there and that she got to see this thing ... preferably I would have wanted to do it alone, but it wasn't possible."

Having run after the father and grabbed hold of him, Nebile lets him go. Why? The police want to know.

What makes me release him? That's when I start to think, but where's Mama now? That's when I loosen my grip, when I came to think where is Mama ... and then he ran.
He flew, like he was flying, you know, and then I went outside ... and I cried and searched behind stones, and behind the bushes, and then I thought, what shall I do now, Mama is gone....

Nebile makes her way back to Songül's apartment and calls her sister Elmas:
"I phoned, I said, she didn't understand a thing ... I said, 'Daddy has shot!' I tried to tell her, but it wasn't possible; I said, 'Daddy has shot Fadime!' I said, 'Mama is gone; Mama has disappeared,' I said...."
Songül needs the phone, she is expecting a message from the police whom she has contacted. Nebile recounts:

I put down the phone, I didn't look at Fadime at all. I saw that she had on a beige jacket, and there were some black spots on it.... It must have been there he shot, though I don't think that it (the bullet) went through for the jacket was quite thick, I think.... I looked at her, at the face, I saw that she got blood in her mouth ... and afterwards I stood there, and then I went around and searched.

"Where are you, Mama?" I said, no, I didn't know where Mama was.

Soon after the mother appears: "She consoled me and said, 'Don't be afraid. It is nothing,' she said; she comforted me and said, 'Don't be afraid; she is not dead,' she said to me."
Nebile does not believe that the murder had been planned.

"They say it was planned this thing, but if he had planned it, then somebody would have stood there and waited for him and helped him to escape. He has not planned this thing."

Nebile leaves no doubt that it is a beloved sister she has lost. But she is also critical of Fadime for the pain she has caused her family:

"We were very close to each other; I loved her, but I'm also very angry because she has lied, truly she did. She lied an awful lot, everything she said, she has lied, for that I'm very disappointed and angry with her, at the same time I love her too."

In Nebile's account, Fadime resorted to lies because she wanted to become a media star. Nebile's understanding accords with the story family members tell, 13 of the 15 who were examined by the police. According to Nebile, Fadime herself admitted that she lied, when Nebile brought it up with her:

I said, "Fadime, why did you do like that?" I said, "Fadime, why did you lie so much on TV?" I said, "Fadime, was it worth it, was it really worth it?" I said, "Was it really worth it going out in the media and … ?" You know … it was all that which made Daddy sick; he got very sick because she went out in the media and above all, because she lied, she described us as a monster family, she truly did.

She lied and lied, and in the end, Daddy went crazy, he got sick; like, she says, she has been on the 20th of December, or when it was, in the Parliament, or where it was, and I heard that she spoke on a tape and said that Daddy had hit her with the rolling pin thirty times…. This rolling pin of ours, let me tell you, it is of wood, you understand, it is made of wood, and she says that Daddy has hit her with it at least thirty times when he hasn't even touched her—thirty times! I mean, my God, if I take it and knock your head thirty times, I don't think your head is going to last; I think it is going to break, your head!

Nebile is on the right track, but gets some of the facts of the case wrong. Fadime did speak in the old Parliament building (not the Parliament) at a conference on November 20, 2001 (not December 20), and her speech was recorded. On another occasion, in her first newspaper interview on February 4, 1998, she told how she had been beaten some thirty times, and once with the rolling pin. But the facts of the case are not important here. What matters is the 13-year-old's trying to come to grips with a catastrophe that has cost her her sister and her father and plunged the family into a turmoil from which they will never escape.

Her sister painted the family as a monster; she lied; her father went mad, became sick; an example is the rolling pin story. (Think for yourself, your head would have been broken if you had been hit thirty times with such an object; it proves Fadime lied; and in Parliament, to make matters worse.)

Fadime is gone, a beloved sister who was also infuriating. The father lives on; and he was a kind man in Nebile's and everyone's account, a gentle man until the day, September 3, 1997, when he spotted his daughter, Fadime, walking with a man on the street. All hell broke loose. When she began her public odyssey the whole family was utterly humiliated, as they saw it. The father sank into despair, and gave up his job. He drank intermittently. How Nebile was affected, we can only intuit.

Let us then not forget that the story we are hearing is one told to the police in a particular context. It is situational; we do not know if the story we hear is the one Nebile tells herself in other contexts, or to friends rather than "the enemy." She must have been out to save her father as much as she could in this account. But her last words to the police are:

"Will I get to see my sister before the funeral?"

"I don't know."

"Because I wanted to put a little something in her hand."

MORALITY, JUDGMENT, CULTURE, AND IDENTITY

In his book *The Culture of Morality* Elliot Turiel (2002, p. 15) launches a view of moral development that can be applied to the story told above:

In contrast with the view of morality as entailing a fixed set of traits reflecting the incorporation of traditional values ... research demonstrates that ... individuals make complex moral, social, and personal judgments that often entail taking into account the context of people's activities. Research also has demonstrated that in their moral decisions people take circumstances into account.... People often weigh and struggle with different and competing moral considerations, as well as try to balance nonmoral with moral considerations.

This proposition has implications for explanations of development: "If morality involves judgments, then it would be expected that moral development would involve a process of constructing such judgments." Turiel's theoretical perspective "is based on the proposition that children construct ways of thinking about welfare, justice, and rights through a variety of social experiences" (p. 16). Research further shows that "children's moral judgments initially revolve around people's welfare" (p. 289).

Nebile is a case in point. She weighs and balances different considerations as she struggles to understand what has come to pass in her family through years of upheaval and pain. A beloved sister, who was like a mother to her, exited the family. Why? It was not because she "fell in love with a Swede," as the media wrote: "He wasn't a Swede, he was Iranian; he was a half-Swede. We tried to get the fucking media to write that, but they wouldn't."

What is at stake here is an identity claim. What does it matter if the media featured Patrik as a Swede or a half-Swede, to use Nebile's word? It makes all the difference to her. She is a Swede, a Swedish-born Swede. But she is also Kurdish. How come the media portrays Patrik as Swedish when his father is actually Iranian? Patrik was a half-Swede, that's the truth, but the media set up a categorical divide between Swede and non-Swede for the better story: Kurdish woman killed because she loved a Swedish boy. In the process, Nebile—and her family—end up as an enemy of "Swedes."

This is a matter of identity: What is the identity of a girl, or a boy, who has grown up in historical circumstances different from those of the parents? Is it the distinct cultural identity of persons that governments have in mind when they pass official policies to the effect that "immigrants shall be able to maintain a separate cultural identity"? Clearly not. In Sweden, as in much of Europe, such policies have been based on the premise that to each people there is one culture and one identity. Thus people were packaged in boxes, which made them easier to contain. But the contents spill over, unruly and angry, for they do not fit the formula. And so we have numerous young people, many of whom suffer because they were prepackaged by the authorities acting in conjunction with parents into "cultures" that did not fit the children's lived experience.

As stated in Wikan (2002, p. 73):

Misconceptions or distorting language that have bedeviled anthropology for decades still ride official European immigration policies, at least in Scandinavia. I refer to those notions known as essentialist in current anthropological theory: that to each people a single culture belongs, which compels all the people to abide by its mores, on which they agree. Thus there is consensus, no contestation, welfare and harmony that "the culture" is supposed to further, or "it" would not be there—or so it is presumed. This notion of culture has timelessness built into it; it is static, unmoving. Nor is identity a problem for the people. It is given, bestowed by culture.

"Culture" is another point of contention for Nebile. She is concerned that Swedes will understand that her family does not practice old-fashioned mores and traditions. Fadime has told the media that brides must be virgins on marriage, and that a bloodstained kerchief must be provided as proof. Nebile is distraught at this. True, a bride should be pure on marriage, she says. But the story of the bloodstained proof is fabricated by Fadime who didn't know anything of their culture:

"Mama says that when she came here (to Sweden) she was hardly … she cannot have known about our culture; she was only four–six years or so and still she says that.…"

"Who says?" asks the police.

Nebile says:

My sister, when she came here. She says that Mama told her, she has written in the newspaper that Mama told her not to go out and play with those Swedish girls; they are whores; all are whores.… Mama has never said anything like that; she was completely shattered when she got to know it. She says, "How can she say anything like that?" It is clear that she thinks like, if they write that in a newspaper and a Swede comes to read this thing that Mama has told her not to go and play with those Swedish whores, of course they will think why the hell have we opened the world to them for? They come here, they eat food, they get everything they need, and yet their parents say, "Don't go and play with those whores." It is easy to understand that they will be angry then. But what we want is to get out the truth so that the people will know what the truth is, that which she has said is not the truth; it is only falsehood.

In Fadime's own account her family stands forth as one committed to the cultural traditions and moral viewpoints from which Nebile is at

pains to distance herself. Fadime's agenda was to throw light on particular lifeways that continued to be practiced and were even reinforced
in certain minority communities, to the detriment of life and health.

Nebile's desire is to be included as "not one of them" and to reha-
bilitate her mother as a decent person respectful of Swedes. Her family
does not want to be seen as ungrateful and they can full well understand that Swedes would want them to get out if the mother said to her
daughters, "Don't go and play with those Swedish whores!"

THE ENEMY: THE MEDIA AND THE POLICE

In her weighing and balancing of judgments, Nebile concludes that the
real rascals are the media who exploited her sister Fadime: "She says,
'they beat me ... I was mistreated; my other siblings were mistreated.'
... We phoned the newspapers, said that we wanted to talk with them,
but they refused because then perhaps they will sell fewer newspapers;
they have exploited my sister."

The police also let the family down: "She says to the police that Daddy
has beaten her and such; why didn't the police think then that there are
other children too in this family; why don't we go and see how they are;
why don't we do that?"

The police agree that Nebile has a point.

Overall Nebile's concern is that her family has been depicted as a
monster in the public space. On why her brother was jailed for attack-
ing Fadime, she says it was because Fadime had provoked him by
talking badly about their parents. On why her father killed her, it was
because he became sick from despair at the public humiliation and disgrace. But these are not easy conclusions. She struggles to understand
and reasons, as we have heard, that if the father had planned the murder, he would have had someone waiting with a car for him outside.
As regards her brother, she is aware that he might have had a hand in
the planning of the murder, and tells the police how she has tested him
out through asking him, indirectly. She does believe, however, that her
brother sensed that Fadime was in Uppsala on that fatal evening when
she was killed.

LIBERTY VERSUS EXILE

I have given an account of a family drama that ended in the worst possible way. For Fadime, the stakes were liberty, equality, and social justice. She regarded that she had the right to choose her own boyfriend;
she was already 21. She regarded that she should have the same rights

as other Swedish girls to choose her own spouse. And to study; as she told her story, her clan was utterly opposed to the idea that a girl needed an education beyond primary school. Girls should marry and be housewives. Such was their lot in life.

Fadime further regarded that she should have freedom of movement: "This is a free country; I have the right to come to where my beloved lies buried!" she said in response to being "exiled" from Uppsala on threats of being murdered if she returned. "This is a free country also for me; I'll get you!" retorted her father.

Fadime was offered a secret identity and declined. "Why should I hide? I have committed no crime."

What the mother thought of Fadime's judgments and acts, we do not know. It appears that Fadime asked forgiveness for the pain she had caused the family, and then mother and child were reunited, secretly. A conspiracy was set up between the mother and three of her children behind the menfolks' backs. This is like a guerrilla movement, a revolt against male power and patriarchy. "I have done it; it was my mistake!" the mother cried to Fidan, her eldest daughter, after the murder. Had not Fadime come to Uppsala, she might have survived.

She broke an exile that is an institutionalized way for families to save their honor without taking a life in eastern Turkey where the Sahindals came from, and also in some other parts of the world. By sending the person into exile, like Fadime was, pride can be salvaged in the best of cases.

CONCLUDING REMARKS

My account here of the Fadime case is microscopic. A macroperspective would deal with honor-based violence in an international and transnational perspective and with the place and position of some non-Western immigrant communities in Sweden and elsewhere in Western and Northern Europe where marginalization, segregation, and "parallel societies" bespeak the failure of so-called integration policies, or policies of inclusion, as they are now increasingly called (Carlbom, 2003; Wikan, 2002). The Swedes have a good word for it, *utanförskap*, which means both being on the outside and beyond the real thing, or what really counts. Of course, many immigrants and some of their children and grandchildren are content to be precisely that: *utanför*, outside and beyond the claims and demands and immoral influences, as they perceive it, of the surrounding society.

From that point of view, being outside and beyond confers protection. It is a desired position, a haven of sorts. But it is also a trap, as females especially come increasingly to realize. Many males too are concerned that traditions and customary ways are being reinforced, even reinvented, in some such communities, to the detriment of all.

Pressure to help relatives back home to enter Europe via marriage—the only legal way now save political asylum or refugee status, which is hard to obtain—is also increasingly contested. Fadime spoke out against forced marriage, and with good reason. At her time, when she was still alive, Sweden even had a law that permitted child marriage of Swedish-born residents of immigrant background. In a misplaced respect for "culture," Sweden as the most "liberal" of the Nordic countries allowed children as young as 15 to be married if the law in the parents' homeland permitted it. This law was only repealed in 2004, making 18 the legal minimum marriage age for all (Bergh, 2004; Wikan, 2004b).

Forced marriage is now an increasing concern in many European countries. Norway, as the first, moved to criminalize forced marriage in 2004; Belgium followed suit in 2005 and Germany in 2006. Other countries are considering making similar legal amendments. The line between arranged and forced marriage is difficult to draw in many cases. But the evidence is overwhelming that hundreds of youngsters in all of these countries fear forced marriage, and hundreds are seeking help or are in hiding. Equality and social justice are not values that are upheld in many of the immigrant communities in the West (as in many native communities, especially among fundamentalist Christians). But it is a sad fact of life that European governments have been late in acknowledging the equal rights of individuals of non-Western background.

A policy of multiculturalism, which has probably for Europe been most pronounced in Sweden, Great Britain, and the Netherlands, has focused attention on the rights and liberties of groups, communities, rather than on individual integrity and liberty. Fear of being accused of racism has been an underlying rationale (or implicit excuse) for such policies that often played up to powerholders at the expense of the weaker members of groups. Identity politics thrived under such conditions. Societies became segmented into ethnic and religious groups that celebrated a unidimensional view of man (or the person). Further segmentation was reinforced as marriage took place within castes, sub-castes, tribes, clans, and religious sects. Fadime was supposed to marry, not a Kurd, but a specific Kurd of a particular clan. All too many youngsters experience that their own interests are sacrificed on the altar of the collective, and that ostracism or outcasting might be the result if they object. In extreme cases, honor killings take place.

A word that could hardly be spoken until after Fadime's death is now part and parcel of public language. The murder of Fadime, although it was far from the first honor killing to take place in Sweden, became a trauma and triggered events that had international and transnational repercussions. In 2003, the United Nations General Assembly passed a resolution against crimes against women committed in the name of honor. The Council of Europe followed suit shortly after. These may sound like small achievements, but they are not. A critical silence has been broken. Admitting to the fact that violence is being perpetrated in the name of honor, and that honor killings or so-called honor killings exist, is a big step forward. Numerous governmental and nongovernmental institutions and organizations are now working worldwide to counter and prevent a particular form of murder that is estimated to take some 5,000 lives annually, one tenth of which are men.

What sets honor killings apart from crimes of passion is the heroic status that is conferred on the murderer and his family or accomplices. The murder confers glory; it redeems honor lost.

What has been less well researched and documented is the pain and sorrow that persons caught in the grip of a cultural tradition that requires them even to kill for honor's sake, short of other solutions, or experience. Nebile's story was for me an eye opener onto a closed world, a child's world that was unhinged in the battle that adults waged. There are no winners or losers here, and no rascals, only deeply vexed human beings. This is the point of the story I have told: To see beyond "culture" and "identity" we need to hear people's voices, both the more powerful, the relatively silent ones, and the voices that cannot speak in the public space. Nebile has spoken in public only because I "rescued" her voice from the police report where it lingered. Would that it was for good, that she will not come to regret my taking advantage of the very special Swedish publicity laws to publish a part of her testimony to the police, and that in a language that cannot do justice to her own way of thinking and speaking.

From what I know from her sister Songül, Nebile is doing well. She lives alone with her mother and is given much more freedom than her elder sisters ever had. Songül has been reconciled with the family. But unlike Nebile, she will not visit her father in jail. Life moves on.

Tradition, not religion, is the culprit in the story I have told. Traditions that justify violence in the name of honor are found across religious communities of Hindus, Muslims, Christians, Confucians, and among secular people as well (see Abdo, 2004; Bearak, 1999; Chakravarti, 2005; Ginat, 1997; Htun, 2000; Kim, 2000; Tsering, 2001). Nor do all Muslims or Hindus support a violent honor code; it is found only in some communities within different religious or secular traditions.

But it does untold damage where it is found, which is why it must be addressed and counteracted.

As this is being written (July 2006) Denmark has just passed a historical verdict: Nine persons were found guilty of being complicit in the murder of an 18-year-old girl, Ghazala Khan. As in Fadime's case, Ghazala had fallen in love with the wrong man. She was Danish–Pakistani, he was Afghani–Danish. Her family had lived in Denmark for 30 years, and was very well off. He was a refugee, a newcomer to the scene, and a poor man at that. They met on a plane to Pakistan, and kept up relations by e-mail and SMS, until Ghazala, panicking that her family would marry her off to a cousin, eloped with Emal Khan and married him. It was a short-lived marriage. She was killed two days later by her brother in broad daylight at a train station. Her husband was shot too, and barely survived.

What is historic about the verdict is that the evidence was found sufficient to convict not just the murderer but also the one who passed the death sentence (Ghazala's father) and seven other persons, including four family members who collaborated in the planning of the murder. The harshest sentence was not given to the murderer (the brother), but to the man who ordered the murder (the father).

Just about the same time, Sweden and Germany failed to have the apparent collaborators in similar cases convicted. A well-known case is that of Hatun Sürücü in Berlin, a 23-year-old mother of a young son who was shot dead by her three brothers: Only the youngest, a minor, was convicted. The victim and culprit were German-born, of Turkish-Kurdish origin. Her offense was having divorced her violent husband from an arranged marriage, who was also her cousin, and of having become "too German"; she dressed like a German and was about to finish her education as an electrician. The verdict has been appealed. Because he was a minor, the murderer received a mild sentence (nine years in a youth institution).

In Sweden, the day before the verdict in the Ghazala case, the verdict was passed in an honor killing where an Afghani boy was murdered in a bestial way by his girlfriend's brother, with the latter's parents watching (or even participating). Again, for lack of evidence, only the young boy was convicted. Again, because he was a minor, the sentence was mild (four years in a youth institution).

The point here is not to go into these cases, but their historical timing so adjacent to the Danish Ghazala case, invites a comparison. What bears mention is that behind the tragedies that are making headlines as honor killings and increasingly treated as such in European courts are people braving resistance and standing up against traditions that truly jeopardize life and liberty. It means, there is hope.

Even a 13-year-old's grappling with issues of right and wrong in the wake of her sister's murder by her beloved father is a voice worth heeding for what it reveals of a sense of justice and compassion. It is the young generation that will shape the face of Europe. Hope lies in their being able increasingly to craft complex identities and to allow others to do so too.

That's where the hope for humanity lies, as writers as eminent as Amin Maalouf (1998) and Amartya Sen (2006) have both urged: in our recognizing the individual integrity and complexity of one another as full-fledged human beings.

REFERENCES

Abdo, N. (2004). Honour killing, patriarchy, and the state: Women in Israel. In S. Mojab & N. Abdo (Eds.), *Violence in the name of honour: Theoretical and political challenges* (pp. 57–90). Istanbul: Bilgi University Press.

Akkoc, N. (2004). The cultural basis of violence in the name of honour. In S. Mojab & N. Abdo (Eds.), *Violence in the name of honour: Theoretical and political challenges* (pp. 113–126). Istanbul: Bilgi University Press.

Älgamo, K. Å. (2004). Confronting honour violence: The Swedish police at work. In S. Mojab & N. Abdo (Eds.), *Violence in the name of honour: Theoretical and political challenges* (pp. 203–210). Istanbul: Bilgi University Press.

Bearak, B. (1999, April 9). A tale of 2 lovers and a taboo recklessly flouted. *New York Times International*.

Begikhani, N. (2005). Honour-based violence among the Kurds: The case of Iraqi Kurdistan. In L. Welchman & S. Hossein (Eds.), *"Honour": Crimes, paradigms, and violence against women* (pp. 209–229). London and New York: Zed Books.

Bergh, L. (2004). Swedish government initiatives to help young people at risk of honour-related violence. In S. Mojab & N. Abdo (Eds.), *Violence in the name of honour: Theoretical and political challenges* (pp. 193–202). Istanbul: Bilgi University Press.

Carlbom, A. (2003). *The imagined versus the real other: Multiculturalism and the representation of Muslims in Sweden.* Lund: Department of Sociology, Lund University.

Chakravarti, U. (2005). From fathers to husbands: Of love, death and marriage in North India. In L. Welchman & S. Hossein (Eds.), *"Honour": Crimes, paradigms, and violence against women* (pp. 308–331). London and New York: Zed books.

Connors, J. (2005). United Nations approaches to "crimes of honour." In L. Welchman & S. Hossein (Eds.), *"Honour": Crimes, paradigms, and violence against women* (pp. 22–41). London and New York: Zed Books.

Das, V. (1995). *Critical events: An anthropological perspective on contemporary India*. New Delhi: Oxford University Press.

Eldén, Å. (2004). Life-and-death honour: Young women's violent stories about reputation, virginity and honour – in a Swedish context. In S. Mojab & N. Abdo (Eds.), *Violence in the name of honour: Theoretical and political challenges* (pp. 91–100). Istanbul: Bilgi University Press.

Ginat, J. (1997). *Blood revenge: Family honor, mediation, and outcasting.* Brighton: Sussex Academic Press.

Hjärpe, J. (2003). Hedersmord. Nationalencyklopedin http://www.ne.se/isp/search/article.isp?i art id=491725

Htun, M. (2000). Culture, institutions and gender inequality in Latin America. In S. Mojab & N. Abdo (Eds.), *Culture Matters* (pp. 189–201). New York: Bantam Books.

Kertzer, D. I. (1993). *Sacrificed for honour: Italian infant abandonment and the politics of reproductive control.* Boston: Beacon Press.

Kim, E. (2000). *Ten thousand sorrows: The extraordinary journey of a Korean War orphan.* London: Bantam Books.

Maalouf, A. (1998). *Les identités meurtrières.* Paris: Grasset & Fasquelle.

Mernissi, F. (1994). *Dreams of trespass: Tales of a harem girlhood.* Reading, MA: Addison-Wesley.

Mojab, S. (2004). The particularity of "honour" and the universality of "killing." In S. Mojab & N. Abdo (Eds.), *Violence in the name of honour: Theoretical and political challenges* (pp. 15–38). Istanbul: Bilgi University Press.

Nussbaum, M. (1999). *Sex and social justice.* New York: Oxford University Press.

Pitt-Rivers, J. (1965). Honour and social status. In J. G. Peristiany (Ed.), *Honour and shame: The values of Mediterranean society* (pp. 9–77). London: Weidenfeld and Nicholson.

Sen, A. (2006). *Identity and violence: The illusion of destiny.* New York: W.W. Norton.

Stewart, F. H. (1994). *Honor.* Chicago: University of Chicago Press.

SVT1 (1998). "Striptease." Samhällsmagasin. Reporter Marianne Spanner. First featured on May 6.

Swanberg, L. K. (2002). *Hedersmordet på Pela: Lillasystern berättar.* Stockholm: Bokförlaget.

Tsering, D. (2001). *Dalai Lama, my son: A mother's story.* London: Virgin.

Turiel, E. (2002). *The culture of morality: Social development, context, and conflict.* New York: Cambridge University Press.

Welchman, L., & Hossein, S. (2005). Introduction: "honour," rights and wrongs. In L. Welchman & S. Hossein (Eds.), *"Honour": crimes, paradigms, and violence against women* (pp. 1–21). London and New York: Zed Books.

Wikan, U. (1984). Shame and honour: A contestable pair. *Man, 19,* 635–652.

Wikan, U. (1991). *Behind the veil in Arabia: Women in Oman.* Chicago: University of Chicago Press.

Wikan, U. (1996). *Tomorrow, God willing: Self-made destinies in Cairo.* Chicago: University of Chicago Press.

Wikan, U. (2002). *Generous betrayal: Politics of culture in the New Europe.* Chicago: University of Chicago Press.

Wikan, U. (2003). *For ærens skyld: Fadime til ettertanke.* Oslo: Universitetsforlaget.

Wikan, U. (2004a). *En fråga om heder.* Stockholm: Ordfront.

Wikan, U. (2004b). Deadly distrust: Honor killings and Swedish multiculturalism. In R. Hardin (Ed.), *Distrust* (pp. 192–204). New York: Russell Sage Foundation.

Wikan, U. (in press). *For honor's sake: Fadime's legacy.* Chicago: University of Chicago Press.

9

IN DEFENSE OF UNIVERSAL VALUES*

Martha Nussbaum

I found myself beautiful as a free human mind.

Mrinal, in Rabindranath Tagore's *Letter From a Wife*

It is obvious that the human eye gratifies itself in a way different from the crude, non-human eye; the human ear different from the crude ear, etc....The sense caught up in crude practical need has only a restricted sense. For the starving man, it is not the human form of food that exists, but only its abstract being as food; it could just as well be there in its crudest form, and it would be impossible to say wherein this feeding activity differs from that of animals.

Karl Marx, *Economic and Philosophical Manuscripts of 1844*

I

Ahmedabad, in Gujarat, is the textile mill city where Mahatma Gandhi organized labor in accordance with his principles of nonviolent resistance. Tourists visit it for its textile museum and its Gandhi ashram. But today it attracts attention, too, as the home of another resistance movement: the Self-Employed Women's Association (SEWA), with

---

* Parts of this chapter were first published in M. Nussbaum (2000), *Women and human development: The capabilities approach*. Cambridge University Press.

more than 50,000 members, which for over 20 years has been helping female workers to improve their living conditions through credit, education, and a labor union. On one side of the polluted river that bisects the city is the shabby old building where SEWA was first established, now used as offices for staff. On the other side are the education offices and the SEWA bank, newly housed in a marble office building. All the customers and all the employees are women.

Vasanti sits on the floor in the meeting room of the old office building, where SEWA members meet to consult with staff. A tiny dark woman in her early thirties, she wears an attractive electric blue sari, and her long hair is wound neatly into a bun on the top of her head. Soft and round, she seems more comfortable sitting than walking. Her teeth are uneven and discolored, but otherwise she looks in reasonable health. Marty tells me later she is a Rajput, that is, of good caste; I've never figured out how one would know that. She has come with her older (and lower-caste) friend Kokila, maker of clay pots and a janitor at the local conference hall, a tall fiery community organizer who helps the police identify cases of domestic violence. Vasanti speaks quietly, looking down often as she speaks, but there is animation in her eyes.

Vasanti's husband was a gambler and an alcoholic. He used the household money to get drunk, and when he ran out of that money he got a vasectomy in order to take the cash incentive payment offered by local government. So Vasanti has no children to help her. Eventually, as her husband became more abusive, she could live with him no longer and returned to her own family. Her father, who used to make Singer sewing machine parts, had died, but her brothers ran an auto parts business in what used to be his shop. Using a machine that used to be her father's, and living in the shop itself, she earned a small income making eyeholes for the hooks on sari tops. Her brothers got her a lawyer to take her husband to court for maintenance—quite an unusual step in her economic class—but the case has dragged on for years with no conclusion in sight. Meanwhile, her brothers also gave her a loan to get the machine that rolls the edges of the sari; but she didn't like being dependent on them, because they were married and had children, and might not want to support her much longer.

With the help of SEWA, therefore, she got a bank loan of her own to pay back the brothers, and by now she has paid back almost all of the SEWA loan. Usually, she says, women lack unity, and rich women take advantage of poor women. In SEWA, by contrast, she has found a sense of community. She clearly finds pleasure in the company of Kokila, a woman of very different social class and temperament.

By now, Vasanti is animated; she is looking us straight in the eye, and her voice is strong and clear. "Women in India have a lot of pain," she says. "And I, I have had quite a lot of sorrow in my life. But from the pain, our strength is born. Now that we are doing better ourselves, we want to do some good for other women, to feel that we are good human beings."

Jayamma* stands outside her hut in the wilting heat of a late March day in Trivandrum. The first thing you notice about her is the straightness of her back, and the muscular strength of her movements. Her teeth are falling out, her eyesight seems clouded, and her hair is thin, but she could be a captain of the regiment, ordering her troops into battle. It doesn't surprise me that her history speaks of fierce quarrels with her children and her neighbors. Her jaw juts out as she chews tobacco. An Ezhava—a lower but not "scheduled" caste—Jayamma loses out two ways, lacking good social standing but ineligible for the affirmative action programs established by government for the lowest castes. She still lives in a squatter's colony on some government land on the outskirts of Trivandrum.

For approximately 45 years, until her recent retirement, Jayamma went every day to the brick kiln and spent eight hours a day carrying bricks on her head, 500 to 700 bricks per day. (She never earned more than five rupees a day, and employment depends upon weather.) Jayamma balanced a plank on her head, stacked 20 bricks at a time on the plank, and then walked rapidly, balancing the bricks by the strength of her neck, to the kiln, where she then had to unload the bricks without twisting her neck, handing them two by two to the man who loads the kiln.

Men in the brick industry typically do this sort of heavy labor for a while, and then graduate to the skilled (but less arduous) tasks of brick molding and kiln loading, which they can continue into middle and advanced ages. Those jobs pay up to twice as much, although they are less dangerous and lighter. Women are never considered for these promotions and are never permitted to learn the skills involved. Like most small businesses in India, the brick kiln is defined as a cottage industry and thus its workers are not protected by any union. All workers are badly paid, but women suffer special disabilities. Jayamma felt she had a bad deal, but she didn't see any way of changing it.

---

* Unlike Vasanti, Jayamma has already been studied in the development economics literature; see Gulati (1981, 1997). I am very grateful to Leela Gulati for introducing me to Jayamma and her family and for translating.

Thus in her middle 60s, unable to perform the physically taxing job of brick carrying, Jayamma has no employment on which to fall back. She refuses to become a domestic servant, because in her community such work is considered shameful and degrading. Jayamma adds a political explanation: "As a servant, your alliance is with a class that is your enemy." A widow, she is unable to collect a widows' pension from the government: The village office told her that she was ineligible because she has able-bodied sons, although in fact her sons refuse to support her. Despite all these reversals (and others), Jayamma is tough, defiant, and healthy. She doesn't seem interested in talking, but she shows her visitors around, and makes sure that they are offered lime juice and water.

Jayamma and Vasanti have been raised in a nation in which women are formally the equals of men, with equal political rights and nominally equal social and employment opportunities. (Discrimination on the basis of sex is outlawed by the Indian Constitution itself.) Both, however, have suffered from deprivations that do arise from sex: problems of discrimination in education and employment, problems of male nonsupport, indolence in the case of Jayamma, and domestic abuse and alcoholism in the case of Vasanti. The problems they face are particular to the social situation of women in particular caste and regional circumstances in India.

One can't understand Jayamma's choices and constraints without understanding, at many different levels of specificity and generality, how she is socially placed: what it means to be an Ezhava rather than a Pulaya, what it means that she lives in Kerala rather than some other state, or what it means that she is in the city rather than a rural area. One can't understand Vasanti without understanding the double bind of being both upper caste—with lots of rules limiting what it's proper to do—and very poor, with few opportunities to do nice proper things that bring in a living. One also can't understand her story without knowing about family planning programs in Gujarat, the progress of the SEWA movement, or the background Gandhian tradition of self-sufficiency on which the Gujarati women's movement draws. No doubt all this particularity shapes the inner life of each, in ways that it's hard for an outsider to begin to understand.

On the other hand, their problems are not altogether and unrecognizably different from problems of many women (and many poor people generally) in many parts of the world. In the intense desire of both women for independence and economic self-sufficiency, the desire of both to have some money and property in their own name, these are efforts common to women in many parts of the world. The body that labors is the same body all over the world, and its needs for food and nutrition and health care are the same, so it's not too surprising that the female manual laborer in Trivandrum is in some ways comparable to a female manual laborer in Beijing or even Chicago, that she doesn't seem to have an utterly alien consciousness or an identity unrecognizably strange, strange though the circumstances are in which her consciousness takes root. Similarly the body that gets beaten is in a sense the same all over the world, concrete though the circumstances of domestic violence are in each society.

Even what is most apparently strange in the circumstances of each is also, at another level, not so unfamiliar. We find it pretty odd that the brick kiln makes women do all the heavy jobs and then pays them less, but many forms of sex discrimination in employment exhibit similar forms of irrationality. Again, the fact that a woman as strong and resourceful as Vasanti doesn't want to go to school seems odd, but of course it isn't so surprising, given that she doesn't see any signs of a better way of life that she could get by becoming educated. How to think well about what is similar and what different in these lives: that is the task I begin to undertake in this chapter.

II

An international feminism that is going to have any critical bite quickly gets involved in making normative recommendations that cross boundaries of culture, nation, religion, race, and class. It will therefore need to find descriptive and normative concepts adequate to that task (for earlier articulations of my views on matters contained in this chapter, see Nussbaum, 1988, 1990, 1992, 1993, 1995a, 1995b, 1998, 1999a). This enterprise is fraught with peril, both intellectual and political. Where do these categories come from, it will be asked. And how can they be justified as appropriate ones for lives in which those categories themselves are not explicitly recognized? The suspicion uneasily grows that the theorist is imposing something on people who surely have their own ideas of what is right and proper. And this suspicion grates all the more unpleasantly when we remind ourselves that theorists often come from nations that have been oppressors, or from classes in poorer nations that are themselves unusually privileged. Isn't all this philosophizing, then, simply one more exercise in colonial or class domination?

Now of course no normative political theory uses terms that are straightforwardly those of ordinary daily life. If it did, it probably could not perform its special task as theory, which involves the systematization and critical scrutiny of intuitions that in daily life are often unexamined. Theory gives people a set of terms with which to criticize abuses that otherwise might lurk nameless in the background. Jayamma's use of the Marxian language of class struggle is just one obvious example of this point.

But even if one defends theoretical abstractions as valuable for practice, it may still be problematic to use concepts that originated in a culture that has colonized and oppressed the culture that one is describing. Attempts by international feminists today to use a universal language of justice and human rights frequently encounter charges of Westernizing and colonizing, even when the universal categories are used by feminists who live and work within the nation in question itself. In one way, the charge of "Westernizing" is obviously a cheap political trick, of the sort involved when Lee Kuan Yew says that "the East" doesn't value freedom: a way of discrediting opponents who are pressing for change.

Applied to India, such a claim about women's rights and liberties is not only cheap, but also unconvincing. It ignores tremendous chunks of reality, including indigenous movements for women's education, for the end of *purdah*, and for women's political participation, that gained strength straight through the 19th and early 20th centuries in both Hindu and Muslim traditions, in some ways running ahead of British and U.S. feminist movements (for overviews, see Ahmad, 1983; Devji, 1994; Metcalf, 1994).* And it ignores the founding of the Indian nation itself, where sex equality was adopted by overwhelming consensus in 1951, as among the Fundamental Rights, something the United States, of course, has been unable to do. We need to remind ourselves that sex equality is an Indian constitutional idea and it is not an American constitutional idea. How condescending to suggest that in striving for it Nehru and Ambedkar were dupes of Western colonial thinking.

On the other hand, when we propose a universal framework to assess women's quality of life, we face three more respectable arguments that deserve to be seriously answered.

First is an argument from culture. A more subtle and sincere version of the anti-Westernizing argument, it says that Indian culture contains powerful norms of female modesty, deference, obedience, and self-sacrifice that have defined women's lives for centuries, in both Hindu

---

* For the special situation of Bengal, which in some ways developed progressive educational ideas earlier than other regions, under the influence of the reforms of Rammohun Roy and the Brahmo movement, see Bardhan (1990) and Sarkar (1979). Both in East and West Bengal, schools for girls were well established by 1850, and Bethune College, which opened in 1849, in 1888 became the first college in India to teach women through the MA level.

and Muslim tradition. Feminists should not assume without argument that those are bad norms, incapable of constructing good and flourishing lives for women. Western women are not so happy, with their high divorce rate and their exhausting careerism. They condescend to third-world women when they assume that only lives like their own can be fruitful.

My full answer to this point emerges from the proposal I make, which certainly does not preclude any woman's choice to lead a traditional life, as long as she does so with certain economic and political opportunities firmly in place. But the objection, once again, oversimplifies tradition, ignoring countertraditions of female defiance and strength, ignoring women's protests against harmful traditions, and in general forgetting to ask women themselves what they think of these norms, which are typically purveyed, in tradition, through male texts and the authority of male religious and cultural leaders, against a background of almost total economic disempowerment for women.

Neither Vasanti nor Jayamma comes close to defending such traditions. Philosopher Uma Narayan had a middle-class upbringing that did endorse traditions of female submissiveness, silence, and purity, and yet, she records, she heard from her mother, all the while, a constant stream of highly articulate protest against the misery such confining traditions had caused. "The shape your 'silence' took," she addresses her mother, "is in part what has incited me to speech." It would be mistaken to describe only the official teaching as Indian tradition, ignoring the protest.

The argument from culture shows us, then, that we should be ready to learn from what we see and to treat seriously any cultural proposal that has serious support. It does not, and could not, show that there is a single norm of modesty and subservience that is "the Indian tradition." Cultures are scenes of debate, so appealing to culture gives us questions rather than answers. It certainly doesn't show that universal norms are a bad answer to those questions.

Let us now consider the argument that I call the argument from the good of diversity. This argument reminds us that our world is rich in part because we don't all agree on a single set of practices and norms. We think the world's different languages have worth and beauty, and that it's a bad thing, diminishing the expressive resources of human life generally, if any language should cease to exist. So too, cultural systems each have a distinctive beauty, and that it would be an impoverished world if everyone took on the value system of America.

Here we should distinguish two claims the objector might be making. She might be claiming that diversity is good as such, or she might simply be saying that there are problems with the value system of America, and that it would be too bad if the rest of the world emulated our materialism and aggressiveness. This second claim, of course, doesn't yet say anything against universal values; it just suggests that their content should be critical of some American values. So the real challenge to our enterprise lies in the first claim. To meet it we must ask how far cultural diversity really is like linguistic diversity, or the diversity of species. The trouble with the analogy is that languages don't harm people, and cultural practices frequently do. We could think that Cornish or Breton should be preserved, without thinking the same about domestic violence.

In the end, then, the objection doesn't undermine the search for universal values, it requires it: for what it invites us to ask is, whether the cultural values in question are among the ones worth preserving, and this entails at least a very general universal framework of assessment, one that will tell us what is and is not beyond the pale. I offer just such a very general framework, one that allows a great deal of latitude for diversity, but one that also sets up some general benchmarks that will tell us when we are better off letting a practice die out. Traditional practices such as the division of labor in Jayamma's brick kiln site, or Vasanti's husband's highly traditional practice of wife-beating are not worth preserving simply because they are there, or because they are old. To make a case for preserving them, we have to assess the contribution they make and the harm they do. And this requires a set of values that gives us a critical purchase on cultural particulars. The argument gives us reasons to preserve types of diversity that are compatible with human dignity and other basic values; but it does not undermine and even supports our search for a general universal framework of critical assessment.

Finally, we have the argument from paternalism. This argument says that when we use a set of universal norms as benchmarks for the world's varied societies, we show too little respect for people's freedom as agents (and, in a related way, their role as democratic citizens). People are the best judges of what is good for them, and if we say that their own choices are not good for them we treat them like children. This is an important point, and one that any viable cross-cultural proposal should bear firmly in mind. But it hardly seems incompatible with the endorsement of universal values. Indeed, it appears to endorse explicitly at least some universal values, such as the value of the political liberties and other opportunities for choice. Thinking about paternalism gives us a strong reason to respect the variety of ways citizens actually choose to lead their lives in a pluralistic society and therefore to prefer a form of universalism that is compatible with freedom and choice of the most significant sorts. But such respect naturally leads us to value religious toleration, associative freedom, and the other major liberties. These liberties are themselves universal values, and they are not compatible with views that many real people and societies hold.

We can make a further claim: Many existing value systems are themselves highly paternalistic, particularly toward women. They treat them as unequal under the law, as lacking full civil capacity, as not having the property rights, associative liberties, and employment rights of males. If we encounter a system like this, it is in one sense paternalistic to say, sorry, that is unacceptable under the universal norms of equality and liberty that we would like to defend. In that way, any bill of rights is "paternalistic" vis-à-vis families, or groups, or practices, or even pieces of legislation, that treat people with insufficient or unequal respect. The Indian Constitution is in that sense paternalistic when it tells people that it is from now on illegal to use caste or sex as grounds of discrimination. But that is hardly a good argument against fundamental constitutional rights or, more generally, against opposing the attempts of some people to tyrannize over others. We dislike paternalism because there is something else that we like, namely liberty of choice in fundamental matters. It is fully consistent to reject some forms of paternalism while supporting those that underwrite these basic values.

Nor does the protection of choice require only a formal defense of basic liberties. The various liberties of choice have material preconditions, in whose absence there is merely a simulacrum of choice. Jayamma in a sense had the choice to go to school, but the economic circumstances of her life made this impossible. Nothing told Vasanti she couldn't have economic independence from her brothers, but in the absence of the SEWA bank, the independence she now enjoys would not have been available to her. Children in the desert areas of Andhra Pradesh have the right to go to school, but there aren't any schools or teachers, because nobody has decided to spend money on creating them. All women in India have equal rights under the Constitution, but in the absence of effective enforcement, and of programs targeted at increasing female literacy, economic empowerment, and employment opportunities, those rights are not real to them. In short, liberty is not just a matter of having rights on paper; it requires being in a position to exercise those rights. And this requires material resources.

The state that is going to guarantee people rights effectively is going to have to recognize universal norms beyond the small menu of basic rights: It will have to take a stand about the redistribution of wealth and income, about employment, land rights, health, and education. That requires yet more universalism and in a sense paternalism, but we could hardly say that the children of rural Andhra Pradesh, living in a state of virtual anarchy, with no water, no buses, and no teacher, are especially free to do as they wish.

The argument from paternalism indicates, then, that we should prefer a universal normative account that allows people plenty of liberty to pursue their own conceptions of value, within limits set by the protection of the equal worth of the liberties of others. It does not give us any good reason not to endorse any universal account, and some strong reasons why we should do so, including in our account, not only the liberties themselves, but also forms of economic empowerment that are crucial in making the liberties truly available to people.

And the argument suggests one thing more: that the account we search for should preserve liberties and opportunities for each and every person, taken one by one, respecting each of them as an end, rather than simply as the agent or supporter of ends of others. Women are too often treated as members of an organic unit such as the family or the community and their interests subordinated to the larger goals of that unit, which means, typically, those of its male members. However, Gujarat's impressive economic growth meant nothing to Vasanti as long as her husband deprived her of control over resources. We need to consider not just the aggregate, whether in a region or in a family; we need to consider the distribution of resources and opportunities to each individual, thinking of each as an end.

Veena Das has claimed that Indian women lack this intuitive idea that each person has her own dignity and well-being, distinct from that of the family. If this claim simply means that Indian women frequently judge sacrifice for the family to be a good thing and frequently subordinate their own well-being to the well-being of others, it is plausible enough, but hardly an objection to the concern for the individual that I recommend; there is no incompatibility between the idea that politics should treat each person as an end and the idea that some people choose to make sacrifices for others.

If, however, Das really means to say that Indian women can't tell their own hunger apart from the hunger of a child or a husband, can't really distinguish their own body and its health from someone else's body and its health, then what she says just seems false. Jayamma certainly in some ways puts others first and herself second. She takes sugar in her tea, for example, while she allows her husband and her children to take the more expensive milk. But even in that act she is distinguishing her own well-being from that of others; in general, she budgets the family account with intense awareness of the separateness of its various people, asking how much shall be spent on each one. Indeed, we might say that the poorer people are the more likely they are to be keenly aware of the separateness of their well-being, for hunger and hard physical labor are great reminders that one is oneself and not someone else. Bengali author Manik Bandyopadhyay (1990) put it this way in his story, "A Female Problem at a Low Level":

> A slum girl and daughter of a laborer cannot mentally depend on her father or brother, like the daughters of the babu families who even as grown women see individual disaster in any family mishap. She is used to fending for herself, relying on her own wits. (p. 155)

In other words, forgetting about distinctions of well-being in the family is an upper middle class privilege, alien to those who are really struggling to survive.

III

Let me recapitulate. The argument from culture reminded us that we should leave space for women who may wish to choose a traditional hierarchical way of life. But it said nothing against using a universal account to criticize unjust cultural practices; indeed, we were reminded that the activity of criticism is deeply internal to Indian culture itself.

The argument from the good of diversity told us something important about any proposal we should endorse: that it ought to provide spaces in which valuably different forms of human activity can flourish. We should not stamp out diversity, or even put it at risk, without a very strong reason. But in light of the fact that some traditional practices are harmful and evil and some actively hostile to other elements of a diverse culture, we are forced by our interest in diversity itself to develop a set of criteria against which to assess the practices we find, asking which are acceptable and worth preserving, and which are not.

As for the argument from paternalism, it nudges us strongly in the direction of what might be called political rather than comprehensive liberalism, in the sense that it urges us to respect the many different conceptions of the good that citizens may have and to foster a political climate in which they will each be able to pursue the good (whether religious or ethical) according to their own lights. In other words, we want universals that are facilitative rather than tyrannical,* that create spaces for choice rather than dragooning people into a desired total mode of functioning. But understood at its best, the paternalism argument is not an argument against cross-cultural universals. For it is all about respect for the dignity of persons as choosers. This respect requires us to defend universally a wide range of liberties, plus their material conditions, and to defend them for each and every person.

Another way of seeing why universal norms are badly needed in the international policy arena is to consider what the alternative has typically been. The most prevalent approach to measuring quality of life in a nation used to be simply to ask about GNP per capita. This approach tries to weasel out of making any universal claims about what has value, although, notice that it does assume the universal value of opulence. What it omits, however, is much more significant. We are not even told about the distribution of wealth and income, and countries with similar aggregate figures can exhibit great distributional variations. Circus girl Sissy Jupe, in Dickens's *Hard Times*, already saw the problem with this absence of normative concern for the individual; she says that the economic approach doesn't tell her "who has got the money and whether any of it is mine."

So too with Jayamma and Vasanti. The fact that Gujarat is in general a much more prosperous state than Kerala is only a part of the story; it doesn't tell us what government has done for each of them, or how they are doing. To know that, we'd need to look at their lives; but then we need to specify, beyond distribution of wealth and income itself, what parts of lives we ought to look at, such as life expectancy, infant mortality, educational opportunities, health care, employment opportunities, land rights, and political liberties. Seeing what is absent from the GNP account nudges us sharply in the direction of mapping out these and other basic goods in a universal way, so that we can use the list of basic goods to compare quality of life across societies.

A further problem with all resource-based approaches, even those that are sensitive to distribution, is that individuals vary in their ability to convert resources into functionings. Some of these differences are straightforwardly physical. Nutritional needs vary with age, occupation, and sex. A pregnant or lactating woman needs more nutrients than a nonpregnant woman. A child needs more protein than an adult. A person whose limbs work well needs few resources to be mobile, whereas a person with paralyzed limbs needs many more resources to

---

* For the charge that international human rights norms are tyrannical, see Brown (1995).

achieve the same level of mobility. Many such variations can escape our notice if we live in a prosperous nation that can afford to bring all individuals to a high level of physical attainment; in the developing world we must be highly alert to these variations in need.

Again, some of the pertinent variations are social, connected with traditional hierarchies. If we wish to bring all citizens of a nation to the same level of educational attainment, we will need to devote more resources to those who encounter obstacles from traditional hierarchy or prejudice: thus, women's literacy will prove more expensive than men's literacy in many parts of the world. If we operate only with an index of resources, we will frequently reinforce inequalities that are highly relevant to well-being.

IV

I now argue that a reasonable answer to all these concerns—capable of giving good guidance to government establishing basic constitutional principles and to international agencies assessing the quality of life—is given by a version of the capabilities approach, an approach to quality of life assessment pioneered within economics by Amartya Sen (1980), and by now highly influential through the *Human Development Reports* of the UNDP (1993, 1994, 1995, 1996). My own version of this approach is in several ways different from Sen's; I simply lay out my view as I would currently defend it.

The central question asked by the capabilities approach is not, "How satisfied is Vasanti?" or even "How much in the way of resources is she able to command?" It is, instead, "What is Vasanti actually able to do and to be?" Taking a stand for political purposes on a working list of functions that would appear to be of central importance in human life, users of this approach ask, "Is the person capable of this, or not?" They ask not only about the person's satisfaction with what she does, but about what she does, and what she is in a position to do (what her opportunities and liberties are). They ask not just about the resources that are present, but about how those do or do not go to work, enabling Vasanti to function.

The intuitive idea behind the approach is twofold: first, that there are certain functions that are particularly central in human life, in the sense that their presence or absence is typically understood to be a mark of the presence or absence of human life. Second, and this is what Marx found in Aristotle, that there is something that it is to do these functions in a truly human way, not a merely animal way. We judge, frequently enough, that a life has been so impoverished that it is not worthy of the dignity of the human being, that it is a life in which one goes on living, but more or less like an animal, not being able to develop and exercise one's human powers.

In Marx's example, a starving person doesn't use food in a fully human way, by which I think he means a way infused by practical reasoning and sociability. He or she just grabs at the food in order to survive, and the many social and rational ingredients of human feeding can't make their appearance. Similarly, the senses of a human being can operate at a merely animal level, if they are not cultivated by appropriate education, by leisure for play and self-expression, by valuable associations with others, and we should add to the list some items that Marx probably would not endorse, such as expressive and associational liberty and the freedom of worship. The core idea seems to be that of the human being as a dignified free being who shapes his or her own life, rather than being passively shaped or pushed around by the world in the manner of a "flock" or "herd."*

At one extreme, we may judge that the absence of capability for a central function is so acute that the person isn't really a human being at all, or any longer, as in the case of certain very severe forms of mental disability, or senile dementia. But I am less interested in that boundary (important though it is for medical ethics) than in a higher one, the level at which a person's capability is "truly human," that is, worthy of a human being. Note that this idea contains, thus, a reference to an idea of human worth or dignity. Marx was departing from Kant in some important respects, by stressing (along with Aristotle) that the major powers of a human being need material support and cannot be what they are without it. But he also learned from Kant, and his way of expressing his Aristotelian heritage is distinctively shaped by the Kantian notion of the inviolability and the dignity of the person.

Notice that the approach makes each person a bearer of value, and an end. Marx, like his bourgeois forebears, holds that it is profoundly wrong to subordinate the ends of some individuals to those of others. That is at the core of what exploitation is, to treat a person as a mere object for the use of others. What this approach is after is a society in

---

* Compare Amartya Sen (1994), "The importance of political rights for the understanding of economic needs turns ultimately on seeing human beings as people with rights to exercise, not as parts of a 'stock' or a 'population' that passively exists and must be looked after" (p. 38).

which individuals are treated as each worthy of regard and in which each has been put in a position to live really humanly.

I think we can produce an account of these necessary elements of truly human functioning that commands a broad cross-cultural consensus. Although this list of basic capabilities is somewhat different in both structure and substance from Rawls's list of primary goods, it is offered in a similar, political-liberal spirit: as a list that can be endorsed for political purposes by people who otherwise have very different views of what a complete good life for a human being would be. (In part, as we show, this is because the list is a list of capabilities or opportunities for functioning, rather than of actual functions; in part it is because the list leaves spaces for people to pursue other functions that they value.) The list is supposed to provide a focus for quality of life assessment and for political planning, and it aims to select capabilities that are of central importance in any human life, whatever else the person pursues or chooses. They therefore have a special claim to be supported for political purposes in a pluralistic society.*

The list represents the result of years of cross-cultural discussion, and comparisons between earlier and later versions will show that the input of other voices has shaped its content in many ways. Thus it represents a type of overlapping consensus on the part of people with otherwise very different views of human life. It remains open-ended and humble; it can always be contested and remade. Nor does it deny that the items on the list are to some extent differently constructed by different societies. Indeed part of the idea of the list is that its members can be more concretely specified in accordance with local beliefs and circumstances. Here is the current version of the list.**

---

* Obviously, I am thinking of the political more broadly than does Rawls, for whom the nation state remains the basic unit. I am envisaging not only domestic deliberations but also cross-cultural quality of life assessments and other forms of international deliberation and planning.

** The current version of the list reflects changes made as a result of my discussions with people in India. The primary changes are a greater emphasis on bodily integrity and control over one's environment, and a new emphasis on dignity and nonhumiliation. Oddly, these features of human "self-sufficiency" and the dignity of the person are the ones most often criticized by Western feminists as "male" and "Western," one reason for their more muted role in earlier versions of the list (see Nussbaum, 1999b).

Central Human Functional Capabilities

1. *Life.* Being able to live to the end of a human life of normal length; not dying prematurely, or before one's life is so reduced as to be not worth living.
2. *Bodily Health.* Being able to have good health, including reproductive health;* to be adequately nourished; to have adequate shelter.
3. *Bodily Integrity.* Being able to move freely from place to place; to be secure against violent assault, including sexual assault and domestic violence; having opportunities for sexual satisfaction and for choice in matters of reproduction.
4. *Senses, Imagination, and Thought.* Being able to use the senses, to imagine, think, and reason, and to do these things in a "truly human" way, a way informed and cultivated by an adequate education, including, but by no means limited to, literacy and basic mathematical and scientific training. Being able to use imagination and thought in connection with experiencing and producing works and events of one's own choice, religious, literary, musical, and so forth. Being able to use one's mind in ways protected by guarantees of freedom of expression with respect to both political and artistic speech, and freedom of religious exercise. Being able to have pleasurable experiences, and to avoid nonnecessary pain.
5. *Emotions.* Being able to have attachments to things and people outside ourselves; to love those who love and care for us, to grieve at their absence; in general, to love, to grieve, to experience longing, gratitude, and justified anger. Not having one's emotional development blighted by fear and anxiety. Supporting this capability means supporting forms of human association that can be shown to be crucial in their development.

---

* The 1994 International Conference on Population and Development (ICPD) adopted a definition of reproductive health that fits well with the intuitive idea of truly human functioning that guides this list: "Reproductive health is a state of complete physical, mental, and social well-being and not merely the absence of disease or infirmity, in all matters relating to the reproductive system and its processes. Reproductive health therefore implies that people are able to have a satisfying and safe sex life and that they have the capability to reproduce and the freedom to decide if, when, and how often to do so." The definition goes on say that it also implies information and access to family planning methods of their choice. A brief summary of the ICPD's recommendations, adopted by the Panel on Reproductive Health of the Committee on Population established by the National Research Council specifies three requirements of reproductive health: "1. Every sex act should be free of coercion and infection. 2. Every pregnancy should be intended. 3. Every birth should be healthy" (see Tsui, Wasserheit, & Haaga, 1997, p. 14).

6. *Practical Reason.* Being able to form a conception of the good and to engage in critical reflection about the planning of one's life. This entails protection for the liberty of conscience.

7. *Affiliation.*
   a. Being able to live with and toward others, to recognize and show concern for other human beings, to engage in various forms of social interaction; to be able to imagine the situation of another and to have compassion for that situation; to have the capability for both justice and friendship. Protecting this capability means protecting institutions that constitute and nourish such forms of affiliation and also protecting the freedom of assembly and political speech.
   b. Having the social bases of self-respect and nonhumiliation; being able to be treated as a dignified being whose worth is equal to that of others. This entails protections against discrimination on the basis of race, sex, religion, caste, ethnicity, or national origin.*

8. *Other Species.* Being able to live with concern for and in relation to animals, plants, and the world of nature.**

9. *Play.* Being able to laugh, to play, to enjoy recreational activities.

10. *Control Over One's Environment.*
    a. Political. Being able to participate effectively in political choices that govern one's life; having the right of political participation, protections of free speech and association.
    b. Material. Being able to hold property (both land and movable goods); having the right to seek employment on an equal basis with others; having the freedom from unwarranted search and seizure.***

The list is, emphatically, a list of separate components. We cannot satisfy the need for one of them by giving a larger amount of another one. All are of central importance, and all are distinct in quality. The irreducible plurality of the list limits the trade-offs that it will be reasonable to make and thus limits the applicability of quantitative cost-benefit

---

* This provision is based on Indian Constitution Article 15, which adds (as I would) that this should not be taken to prevent government from enacting measures to correct the history of discrimination against women and against the scheduled tribes and castes.

** In terms of cross-cultural development, this has been the most controversial item on the list. It also properly raises the question whether the list ought to be anthropocentric at all, or whether we should seek to promote appropriate capabilities for all living things. I leave these important questions for another occasion.

*** Property rights are distinct from, for example, speech rights, in the sense that property is a tool of human functioning and not an end in itself (Nussbaum, 1990).

analysis. At the same time, the items on the list are related to one another in many complex ways. One of the most effective ways of promoting women's control over their environment and their effective right of political participation, is to promote women's literacy. Women who can seek employment outside the home have more resources in protecting their bodily integrity from assaults within it. Such facts give us still more reason not to promote one capability at the expense of the others.

Among the capabilities, two, practical reason and affiliation, stand out as of special importance, because they both organize and suffuse all the others, making their pursuit truly human. To use one's senses in a way not infused by the characteristically human use of thought and planning is to use them in a merely animal manner (Nussbaum, 1990, 1995a). Tagore's heroine describes herself as "a free human mind," and this idea of oneself infuses all one's other functions. At the same time, to reason for oneself without at all considering the circumstances and needs of others is, again, to behave in a not fully human way.

The basic intuition from which the capability approach begins, in the political arena, is that human abilities exert a moral claim that they should be developed. Human beings are creatures such that, provided with the right educational and material support, they can become fully capable of these human functions. That is, they are creatures with certain lower-level capabilities (which I call "basic capabilities")* to perform the functions in question. When these capabilities are deprived of the nourishment that would transform them into the high-level capabilities that figure on my list, they are fruitless, cut off, in some way but a shadow of themselves. If a turtle were given a life that afforded a merely animal level of functioning, we would have no indignation, no sense of waste and tragedy. When a human being is given a life that blights powers of human action and expression, that does give us a sense of waste and tragedy, the tragedy expressed, for example, in Mrinal's statement to her husband, in Tagore's story, when she says, "I am not one to die easily." In her view, a life without dignity and choice, a life in which she can be no more than an appendage, was a type of death.

We begin, then, with a sense of the worth and dignity of basic human powers, thinking of them as claims to a chance for functioning, claims that give rise to correlated social and political duties. And in fact there are three different types of capabilities that play a role in the analysis.**

---

* See Nussbaum (1988) with reference to Aristotle's ways of characterizing levels of *dunamis*.

** See Nussbaum (1988) referring to Aristotle's similar distinctions; and, on the basic capabilities, see Nussbaum (1995b). Sen does not use these three levels explicitly, although in practice many of his statements assume related distinctions.

First, there are basic capabilities: the innate equipment of individuals that is the necessary basis for developing the more advanced capability, and a ground of moral concern. Second, there are internal capabilities: that is, states of the person herself that are, as far as the person herself is concerned, sufficient conditions for the exercise of the requisite functions. A woman who has not suffered genital mutilation has the internal capability for sexual pleasure; most adult human beings everywhere have the internal capability for religious freedom and the freedom of speech. Finally, there are combined capabilities,* which may be defined as internal capabilities combined with suitable external conditions for the exercise of the function. A woman who is not mutilated but who has been widowed as a child and is forbidden to make another marriage has the internal but not the combined capability for sexual expression (and, in most such cases, for employment and political participation; see Chen, 1995, 2000). Citizens of repressive nondemocratic regimes have the internal but not the combined capability to exercise thought and speech in accordance with their conscience.

The list, then, is a list of combined capabilities. To realize one of the items on the list entails not only promoting appropriate development of people's internal powers, but also preparing the environment so that it is favorable for the exercise of practical reason and the other major functions. In other words, its liberties and opportunities correspond to Rawls's ideas of "the equal worth of liberty" and "truly fair equality of opportunity," rather than to his thinner notions of "formally equal liberty" and "formal equality of opportunity."

A focus on capabilities as social goals is closely related to a focus on human equality, in the sense that discrimination on the basis of race, religion, sex, national origin, caste, or ethnicity is taken to be itself a failure of associational capability, a type of indignity or humiliation. And making capabilities the goals entails promoting for all citizens a greater measure of material equality than exists in most societies, because we are unlikely to get all citizens above a minimum threshold of capability for truly human functioning without some redistributive policies.

On the other hand, it is possible for supporters of the general capability goal to differ about the amount of material equality a society focused

---

* In earlier papers I called these "external capabilities" (Nussbaum, 1988), but David Crocker persuaded me that this misleadingly suggested a focus on external conditions rather than internal fitness.

on capability should seek. Complete egalitarianism,* a Rawlsian difference principle, and a weaker focus on a (rather ample) social minimum would all be compatible with the proposal as so far advanced. Where women are concerned, almost all world societies are very far from even providing the basic minimum of truly human functioning.

V

I have spoken both of functioning and of capability. How are they related? Getting clear about this is crucial in defining the relation of the "capabilities approach" both to Rawlsian liberalism and to our concerns about paternalism and pluralism. For if we were to take functioning itself as the goal of public policy, the liberal pluralist would rightly judge that we were precluding many choices that citizens may make in accordance with their own conceptions of the good, and perhaps violating their rights. A deeply religious person may prefer not to be well-nourished, but to engage in strenuous fasting. Whether for religious or for other reasons, a person may prefer a celibate life to one containing sexual expression. A person may prefer to work with an intense dedication that precludes recreation and play. Am I declaring, by my very use of the list, that these are not fully human or flourishing lives? And am I instructing government to nudge or push people into functioning of the requisite sort, no matter what they prefer?

It is important that the answer to this question is "No." Capability, not functioning, is the political goal. This is so because of the very great importance the approach attaches to practical reason, as a good that both suffuses all the other functions, making them human rather than animal (see Nussbaum, 1995a) and figures, itself, as a central function on the list. It is perfectly true that functionings, not simply capabilities, are what render a life fully human: If there were no functioning of any kind in a life, we could hardly applaud it, no matter what opportunities it contained.

Nonetheless, for political purposes it is appropriate for us to shoot for capabilities, and those alone. Citizens must be left free to determine their course after that. The person with plenty of food may always choose to fast, but there is a great difference between fasting and starving, and it is this difference that we wish to capture. Again, the person

---

* Notice, however, that capability equality wouldn't necessarily entail equality of resources: that all depends on how resources affect capabilities once we get well above the threshold. Aristotle thought that we reach a point of negative returns: After a certain "limit," wealth becomes counterproductive, a distraction from the things that matter.

who has normal opportunities for sexual satisfaction can always choose a life of celibacy, and we say nothing against this. What we do speak against (for example) is the practice of female genital mutilation, which deprives individuals of the opportunity to choose sexual functioning (and indeed, the opportunity to choose celibacy as well; Nussbaum, 1996, 1997). A person who has opportunities for play can always choose a workaholic life; again, there is a great difference between that chosen life and a life constrained by insufficient maximum-hour protections or the "double day" that makes women unable to play in many parts of the world.

The approach does not rest content with internal capabilities, indifferent to the struggles of individuals who have to try to exercise these in a hostile environment. In that sense, it is highly attentive to the goal of functioning and instructs governments to keep it always in view. On the other hand, it does not push individuals into functioning; once the stage is fully set, the choice is up to them. Another way in which the list respects choice is in the prominent place it gives to the political liberties and the liberty of conscience, and the personal capability for practical reasoning and life-planning.

VI

I have argued that legitimate concerns for diversity, pluralism, and personal freedom are not incompatible with the recognition of universal norms, and indeed that universal norms are actually required if we are to protect diversity, pluralism, and freedom, treating each human being as an agent and an end. The best way to hold all these concerns together, I have argued, is to formulate the universal norms as a set of capabilities for fully human functioning, emphasizing the fact that capabilities protect, and do not close off, spheres of human freedom.

Let us now return to Vasanti and Jayamma. The script of Vasanti's life has been largely written by men on whom she has been dependent: her father, her husband, the brothers who helped her out when her marriage collapsed. This dependency put her at risk with respect to life and health, denied her the education that would have developed her powers of thought, and prevented her from thinking of herself as a person who has a plan of life to shape and choices to make. In the marriage itself she fared worst of all, losing her bodily integrity to domestic violence, her emotional equanimity to fear, and being cut off from meaningful forms of affiliation, familial, friendly, and civic. For these reasons, she did not really have the conception of herself as a free and dignified being whose worth is equal to that of others.

We should note that mundane matters of property, employment, and credit play a large role here: The fact that she held no property in her own name, no literacy and no employment-related skills, and no access to a loan except from male relatives, all this cemented her dependent status and kept her in an abusive relationship far longer than she would otherwise have chosen. We see here how closely all the capabilities are linked to one another, and how the absence of one, bad in itself, also erodes others. Vasanti also had some good luck: She had no abusive in-laws to put up with, and she had brothers who were more than usually solicitous of her well-being. Thus she could and did leave the marriage without turning to any physically dangerous or degrading occupation. But this good luck created new forms of dependency; Vasanti thus remained highly vulnerable, and lacking in confidence.

The SEWA loan changed this picture. Vasanti now had not only an income, but also independent control over her livelihood. Even when she still owed a lot of money, it was better to owe it to SEWA than to her brothers; being part of a mutually supportive community of women was crucially different, in respect of both practical reason and affiliation, from being a poor relation being given a handout. Her sense of her dignity increased as she paid off the loan and began saving. By the time I saw her, she had achieved considerable self-confidence and sense of worth, and her affiliations with other women, in both groups and personal friendships, were a new source of both pleasure and pride to her. Her participation in political life had also gone way up, as she joined in Kokila's project to prod the police to investigate more cases of domestic violence. Interestingly, she now felt that she had the capacity to be a good person by giving to others, something that the narrow focus on survival had not permitted her to do. Reflecting on her situation, we notice how little the public sector did for her and how lucky she was that one of the best women's NGOs in the world was right in her back yard. Government failed to ensure her an education; it failed to prosecute her husband for abuse, or to offer her shelter from that abuse;* it failed to secure her equal property rights in her own family; it failed to offer her access to credit. Indeed, the only strong role government played in Vasanti's life was negative, the cash payment for her husband's vasectomy, which made her vulnerable position still more so.

Jayamma's situation provides an interesting contrast. She had a much worse start in life than Vasanti, and has done worse throughout her life on some of the measures of capability. She has had to worry constantly about hunger, and she has at times suffered from malnutrition; she has

---

* The number of women's shelters in India is extremely small, indeed close to zero.

engaged in extremely dangerous and taxing physical labor. She has had no supportive male relatives, and, although she has had children as Vasanti has not, they have been more of a liability than an asset. She has no savings and has never had a loan; her property rights to the land on which she squats are unclearly established. She has suffered from discrimination in employment, with no chance of rectification. And she has had to do what countless women in developing countries routinely do, but Vasanti did not, that is to shoulder all the burden of running a household with children, while working a full day at a demanding job.

On the other hand, Jayamma has in some ways done better than Vasanti. Her health has been good, no doubt on account of her impressive physical strength and fitness, and she has never suffered physical abuse from her husband, who seems to have been a lot weaker than she was. She does not seem to be intimidated by anyone, and she has a consciousness of political issues that Vasanti developed only recently. Unlike Vasanti, she has never been encouraged to be submissive, and she certainly isn't; through the years she has fought effectively to keep her family together and to improve its standing.

Government has done much more for Jayamma than for Vasanti. The squatters on government land now have been given property rights in the land, although they will need to go to court to establish their claim clearly. Services provided by government are invaluable aids in Jayamma's taxing day. Water now comes into the squat itself, and a government program built her an indoor toilet. Government medical services are nearby, good, and available free of charge. Even though Jayamma did not take advantage of educational opportunities for her own children, her grandchildren have profited from government's aggressiveness against traditions of noneducation. Government certainly failed to eradicate sex discrimination in her place of employment. But in many respects the government of Kerala can be given good marks for promoting human capabilities.

Used to evaluate these lives, the capabilities framework does not look like an alien importation: It squares pretty well with the things these women are already thinking about, or start thinking about at some time in their lives. Insofar as it entails criticism of traditional culture, these women are already full of criticism; indeed, any framework that did not suggest criticism would not be adequate to capture what they want and aim for. In particular, the ideas of practical reason, control over environment, and nonhumiliation seem especially salient in their thought, alongside more obvious considerations of nutrition, health, and freedom from violence. Even where the list doesn't exactly echo their thoughts—as, for example, in the value it ascribes to education—it still seems to capture well, for normative political purposes, aspects of life that stand between these women and the general goals of independence, dignity, and mastery for which they are both intensely striving.

Vasanti and Jayamma, like many women in India and in the rest of the world, have lacked support for central human functions, and that lack of support is to some extent caused by their being women. But women, unlike rocks and trees, have the potential to become capable of these human functions, given sufficient nutrition, education, and other support. That is why their unequal failure in capability is a problem of justice. It is up to all human beings to solve this problem. I claim that a universal conception of human capability gives us good guidance as we pursue this difficult task.

REFERENCES

Ahmad, I. (Ed.) (1983). *Modernization and social change among Muslims in India*. Delhi: Manohar.

Bandyopadhyay, M. (1990). A female problem at a low level. In K. Bardhan (Ed.), *Of women, outcastes, peasants and rebels: A selection of Bengali short stories* (pp. 152–157). Berkeley: University of California Press.

Bardhan, K. (1990). Introduction. In K. Bardhan (Ed.), *Of women, outcastes, peasants and rebels: A selection of Bengali short stories* (pp. 1–49). Berkeley: University of California Press.

Brown, W. (1995). *States of injury: Power and freedom in late modernity*. Princeton, NJ: Princeton University Press.

Chen, M. A. (1995). A matter of survival: Women's right to employment in India and Bangladesh. In M. Nussbaum & J. Glover (Eds.), *Women, culture, and development* (pp. 61–104). Oxford, UK: Clarendon Press.

Chen, M. A. (2000). *Perpetual mourning: Widowhood in rural India*. New York: Oxford University Press.

Devji, F. F. (1994). Gender and the politics of space: The movement for women's reform, 1857–1900. In Z. Hasan (Ed.), *Forging identities: Gender, communities and the state in India* (pp. 22–37). Delhi: Kali for Women and Boulder, CO: Westview Press.

Gulati, L. (1981). *Profiles in female poverty: A study of five poor working women in Kerala*. Delhi: Hindustan.

Gulati, L. (1997). Female labour in the unorganised sector: The brick worker revisited. *Economic and Political Weekly, 32*(18), 968–971.

Human Development Reports: 1993, 1994, 1995, 1996. New York: United Nations Development Programme.

Metcalf, B. D. (1994). Reading and writing about Muslim women in British India. In Z. Hasan (Ed.), *Forging identities: Gender, communities and the state* (pp. 1–21). Delhi: Kali for Women and Boulder, CO: Westview Press.

Nussbaum, M. (1988). Nature, function, and capability: Aristotle on political distribution. In J. Annas & R. H. Grimm (Eds.), *Oxford studies in ancient philosophy, Supplementary Volume* (pp. 145–184). Oxford, UK: Clarendon Press.

Nussbaum, M. (1990). Aristotelian social democracy. In R. B. Douglass, G. M. Mara, & H. S. Richardson (Eds.), *Liberalism and the good* (pp. 203–252). New York: Routledge.

Nussbaum, M. (1992). Human functioning and social justice: In defense of Aristotelian essentialism. *Political Theory, 20,* 202–246.

Nussbaum, M. (1993). Non-relative virtues: An Aristotelian approach. In M. Nussbaum & A. Sen (Eds.), *The quality of life* (pp. 1–6). Oxford, UK: Clarendon Press.

Nussbaum, M. (1995a). Aristotle on human nature and the foundations of ethics. In J. E. J. Altham & R. Harrison (Eds.), *World, mind and ethics: Essays on the ethical philosophy of Bernard Williams* (pp. 86–131). Cambridge and New York: Cambridge University Press.

Nussbaum, M. (1995b). Human capabilities, female human beings. In M. Nussbaum & J. Glover (Eds.), *Women, culture, and development* (pp. 61–104). Oxford, UK: Clarendon Press.

Nussbaum, M. (1996). Double moral standards? A response to Yael Tamir's "Hands off clitoridectomy." *Boston Review, 21*(5), 28–30.

Nussbaum, M. (1997). Religion and women's human rights. In P. J. Weithman (Ed.), *Religion and contemporary liberalism* (pp. 1–37). Notre Dame, IN: Notre Dame University Press.

Nussbaum, M. (1998). The good as discipline, the good as freedom. In D. A. Crocker & T. Linden (Eds.), *Ethics of consumption: The good life, justice, and global stewardship* (pp. 312–341). Lanham, MD: Rowman and Littlefield.

Nussbaum, M. (1999a). *Sex and social justice.* New York: Oxford University Press.

Nussbaum, M. (1999b). The feminist critique of liberalism. In A. Jeffries (Ed.), *Women's voices, women's rights* (pp. 13–56). Boulder, CO: Westview Press.

Sarkar, S. (1979). *On the Bengal renaissance.* Calcutta: Papyrus.

Sen, A. (1980). Equality of what? In S. Mc Murrin (Ed.), *Tanner lectures on human values: 1980, vol. 1* (pp. 195–220), Cambridge, UK: Cambridge University Press.

Sen, A. (1994, January 10/17). Freedoms and needs. *The New Republic,* 31–38.

Tsui, A. O., Wasserheit, J. N., & Haaga, J. G. (Eds.) (1997). *Reproductive health in developing countries.* Washington: National Academy Press.

AUTHOR \ INDEX

SUBJECT \ INDEX